QUANTITATIVE ANALYSIS OF QUESTIONNAIRES

Bringing together the techniques required to understand, interpret and quantify the processes involved when exploring structures and relationships in questionnaire data, *Quantitative Analysis of Questionnaires* provides the knowledge and capability for a greater understanding of choice decisions. The ideal companion for non-mathematical students with no prior knowledge of quantitative methods, it highlights how to uncover and explore what lies within data that cannot be achieved through descriptive statistics. This book introduces significance testing, contingency tables, correlations, factor analysis (exploratory and confirmatory), regression (linear and logistic), discrete choice theory and item response theory.

Using simple and clear methodology, and rich examples from a range of settings, this book:

- provides hands-on analysis with data sets from both SPSS and Stata packages;
- explores how to articulate the calculations and theory around statistical techniques;
- offers workable examples in each chapter with concepts, applications and proofs to help produce a higher quality of research outputs;
- discusses the use of formulas in the appendix for those who wish to explore a greater mathematical understanding of the concepts.

Quantitative Analysis of Questionnaires is the ideal introductory textbook for any student looking to begin and or improve statistical learning as well as interpretation.

Steve Humble MBE is a senior lecturer and Head of Education at Newcastle University, UK. He teaches undergraduate and graduate advanced quantitative methods and is an expert around collecting and analysing data from large samples using advanced statistical techniques in both SPSS and Stata.

QUANTITATIVE ANALYSIS OF QUESTIONNAIRES

Techniques to Explore Structures and Relationships

Steve Humble

LONDON AND NEW YORK

First published 2020
by Routledge
2 Park Square, Milton Park, Abingdon, Oxon, OX14 4RN

and by Routledge
52 Vanderbilt Avenue, New York, NY 10017

Routledge is an imprint of the Taylor & Francis Group, an informa business

© 2020 Steve Humble

The right of Steve Humble to be identified as author of this work has been asserted by him in accordance with sections 77 and 78 of the Copyright, Designs and Patents Act 1988.

All rights reserved. No part of this book may be reprinted or reproduced or utilised in any form or by any electronic, mechanical, or other means, now known or hereafter invented, including photocopying and recording, or in any information storage or retrieval system, without permission in writing from the publishers.

Trademark notice: Product or corporate names may be trademarks or registered trademarks, and are used only for identification and explanation without intent to infringe.

British Library Cataloguing-in-Publication Data
A catalogue record for this book is available from the British Library

Library of Congress Cataloging-in-Publication Data
A catalogue record has been requested for this book

ISBN: 978-0-367-02279-2 (hbk)
ISBN: 978-0-367-02283-9 (pbk)
ISBN: 978-0-429-40046-9 (ebk)

Typeset in Times New Roman
by Swales & Willis, Exeter, Devon, UK

Images from Strata courtesy of StataCorp. 2017. Stata Statistical Software: Release 15. College Station, TX: StataCorp LLC.

IBM, the IBM logo, ibm.com, and SPSS are trademarks or registered trademarks of **International Business Machines Corporation**, registered in many jurisdictions worldwide. Other product and service names might be trademarks of IBM or other companies. A current list of IBM trademarks is available on the Web at "IBM Copyright and trademark information" at www.ibm.com/legal/copytrade.shtml.

TABLE OF CONTENTS

List of illustrations viii
About the author xiii
About the book xiv

1 **Introduction** 1
Criteria for statistical testing 4
Types of data 5
Data sets used as example studies 6
Missing data 16

2 **Statistical significance and contingency tables** 20
Statistical significance 20
Contingency tables 21
How to report contingency tables 27

3 **Factor analysis: Exploratory** 30
Exploratory factor analysis 31
Discovering latent factors 32
Factor analysis for data reduction 41
Calculating and using latent factors in future analysis 44
Missing values 46
How to report factor analysis 47

4 **Correlation and linear regression** 51
Scatter diagram 51
Correlation 54
Spearman's rank correlation coefficient (Spearman's rho) 64
Kendall's Tau correlation (τ) 64
Correlations between two variables of different scales 65

CONTENTS

How to report correlations 65
Calculating correlation with Stata and SPSS 66
Linear regression 67
Multicollinearity 71
Multivariate linear regression 71
Linear regression sample size conditions 77
How to report linear regression 77

5 Factor analysis: Confirmatory   79

Constructing First Order CFA Models 80
More complex CFA models 87
Uncovering structures in questionnaires 90
Longitudinal measurement invariance 95
How to report confirmatory factor analysis 96

6 Regression: Logistic   100

Simple logistic regression 100
Multivariable analysis 110
Complex multinomial models 117
How to report logistic regression 120

7 Making choices: Discrete choice theory   123

Stated and revealed preference 124
A simple consumer choice model 124
Multinomial logistic regression model with socio-economic factors 132
Ordered logit choice model 138
The range of discrete choice models 147
How to calculate ordered and ordinal regression 148

8 Item response theory   150

Item response model 151
Differential item testing 157
Graded Response Model (GRM) 159
Partial Credit Models (PCM) 161
Information function 161
Reliability of measures when collapsing Likert scale categories 166

Appendix   172

Multiple imputation 172
Distribution fitting 173

■ ■ ■ ■ **CONTENTS**

Factor analysis 176
Correlation 180
Linear regression 184
Sample size 188
Confirmatory Factor Analysis (CFA) 189
Logistic regression 190
Marginal effects 196
Discrete choice theory 197
Longitudinal data analysis 199
Item response theory 201

References   205
Index   214

ILLUSTRATIONS

FIGURES

2.1	Stata two-way contingency table	28
2.2	SPSS crosstabs contingency table	28
2.3	SPSS cell statistics	29
2.4	SPSS crosstabs statistics	29
3.1	Scree plot	37
3.2	Stata factor analysis: select model	48
3.3	Stata Varimax or Promax rotation	48
3.4	SPSS factor analysis	48
3.5	SPSS extraction window	49
3.6	SPSS rotation window	49
3.7	SPSS factor scores	49
3.8	SPSS options window	50
4.1	Positive correlation	52
4.2	Negative correlation	53
4.3	No clear correlation	53
4.4	Estimated linear relationship	55
4.5	SPSS scatterplot	66
4.6	Stata scatterplot	66
4.7	SPSS correlation	67
4.8	Stata correlation	67
4.9	Regression line for child invitations	69
4.10	Stata linear regression	77
4.11	SPSS linear regression	78
5.1	CFA for happiness items	81
5.2	Model 1 Two latent structure	83
5.3	Model 2 Two latent structure with covariance	84
5.4	Complex CFA structure for Roets leadership study	89
5.5	Simple factor structure for parental involvement study	91
5.6	Higher order CFA model for parental involvement study	95
5.7	Longitudinal measurement invariance	96
5.8	Stata drawing palette icons	98
5.9	Stata defining the factor structure	98

■ ■ ■ ■ **ILLUSTRATIONS**

5.10	Stata goodness of fit	99
5.11	Stata goodness of fit statistics	99
6.1	Margin plot: university aspirations	110
6.2	Stata logistic regression	122
6.3	SPSS binary logistic regression	122
7.1	School choice by family income decile	132
7.2	Cut-off points for decisions	141
7.3	Stata ordered logistic regression	149
7.4	SPSS ordinal regression	149
8.1	Item characteristic curve: health	151
8.2	Category characteristic curve: health	152
8.3	Item characteristic curve: health and environment	153
8.4	Item characteristic curve: health and appearance	155
8.5	Item characteristic curve: price and health	156
8.6	Boundary characteristic curve: energetic	160
8.7	Category characteristic curve: energetic	160
8.8	Item information function: mood categories	162
8.9	Item information function: organic food	162
8.10	Item information function: Roets leadership study	163
8.11	Non-uniform boundary curves: gender in Roets leadership study	165
8.12	Test information function for models	167
8.13	Item information function for models	168
8.14	Stata item response theory	171
A.1	Stata imputation screenshot	173
A.2	Factor model	177
A.3	Factor loading	178
A.4	Regression line with errors	185
A.5	Histograms illustrating excellent discrimination	195
A.6	ROC curve	195
A.7	Stata margins plot	196

TABLES

1.1	Responses to the happiness study	7
1.2	Responses to the parental involvement study	8
1.3	Responses to the Roets leadership study	10
1.4	Responses to the students' aspirations study	11
1.5	Responses to food insecurity study	12
1.6	Responses to the organic foods study	13
1.7	Responses to the school choice study	14
1.8	Responses to the transportation study	16
1.9	Responses to the intrinsic motivation study	17
2.1	Contingency table: Monday coffee consumers	22
2.2	Gender responses to drinking coffee on Monday	22
2.3	Male responses to drinking coffee on Monday	23

ILLUSTRATIONS

2.4	Male and yes to drinking coffee on Monday	23
2.5	Coffee consumers observed and expected on Monday	23
2.6	Coffee consumers observed and expected on Wednesday	24
2.7	Coffee consumers observed and expected on Friday	24
3.1	Simplistic Likert scale scoring	31
3.2	Happiness scale	33
3.3	Responses to the happiness study	34
3.4	Communalities	34
3.5	KMO and Bartlett's test	35
3.6	Total variance explained	36
3.7	Pattern Matrix	38
3.8	Skewness and Kurtosis statistics	39
3.9	Comparison of extraction methods	40
3.10	Socio-economic data	41
3.11	Frequencies for socio-economic data	42
3.12	Eigenvalues: socio-economic data	42
3.13	Three factor rotated PCA solution	43
3.14	Two factor rotated PCA solution	44
3.15	Linear regression for positive happiness	45
3.16	Factor scores: positive attitude to life	45
4.1	Role activity beliefs	57
4.2	Parents self-efficacy	57
4.3	General school invitations	58
4.4	Specific teacher invitations	58
4.5	Specific child invitations	59
4.6	Skills and knowledge	59
4.7	Time and energy	60
4.8	Home based items	61
4.9	School based items	61
4.10	Pearson correlations	63
4.11	Linear regression	68
4.12	Home support regression	70
4.13	Home support multivariate regression	72
4.14	School support multivariate regression	73
4.15	Purposeful selection	76
5.1	Exploratory factor structure for happiness study	80
5.2	Proportion of variance explained calculations	82
5.3	Table of fit indices	85
5.4	Pattern matrix for Roets leadership study	88
5.5	Pearson correlations for Roets leadership study	88
5.6	Fit indices for Roets leadership study	89
5.7	Fit indices for parental involvement study	91
5.8	Coefficient for parental involvement study	92
5.9	R^2 values for parental involvement	93
5.10	Correlations for parental involvement study	94

ILLUSTRATIONS

5.11	Fit indices for longitudinal measurement invariance	96
6.1	Contingency table: education aspirations	101
6.2	Logistic regression: education aspiration	102
6.3	Contingency table: work hard at school	103
6.4	Reference cell coding: work hard at school	104
6.5	Logistic regression: work hard at school	104
6.6	Logistic regression: doing well at school	105
6.7	Logistic regression: work hard and doing well at school	105
6.8	Contingency table: family attitudes to school	107
6.9	Reverse coding: school is important	107
6.10	Logistic regression: school is important	107
6.11	Linear regression: continuous independent variable	108
6.12	Multivariate logistic regression	111
6.13	Logistic regression with multiple independent variables	111
6.14	Model 1 continuous approximations to ordinal variables	112
6.15	Model 2 continuous approximations to ordinal variables	112
6.16	Odds ratio calculations	113
6.17	Hunger scale	114
6.18	Contingency table: hunger scale and energetic mood	115
6.19	Multinomial logistic regression: energetic mood	116
6.20	Model 1 multinomial logistic regression: hunger scale	118
6.21	Model 2 multinomial logistic regression: hunger scale	119
6.22	Model 3 reduced multinomial logistic regression: hunger scale	120
7.1	Code for variables in the organic food study	125
7.2	Contingency table: organic food choice	126
7.3	Model 1 multinomial logistic regression: organic food choice	128
7.4	Model 2 multinomial logistic regression: organic food choice	129
7.5	Empirical model: organic food choice	130
7.6	Parents' preferences: school characteristics	133
7.7	Data reduction: wealth factors	135
7.8	Odds ratio calculations for significant variables	136
7.9	Multinomial logistic regression: school choice study	136
7.10	Questionnaire for commuters	139
7.11	Logistic regression: choice and cost	140
7.12	Model 1 ordinal logit regression: choice and cost	141
7.13	Contingency table: choice of transport	143
7.14	Ordered logit model predictions	143
7.15	Model 2 ordinal logit regression: choice, cost and clean	144
7.16	Multivariable model: estimated response probabilities (choice =1 (Bus))	146

ILLUSTRATIONS

7.17	Multivariable model: estimated response probabilities (choice =0 (Rail))	146
7.18	Model 3 ordinal logit regression: choice, cost, clean available, crowding	147
8.1	Partial credit model: organic food study	154
8.2	Discrimination values	154
8.3	GRM model: organic food study	155
8.4	Differential item test: purchasing groups	157
8.5	Contingency table: knowledge	158
8.6	Differential item test: gender	158
8.7	GRM model: energetic	159
8.8	Differential item test: gender in Roets leadership study	164
8.9	Non-uniform difficulty: gender in Roets leadership study	165
8.10	Factor analysis comparison of models	167
8.11	Graded response model comparison	169
A.1	One sample Kolmogorov-Smirnov distribution test of normality	174
A.2	Two sample Kolmogorov-Smirnov test	175
A.3	Stata Model 1: two sample Kolmogorov-Smirnov test	175
A.4	Kolmogorov-Smirnov test calculation	176
A.5	Stata Model 2: two sample Kolmogorov-Smirnov test	176
A.6	Correlations for parental education motivation	178
A.7	Worked example Pearson correlation calculation	181
A.8	Worked example of Spearman rank correlation	183
A.9	Worked example of Kendall correlation	184
A.10	Calculating regression residuals	185
A.11	Expected distribution contingency table	191
A.12	Example data for expected distribution contingency table	191
A.13	Intent to treat	200
A.14	Calculating likelihoods and trait levels	203

ABOUT THE AUTHOR

Dr Steve Humble MBE is a senior lecturer and Head of Education at Newcastle University in the United Kingdom. He carries out research in sub-Saharan Africa, South America and India concerning parental choice and schooling. He is an expert around collecting and analysing data from large samples using advanced statistical techniques in both Stata and SPSS. He teaches undergraduate and graduate courses in advanced quantitative methods, such as multivariate analysis, item response theory, structural equation modelling, factor analysis, multilevel modelling, longitudinal data analysis and discrete choice theory. His PhD looked at children's ability, creativity and motivation in poor parts of Kinondoni, Tanzania. The research investigated the cross-cultural transferability of Renzulli's three-ring concept to an African setting. Humble has acted as a statistician on several developing country projects (India, Liberia, Sierra Leone, Nigeria and Ghana) undertaking analysis with big data sets. He has worked with the British government on several committees and initiatives to investigate, support and develop educational improvements and social equity policy. He is a fellow of The Institute of Mathematics and its Applications (IMA).

Humble's book *How to be Inventive when teaching Primary Maths*, was published by Routledge (2015) and this earned him Routledge's education author of the month for March 2015. He was an editor on the *Handbook of International Development and Education* (2015) and *50 Visions of Mathematics* (2014). Steve was awarded an MBE, a grade within the British order of chivalry – Member of the Most Excellent Order of the British Empire – for Services to Education in the Queen's 2016 New Year's Honours List.

ABOUT THE BOOK

This book aims to provide the reader with an understanding of the thinking process involved when exploring structures and relationships in questionnaire data. Questionnaires are the underpinning of any empirical research data gathering. For students, researchers and faculty it is imperative to understand and interpret analysis and findings that are possible using a range of different techniques. Examples will be given in the book using data sets from empirical research topics in humanities and social sciences. These will include looking at specific projects along with peer-reviewed journal articles and reports. The main body of the book deliberately tries to avoid the use of formulas and these, on the whole, are left to the appendix for those readers who wish to have a greater mathematical understanding of the concepts explored. The emphasis throughout the main body of the chapters is placed on deciding which statistical techniques would be useful to apply in particular situations and how to interpret and report the output from Stata and IBM® SPSS® Statistics software ("SPSS")[1]. The aim of the book is to provide support to those carrying out research in the humanities and social sciences who would like to understand the principles, techniques and applications of questionnaire statistical analysis. Students undertaking research dissertations at undergraduate or masters level and those studying for higher degrees, such as a doctorate, will find this book invaluable.

In a user-friendly style the book introduces significance testing, contingency tables, correlations, factor analysis (both exploratory and confirmatory), regression (both linear and logistic), discrete choice theory and item response theory. Opening up the world of quantitative analysis to students who wish to know more and often from a standing start is the aim of this book. The author hopes that this book will help and welcomes your comments and questions.

email:
steve.humble@ncl.ac.uk

NOTES

1   SPSS Inc. was acquired by IBM in October, 2009.

Betwixt and between Utopia and Dystopia is the happenstance of choice.

CHAPTER 1

INTRODUCTION

In today's world, choice has become part of our daily routine. From which coffee to order, which mode of transport to use to get to work or which university to attend the multitude of options makes for exciting decision-making processes. Buying online has brought about the emergence of rating providers, sellers and products. This informs future would-be market participants around quality, reliability and appropriateness. Therefore completing rating scales and questionnaires has become commonplace.

As a researcher, having the knowledge and capability to understand, interpret and quantify why and how answers are given when there are choices to be made allows for a greater understanding of the structures around choice. When collecting data the questionnaire is one protocol that can provide rich data relatively easily and simply.

This book works for all types of researchers from those with no prior knowledge of quantitative methods to those who wish to expand their range of statistical techniques. It provides statistical approaches that are appropriate for in-depth analysis of questionnaires. These include questionnaires that can be simple dichotomous, Likert scale, or stated and revealed preference choice.

A range of techniques highlights how to explore and uncover what lies within the data to reveal structures and relationships that are not discovered through descriptive statistics. This accessible book will both illustrate and expand the reader's understanding of the statistical techniques used in this area.

Each of the chapters in this book introduces a specific statistical concept required to evaluate questionnaire data. All the chapters contain illustrative data sets for the reader to explore while learning. These sections provide students undertaking research dissertations at masters or undergraduate level or those studying for higher degrees such as a doctorate in the humanities and social sciences the basic principles, techniques and applications of questionnaire statistical analysis. The text guides the reader through hands-on analysis with data sets and support for using both SPSS and Stata packages for these statistical concepts. The book hopes to bridge a gap between theoretical understanding and easy to use statistical packages. The chapters all detail how to use statistical package calculations and give

INTRODUCTION

reasons why the statistical techniques are explored and articulated through a range of relevant data sets for humanities and social science students.

Chapter 2 examines statistical significance and the use of contingency tables. The chapter begins by providing a brief introduction to statistical significance and p-values. Data on coffee-drinking habits is explored to illustrate how to use contingency tables, Chi-square test, Cramer's V test and how to calculate odds ratios. The concluding part of the chapter looks at how to report and calculate contingency tables when using SPSS and Stata.

Chapter 3 considers exploratory factor analysis and why this is an important tool when exploring structures and relationships in Likert scale data. This chapter sets out the principles and procedures that are involved when carrying out exploratory factor analysis describing and justifying the different possible methods of selection that can be performed when using factor analysis. The first part of this chapter discusses essentials that need to be considered in order to decide whether factor analysis is suited to your data. The chapter explains how communality, Kaiser-Meyer-Olkin test, Bartlett test of Sphericity and Scree plots can all be used to help inform the factor model. Example data sets are used to illustrate the difference between principal factor analysis and principal component analysis. The chapter concludes by discussing when to use a particular latent factor score extraction method. The three methods considered are the Regression method, Bartlett method, and the Anderson-Rubin method.

The statistical procedures correlation and regression are examined in Chapter 4. The chapter first explores how we can visually understand correlation through scatter diagrams and moves on to appreciate why more rigorous statistical techniques are required to prove correlations in data. The chapter then explains how to carry out Pearson Correlation, Spearman's Rank Correlation and Kendall's Tau Correlation illustrating these techniques through a parental motivation study. The second part of the chapter explores linear and multivariate regression. The chapter goes on to describe how the technique of purposeful selection can be used to aid the researcher when deciding on which variables are to be included in the model.

Confirmatory factor analysis is explored in Chapter 5. This chapter takes forward the concepts from Chapters 3 and 4 to show how we can confirm latent structures in a questionnaire. Firstly the chapter explains how a model can be constructed. The happiness study is used to illustrate how to carryout confirmatory factor analysis using Structural Equation Modeling (SEM). The chapter then shows how to assess hypothesized fit structures of items in grouped constructs using fit and comparison indices. Following on from this example two further studies are explored to illustrate the depth of complex themed structures that can be uncovered when confirmatory factor analysis is applied to questionnaire data. The chapter ends with details on how to build, calculate, assess and report confirmatory factor analysis.

■ ■ ■ ■ INTRODUCTION

Chapter 6 explores the use of logistic regression for discrete dependent variables having two or more possible values. This chapter acts a precursor to Chapter 7 on discrete choice theory where the techniques learnt in Chapter 6 will be explored in greater depth. The chapter starts by looking at how to perform simple logistic regression when the independent variable is either dichotomous, polychotomous, or continuous. The chapter then uses two studies to demonstrate how to perform logistic regression. The studies are children's aspiration and food insecurity. The chapter concludes with a section on multinomial logistic regression to illustrate how this technique can be extended to incorporate models that have a dependent variable with three categories and a number of independent variables. As throughout the book the chapter closes with a section on how to calculate logistic regression using SPSS and Stata.

A brief background to discrete choice theory is discussed at the start of Chapter 7. Organic food and school choice studies are then used illustrate how discrete choice techniques can be applied to reveal sophisticated structures and relationships in questionnaires. Within these illustrations we use techniques from previous chapters in the book to organize, calculate and report findings. The chapter then discusses a multivariable ordered logit model as an alternative statistical technique to that of multinomial logistic regression in order to obtain greater detail around revealed preferences. A transport study is used to illustrate this method and how we can obtain estimated response probabilities for different choices. The chapter concludes with a section describing different types of discrete choice models and the most applicable situations in which to use them.

Chapter 8 explores the use of item response theory as a means of assessing questionnaires in relation to their latent traits. The first part of the chapter uses the organic food study to illustrate how 1-parameter and partial credit models (1PL and 2PL) can be used to calculate category and item characteristic curves. In the next section mood items from the food insecurity study are used to show how the item information function checks the reliability of items in relation to latent model structures. The chapter closes by investigating differential item testing using the Roets leadership and intrinsic motivation studies.

Bringing the book to its close is the appendix that gives further depth of understanding into the statistical theory employed during the chapters within the book. This is both for completeness and to answer additional background questions that the reader may have in relation to the statistics employed in the book. The reading of the appendix may be considered as supplementary to the rest of the book and is not required for the user to be able to perform any of the statistical techniques carried out in the book. The appendix gives greater detail on the statistical methods employed offering the reader mathematical equations, proofs and calculations on regression, correlation, factor analysis, discrete choice theory, item response theory and details on a range of statistical tests.

INTRODUCTION

CRITERIA FOR STATISTICAL TESTING
Acceptable deviations from normality

Data that are generated from questionnaires can exhibit a normal distribution structure. For small samples (typically less than 20 to 30) most statistical methods require distributional assumptions. For data sets larger than 30, most statistical methods can rely on the Central Limit Theorem. The theorem states that the average of a large number of independent random variables is approximately normally distributed around the true population mean. It is this normal distribution of an average that underlies the validity of most statistical tests (Lumley et al., 2002; Carifio and Perla, 2008).

Where data samples are large enough, acceptable deviations from normality for distributions can be found by looking at scores for skewness and *excess* kurtosis. Skewness is a measure of how much a distribution's symmetry deviates around the mean. If the skewness value is zero this implies that the distribution is symmetric about the mean. Data that is positively skewed tends to cluster to the left and the curve has a long tail to the right with values reducing. The opposite is the case when the data is negatively skewed tending to cluster to the right.

If data in a distribution is clustered in the tail ends, either right or left or both, this property is called kurtosis. Kurtosis is the measure of flatness or steepness. A value near zero indicates that the shape of the distribution is close to normal. A negative value indicates the shape has a greater steepness. A positive value implies a flatter shape than a normal distribution.[1] How big can the deviation for skewness and *excess* kurtosis be from zero for your dataset to be acceptable given that a value of zero is said to be perfectly normal? Deviations of less than ±1 from zero are considered very good. Values lying outside of this range between ±1 and ±2 considered acceptable (Field, 2000; Trochim and Donnelly, 2006; Muijs, 2010; Gravetter and Wallnau, 2014).

Parametric or non-parametric

The use of either parametric or non-parametric tests are said to be dictated by whether your data are normally distributed or not; hence the section above on examining the skewness and kurtosis of your dataset. Typically research studies take a sample of data from the total population of interest, as it is not usually possible to sample all of the population. Parametric tests make the assumption that the whole population that the sample data has been drawn from is normally distributed.

It has been argued that sample size is not the issue for parametric or non-parametric tests and that the issue is the fact that as the sample size reduces then validity becomes an issue (Hunter and Schmidt, 1990; Suissa, 1991). In fact as long as there is an adequate sample size (at least 5–10

■ ■ ■ ■ INTRODUCTION

observations per group) and the data are normally distributed (or nearly normal), then parametric tests can be used with Likert scale ordinal data (Glass et al., 1972; Johnson and Creech, 1983; Zimmerman and Zumbo, 1993; Dolan, 1994; Jamieson, 2004; Lubke and Muthen, 2004; Norman, 2010; Sullivan and Artino, 2013).

The controversy around using parametric tests for discrete data has been continuing for more than half a century. According to evidence given by a professor of Clinical Epidemiology and Biostatistics, Geoff Norman, parametric tests can be used with ordinal data, such as data from Likert scales. Norman's research shows that parametric tests are generally more robust than nonparametric tests on Likert scale data (Norman, 2010). The work also shows that parametric tests tend to give better results even when statistical assumptions, such as the data needing to be normally distributed, are violated to an extreme degree, showing that Pearson correlation is robust with respect to skewness and non-normality (Havlicek and Peterson, 1976). When analyzing Likert scale responses parametric tests are sufficiently robust to produce high quality results. Norman ends his paper with the following reassuring statement in summary that parametric tests can be used with Likert data.

> Parametric statistics can be used with Likert data, with small sample sizes, with unequal variances, and with non-normal distributions, with no fear of 'coming to the wrong conclusion.'
>
> (Norman, 2010, p.631)

TYPES OF DATA

There are various thoughts around the categorization of data. Definitions and examples of types and sub-types typically depend upon where the author's initial expertise lies (Stevens, 1946). For mathematicians, such as myself, quantitative data in questionnaires can be classified into two main overarching categories – discrete and continuous. It is important to know the categories one is working with in order to determine the appropriate type of statistical analysis to be used to interpret the data. Thinking about data in these two broad categories has always been helpful to me when exploring structures and relationships within questionnaires.

Continuous data can take on any value within a given range, for example height, weight, and blood pressure. Typically continuous data can be measured on a scale. One way of thinking about this is that data collected through measuring rather than counting is continuous (Owen and Jones, 1982).

Discrete data take values that are finite. Data that are discrete can only be increased in uniform steps of 1. Some examples may include the number of children in the family, as this would be a finite value, and a selection rating such as a Likert scale. If the questionnaire codes a variable using

INTRODUCTION

a finite number this also is classified as discrete. One type of discrete data is categorical data. The data are put into categories. Such categories could include professions, degree classification, and gender. Sub types of categorical data are:

- Nominal where the data have no natural ordering such as professions (e.g. butcher =1, baker=2, tailor =3, etc.,).
- Ordinal data that have a natural ordering based on a scale such as a university degree classification or a Likert scale (e.g. distinction=3, merit=2, pass=1; disagree=1, agree=2, strongly agree=3). Binary data is a special case of ordinal data with only two categories as in the example of gender (e.g. male=0, female=1).

When analysing data from questionnaires having an understanding of what type of data you have is important. Although social scientists may add more terms and think about sub categories in multiple ways, if you remember the terms discrete data and continuous data then this will set you on your way. It will inform your understanding, as to which statistical methods you'll need to gain the best out of your data. As we go through the book these terms will crop up again when thinking about techniques to analyse your data.

DATA SETS USED AS EXAMPLE STUDIES

A range of different data sets are used throughout the book to help demonstrate the various statistical techniques explored. All of the data sets that are included in this book are fictitious and should not be taken as original research. Any resemblance to real data is purely by chance. They have all been developed by the author in order to illustrate the relevant statistical procedure under investigation in that specific chapter. Next in this section we will explore descriptive information on the nine major data sets that are used to illustrate the statistical techniques in this book. All of these data sets may be downloaded from the link to the web site at https://www.routledge.com/Quantitative-Analysis-of-Questionnaires-Techniques-to-Explore-Structures/Humble/p/book/9780367022839.

Oxford happiness questionnaire

The Oxford happiness questionnaire data set consists of 500 subjects' answers. Only ten items are used, taken from the original 29-item happiness questionnaire (Argyle and Hills, 2002). All of the items are measured on a five-point Likert scale. Table 1.1 shows that this data set reports responses from a group of 500 pupils who are relatively happy, but not particularly healthy or in control of their own lives. Analysis of this data set is explored in Chapters 3 and 5.

INTRODUCTION

Table 1.1 Responses to the happiness study

	Strongly disagree (1)	Disagree (2)	Neutral (3)	Agree (4)	Strongly agree (5)
I am very happy (Happy)	40	35	40	77	308
I laugh a lot (Laugh)	29	37	62	88	284
Life is good (Goodlife)	32	31	38	93	306
I feel I have a great deal of energy (Energy)	40	39	61	80	280
I am always committed and involved (Commit)	79	65	74	85	197
I feel that life is very rewarding (Reward)	166	96	78	75	85
I feel able to take anything on (Anything)	81	82	116	107	114
I feel that I am not especially in control of my life (Control)	38	54	107	118	183
I don't feel particularly healthy (Health)	50	55	72	120	203
I don't have particularly happy memories (Memory)	126	96	120	81	77

Parental involvement in education

The questions used in this study are taken from the work of Hoover-Dempsey and Sandler (Hoover-Dempsey and Sandler, 1995, 1997, 2005; Walker et al., 2005; Green et al., 2007). To illustrate how parental involvement is associated with education and schooling this data set contains a sample of 500 parent's responses. All of the measures are given on a four point Likert scale, with 1 strongly disagree, 2 disagree, 3 agree and 4 strongly agree. The latent factors are grouped into the three main themed categories in this study. The first group is called psychological motivators. In this category there are two sets of questions. These focus on role activity beliefs and questions on parental self-efficacy. The second themed group of questions relates to invitations to involvement and in this category there are three groups of questions. These are general school invitation, specific teacher invitations and specific child invitations. The final group of questions are termed life context and contains two groups of questions. These categories are called skills and knowledge, and time and energy. The responses to all seven of these areas are shown in Table 1.2. Analysis of this data set is explored in Chapters 4 and 5.

Table 1.2 Responses to the parental involvement study

	Strongly disagree (1)	Disagree (2)	Agree (3)	Strongly agree (4)
Role activity beliefs				
Communicate with my child's teacher regularly (School)	16	43	406	35
Talk with my child about the school day	14	61	306	119
Volunteer at the school (School)	21	164	285	30
Parental self-efficacy				
I feel successful about my efforts to help my child learn	3	16	175	306
I know how to help my child to do well in school (Home)	4	14	134	348
I do know if I'm getting through to my child	85	174	188	53
General school invitations				
I feel welcome at the school (School)	48	98	100	254
The school lets me know about special school events and meetings (School)	11	32	182	275
The teachers at the school keep me informed about my child's progress in school (School)	21	182	267	30
Specific teacher invitations				
My child's teacher asked me to talk with my child about the school day (Home)	206	67	137	90
My child's teacher asked me or expected me to help my daughter with her homework (Home)	115	64	106	215
My child's teacher asked me to attend a special event at school (School)	99	244	147	10
My child's teacher asked me to help out at the school (School)	235	208	52	5

	Strongly disagree (1)	Disagree (2)	Agree (3)	Strongly agree (4)
Specific child invitations				
My child asked me about her homework (Home)	4	14	134	348
I know how to supervise my child's homework (Home)	8	21	153	318
My child asked me to explain things about her homework (Home)	11	52	360	77
Skills and knowledge				
I know enough about subjects to help my child with homework	0	122	191	187
To be able to look for more information about subjects if required	0	138	131	231
To believe that she can learn new things	77	111	141	171
Time and energy				
I have enough time and energy to help out at my child's school (School)	5	13	153	329
I have enough time and energy to help my child with homework (Home)	14	25	194	267
I have enough time and energy to attend special events at school (School)	29	116	338	17
I have enough time and energy to communicate effectively with my child's teacher (School)	30	98	343	29
I have enough time and energy to supervise my daughter's homework (Home)	15	37	356	92

INTRODUCTION

Table 1.3 Responses to the Roets leadership study

	Not very often like me (0)	Quite often like me (1)
Confidence		
Have strong convictions (C1)	319	181
Have self-confidence (C2)	413	87
Promote what is believed (C3)	406	94
Can say opinions in public (C4)	406	94
Leadership		
Act for what one is convinced of (L1)	279	221
Like to be in charge (L2)	250	250
Think one can do well as a leader (L3)	154	346
Lead on projects (L4)	339	161
Ambition and desire		
Dream of a time of accomplishment (A1)	24	476
Admire those who have achieved (A2)	23	477
Can speak with authority (A3)	57	443
Team work		
Can be a peacemaker (T1)	422	78
Listen to both sides (T2)	360	140
Gender	245 (Male = 0)	255 (Female = 1)

Roets Rating Scale for Leadership

The self-reporting assessment leadership scale, called the Roets Rating Scale for Leadership, is intended to measure leadership, confidence, ambition, desire and team work (Roets, 1997). In this study the data set contains a sample of 500 prospective leaders' responses to thirteen questions. The responses were given on a binary scale, either 'not very often like me' (0) or that is 'quite often like me' (1), for each of the questions. In Chapter 5 we analyse the latent factor structure of this study and reveal that there are four main themed categories. These categories are confidence (C1, C2, C3, C4), leadership (L1, L2, L3, L4), ambition and desire (A1, A2, A3) and team work (T1, T2). Analysis of this data is also explored in Chapter 8 when looking at item response theory. The responses to all thirteen questions are shown in Table 1.3.

Aspirations to attend university

In Chapter 6 we consider students' aspirations to attend university using logistic regression. Research in the area of students' aspirations has found that there are a number of factors that need to be considered when

■ ■ ■ ■ INTRODUCTION

Table 1.4 Responses to the students' aspirations study

	Least like me (1)	A little like me (2)	Very much like me (3)	Most like me (4)
I work hard at school (Workhard)	18	46	140	296
Workhard1	454 (=0)	46 (=1)		
Workhard2	360 (=0)	140 (=1)		
Workhard3	204 (=0)	296 (=1)		
My friends think that doing well at school is important (Doingwell)	12	16	88	384
Doingwell1	484 (=0)	16 (=1)		
Doingwell2	412 (=0)	88 (=1)		
Doingwell3	116 (=0)	384 (=1)		
Family members do not feel that school is very important (Schoolimport)	279	65	82	74
Schoolimport1	418 (=0)	82 (=1)		
Schoolimport2	435 (=0)	65 (=1)		
Schoolimport3	221 (=0)	279 (=1)		
Gender				
Education aspiration to go to University	135 (=0)	365 (=1)		
English	Mean = 50.974	SD = 14.189		

investigating aspirations. The aspirations of 500 children are analysed. The independent variables considered are attitudes to work at school (Workhard), peer aspirations (Doingwell), family attitudes (Schoolimport), English academic attainment (English) and gender. Research has shown that all of these factors significantly influence student aspirations to attend university (Pottorff et al., 1996; Trusty et al., 2000; Chenoweth, 2003; Khoo and Ainley, 2005; Strand and Winston, 2008; Archer et al., 2014; David-Kacso et al., 2014)

Food insecurity

This data set is used in Chapter 6 to illustrate how logistic regression can be used in more complex cases of analysis. The data set contains 500 children's responses to a mood questionnaire and a hunger scale. These are explored to illustrate the relationships between hunger and its effect on children's

INTRODUCTION

Table 1.5 Responses to food insecurity study

	I do not feel like this (1)	Undecided (2)	I feel like this (3)
Energetic	96	188	216
Enthusiastic	159	148	193
Tired	304	152	44
Drowsy	42	200	258
Worried	237	93	170
Stressed	122	118	260
Calm	56	41	403
Quiet	192	217	91
Hungry Scale	143 (=0)	218 (=1)	139 (=2)
Hunger	Mean= 5.096	SD = 3.502	

moods. The study uses data from a modified eight-item version of the mood checklist. This questionnaire is split into the four latent components of energy, tiredness, tension, and calmness with each of these components being subdivided into two mood items as follows:

- Energy – energetic and enthusiastic;
- Tiredness – tired and drowsy;
- Tensions – worried and stressed;
- Calmness – calm and quiet.

A number of research studies have been carried out in this area to investigate children's breakfast consumption and its effects on their mood once they arrive at school (Thayer, 1989; Cromer et al., 1990; Kanarek, 1997; Siega-Riz et al., 1998; Dwyer et al., 2001; Mahoney et al., 2005; Pearson et al., 2009).

Organic foods

This study investigates 500 consumers' knowledge of organic food products. This data set is used in Chapter 7 and 8. Consumers are asked questions related to their knowledge of organic foods, how often they bought organic food, price, quality, health benefits, food attributes and socio-demographics (gender, age, education level and income). The variables used in the study have been shown to be important factors in determining consumer food choices (Huang, 1996; Verhoef, 2005; Yiridoe et al., 2005; Tsakiridou et al., 2006).

■ ■ ■ ■ **INTRODUCTION**

■ **Table 1.6** Responses to the organic foods study

	Otherwise (0)	(1) if the consumer feels that		
Organic food products are beneficial for your health (Health)	127	373		
Organic food products are higher quality than other similar products (Quality)	259	241		
Taste is important in their organic food purchase (Taste)	137	363		
Appearance is important in their organic food purchase (Appearance)	387	113		
They were knowledgeable about organic food (Knowledge)	139	361		
Their organic food purchase is beneficial to the environment (Environ)	397	103		
Price is important in their organic food purchase (Price)	82	418		
Choice	If they do not buy organic food (0)	If they buy at least some organic food (1)	If the consumer buys organic food on a regular basis (2)	
	56	248	196	
If the consumer earns more than an average yearly wage (Income)	256 (=0)	244 (=1)		
If the consumer has completed higher studies (Higheduc)	345 (=0)	155 (=1)		
If the consumer who answered the questionnaire was female (Female)	259 (=0)	241 (=1)		
1 if under 21 years of age;	(2) if reported to be 21 and up to 25 years	(3) if 25 and up to 40	(4) if 40 and up to 55	(5) if 55 and over
194	101	91	55	59

13 ■

INTRODUCTION

School choice in the global south

Recent research has revealed that in many sub-Saharan African countries a range of school management types exist and are offering educational choices to all parents, including the very poor living in informal settlements (Dixon and Humble, 2017; Humble and Dixon, 2017). The 500 parents in this study state their school choice preference for government, faith-based or community schools. The data in this study also contains information on the household's socio-economic background. The analysis of this data is explored in Chapter 7.

Table 1.7 Responses to the school choice study

Parents preferences	Not important (0)	Important (1)
Affordability	375	125
Strong discipline	260	240
Safe and close to home	317	183
School reputation	150	350
Academic performance	169	331
Quality of teaching	109	391
Wealth indicators	No (=0)	Yes (=1)
TV	379	121
Generator	392	108
DVD player	425	75
Laptop or computer	473	27
Car	484	16
Motorbike	478	22
Smart phone	485	15
Fridge	494	6
Gas stove	496	4
Freezer	490	10
Family income	Less than the mean LRD 6943 (£59.85)= 0	Greater than the mean LRD 6942 (£59.85)= 1
	201	299
Family expenditure	Less than the mean of LRD 4829 (£41.63)= 0	Greater than the mean of LRD 4829 (£41.63)= 1
	367	133
Family education	No education or primary level only (0)	Above primary level (1)

■ ■ ■ ■ **INTRODUCTION**

Parents preferences	Not important (0)	Important (1)	
	221	279	
Occupation	Unemployed (0)	Employed (1)	
	124	376	
Gender	228 (boy=0)	272 (girl=1)	
Child's age	Mean=10.22	SD=3.328	
Number of children in the family	Mean=3.232	SD=2.235	
School choice	Government (0)	Faith-Based Mission (1)	Community (2)
	272	106	122

Transportation on the commute to work

This study investigates a group of 500 commuters' revealed preferences around transportation on the commute to work. The choice given in this study was between a city center bus and underground rail transport system. The study also asked what were the important reasons why the commuters make the decision to travel to work using either the bus or underground system. Rating these choices on a five point Likert scale around how important it was to them that the transport was affordable, reliable, clean and safe. The data set also contains questions related to whether the chosen service was not over-crowded and that there was a bus stop or rail station close to their home. The analysis of this data is explored in Chapter 7.

Intrinsic motivation

The study on intrinsic motivation is used in Chapter 8 to compare the structural differences between four and two point item Likert scales. Intrinsic motivation arises when a person feels both self-determined and knowledgeable to pursue an area of interest, when feeling both challenged by the task but also looking forward to the work (de Charms, 1968; Barron, 1969; Zuckerman, 1979; Renzulli, 1986, 2012; Hennessey and Amabile, 1998). The enjoyment and challenge intrinsic motivation items in the 500 data set are taken from the Work Preference Inventory (WPI) created by Amabile et al. (1994).

In the next section we consider the issues that can occur with missing data and possible approaches that are available in SPSS and Stata packages to deal with this.

INTRODUCTION

Table 1.8 Responses to the transportation study

	Unimportant (0)	Slightly unimportant (1)	Neither (2)	Slightly important (3)	Important (4)
Cost affordability (Cost)	69	66	80	134	151
Service frequency and reliability (Reliable)	99	62	59	23	257
Level of overcrowding on the service (Crowding)	116	109	99	93	83
Cleanliness and maintenance of service (Clean)	108	110	95	88	99
Safety on board (Safety)	94	90	102	74	140
Availability of bus stop/rail station near home (Available)	155	88	76	79	102
Choice	Rail (0) 214	Bus (1) 286			

MISSING DATA

Cases will not be included where there are missing data on a variable that is being analysed in SPSS and Stata. Only existing data are analysed. When analysing multiple variables a respondent's data will be completely removed automatically if it contains any missing values. This is performed by one of two methods, both assume missing completely at random (MCAR). This absolute exclusion is called 'listwise'. In some extreme cases it can result in the loss of a considerable proportion of the original data, as the analysis will only be performed on respondent's data that are complete. Some statistical procedures allow the 'listwise' setting to be changed to 'pairwise'. The pairwise setting only excludes the variables for an individual respondent that include missing cases. In this setting all of the other variables for this respondent are still used. There are benefits to this approach as it allows for more of the data to be analysed and it has been shown that in fairly unbiased large samples to produce consistent parameter estimates. However 'pairwise' can be problematic as specific statistical routines may use different subsets of data and hence the reason why 'listwise' is set as the default (Allison, 2002; Schafer and Graham, 2002; Brown, 2006).

Table 1.9 Responses to the intrinsic motivation study

	Almost never true of you (1)	Sometimes true of you (2)	Often true of you (3)	Always true of you (4)
Challenge 1: The more difficult the problem, the more I enjoy trying to solve it. (Chal1)	57	111	127	205
Challenge 2: I enjoy tackling problems that are completely new to me. (Chal2)	104	110	124	162
Challenge 3: I prefer work I know I can do well over work that stretches my abilities. (Chal3)	111	123	140	126
Challenge 4: I enjoy trying to solve complex problems. (Chal4)	10	73	101	316
Enjoyment 1: I prefer to figure things out for myself. (Enj1)	17	31	113	339
Enjoyment 2: Curiosity is the driving force behind much of what I do. (Enj2)	50	131	163	156
Enjoyment 3: It is important for me to be able to do what I most enjoy. (Enj3)	37	56	122	285
Enjoyment 4: I want my work to provide me with opportunities for increasing my knowledge and skill. (Enj4)	78	97	111	214

(Continued)

Table 1.9 *(Continued)*

	Not true of you (0)	True of you (1)
Challenge 1: The more difficult the problem, the more I enjoy trying to solve it. (Bch1)	168	332
Challenge 2: I enjoy tackling problems that are completely new to me. (Bch2)	214	286
Challenge 3: I prefer work I know I can do well over work that stretches my abilities. (Bch3)	234	266
Challenge 4: I enjoy trying to solve complex problems. (Bch4)	83	417
Enjoyment 1: I prefer to figure things out for myself. (BEj1)	48	452
Enjoyment 2: Curiosity is the driving force behind much of what I do. (BEj2)	181	319
Enjoyment 3: It is important for me to be able to do what I most enjoy. (BEj3)	93	407
Enjoyment 4: I want my work to provide me with opportunities for increasing my knowledge and skill. (BEj4)	175	325
Gender	303 (Boys=0)	197 (Girls=1)

■ ■ ■ ■ INTRODUCTION

Alternatively, there is a range of techniques that allow the researcher to replace missing data. These techniques vary from very simple routines using the mean value of the variable to sophisticated multiple imputation methods.

Missing values can be replaced with a mean, median, mode or linear interpolation that relates to the particular variable or set of variables for a particular participant. The simplest method is to replace missing values with the mean (or median or mode) of that variable. Alternatively, and if appropriate to your data, a linear interpolation method replaces missing values by using the values before and after the missing numbers to create a straight line approximation. The issue with all of these techniques is that they alter the true standard deviation. For example in the case of using mean values to replace missing data this has a tendency to reduce the spread of values for that particular variable.

When a small number of missing values are replaced for non-systematic omissions then future analysis estimates can be made with relative accuracy. As the number of missing values grows there is a greater tendency towards reducing standard errors in future analysis and hence this 'missing' added data can cause spurious significant results (Roderick et al., 1995).

A more sophisticated method that deals with missing data is multiple imputation. The underlying assumption of this technique is that the missing data are 'Missing at Random' (MAR). Note that the MARs assumption assumes that the missing values depend on the observed (collected) and not the unobserved data. Imputation works by creating a number of different possible solution sets through probability predictions of the missing data. These solution data sets are analysed individually and results are then combined to produce a summary estimate for the model. In Appendix 1 an example is given to demonstrate how multiple imputation is performed.

Great care should be taken when 'filling in gaps' in data without the help of the participant who initially answered the survey, as replacing missing data can cause bias. Even when using multiple imputation techniques the recommendation is that they should be used when there is only a small amount of missing data and that the assumption of 'missing at random' is met. The best advice is on the day to collect as much data as you can and double check to make sure participants in your survey have answered all the questions they can (or are willing to do so). Once data collection has finished going back and filling in the gaps may not only be difficult but can also cause statistical inference problems for the future (Roderick et al., 1995).

NOTES

1 Note that SPSS normalize Kurtosis to a value of 0, not 3. This is called *excess* Kurtosis.

CHAPTER 2

STATISTICAL SIGNIFICANCE AND CONTINGENCY TABLES

STATISTICAL SIGNIFICANCE

When you start looking at quantitative methods and statistical techniques you will hear the words 'p-values', '5% significance' and '0.05 values'. It is important that you have an understanding of these terms, as this will help you to interpret outputs from SPSS and Stata.

A p-value is a probability value. A probability value can range from 0 to 1. When a statistical package gives you a result it will give a p-value significance related to the evidence of the data analysed. In statistical tests the most common cut-off point for statistical significance is at the 5% (0.05) level p-value. This implies that if you get a result that has less than 5% significance then the effect you are looking for exits in your data. Greater than this 5% significance then the effect you are looking for cannot be detected.

You may ask why 5%? A p-value with a level of significance of 0.05 is another way for example of saying that in 19 out of 20 cases (19/20 = 0.95) our result would be supported. The 5% p-value significant level means that you are 95% (0.95) confident in whatever question you are asking is true. This probability is based on an assumption that only 5% of the time you would be making an error by assuming that this is true.

If as a researcher you want greater reassurance than the 5% level then you could set your significance level lower and accept results at the 1% (0.01) level. At the 1% level 99 cases in 100 are true and we are 99% sure you have reached the correct decision. Similarly, just as a p-value of 0.01 significance means that you are 99% confident, then a p-value of 0.001 suggests we are 99.9% confident in whatever question we are asking is true.

Let's consider an example. If your research question looks at the difference between two means in your data, for example marathon running

■ ■ ■ ■ SIGNIFICANCE AND CONTINGENCY TABLES

times for men and women, you may wish to know if the mean times are statistically significantly different. If you carry out an independent sample t-test and the result provides a p-value of 0.05 then you are 95% confident that there is a difference between the means for men and women's race times. The confidence level can be increased as suggested above to 99% and 99.9%. The p-value would then need to be less than 0.01 or 0.001. In statistics we can never be 100% certain but can obtain levels of confidence and therefore an understanding around the likelihood of situations occurring.

We now move on to explore the use of contingency tables. Contingency tables are a useful tool in allowing the researcher to become familiar with their data. In SPSS contingency tables are called 'crosstabs' and in Stata 'two-way tables'.

CONTINGENCY TABLES

Contingency means dependence. You will be familiar with the phase 'planning for all contingences' meaning that you would have a plan on how to react depending on a range of different outcomes.

To look at how contingency tables can be used to help gain a greater understanding of data this chapter will explore a social science research student's study on the drinking habits of customers in coffee shops.

A researcher collected data around consumer drinking habits. The data were collected on three different days of the week – Monday, Wednesday and Friday. The researcher used an explanatory sequential mixed methods research design, firstly, by collecting quantitative data to help inform their qualitative data collection (Ivankova et al., 2006; Creswell and Plano Clark, 2011). Collecting data through a mixed methods approach can help the researcher to examine their data to a higher level of detail and triangulate it for the phenomenon to be explored from different vantage points (Cohen and Manion, 2000; Creswell, 2002; Johnson et al., 2007).

There are great advantages to collecting your own data. These include your own personal connection with respondents and the subtle nuances you gain during the process. An example of this is recounted here when the researcher was gathering data around people's coffee-drinking habits. During the collection of this data the researcher felt that the coffee-drinking habits of the consumers were different for men and women. In total 500 consumers were asked about their coffee-drinking habits, with 51.6% being males (n=258) and 48.4% females (n=242). A contingency table can be a useful tool for a researcher to explore the question of gender differences. The researcher in this specific study asked the following question – 'are males more likely to drink certain types of coffee drinks?'

The researcher classified the coffee drinks offered by the shop into two categories. The first group defined as drinking Americano, latte and

SIGNIFICANCE AND CONTINGENCY TABLES

Table 2.1 Contingency table: Monday coffee consumers

Coffee	Gender		Total
	Male	Female	
No	55	72	127
Yes	203	170	373
Total	258	242	500

espresso with the second group being all other types of coffee drinks. Table 2.1 shows the number of people who drank Americano, latte and espresso (yes = 373, 74.6%) and those who drank other coffees, i.e., not Americano, latte or espresso (no = 127, 25.4%). The survey data in the contingency table (Table 2.1) shows the output from the statistical package.

It looks from the contingency table that it could be true that males are more likely to drink certain types of coffee on a Monday. Yet we cannot be sure as the values for males and females are similar in each category. From Table 2.1 it can be seen that there are 203 males and 170 females reporting that they are in the category that drink Americano, latte and espresso. But there are more males in the sample. The researcher needs to think is this bias being caused by more males choosing this category or is it merely that there are more males in the sample.

To explore this question we will look at expected values. Statistical packages calculate these expected values automatically. However, to give a greater understanding of where these values come from we will undertake this calculation by hand. We know that in 373 cases out of the 500 (373/500 = 0.746) the consumers are saying that they would drink Americano, latte or expresso on a Monday. So that's 74.6% of the whole sample. In Table 2.2 these numbers have been shaded.

The number of people in this sample who are male is 258 out of 500, which gives a percentage 51.6% (shaded numbers in Table 2.3).

Therefore the expected number out of this sample, that drink Americano, latte and espresso and are male is 74.6% of 51.6% this is around 38.5% of the 500.

Table 2.2 Gender responses to drinking coffee on Monday

Coffee	Gender		Total
	Male	Female	
No	55	72	127
Yes	203	170	373
Total	258	242	500

■ ■ ■ ■ SIGNIFICANCE AND CONTINGENCY TABLES

Table 2.3 Male responses to drinking coffee on Monday

Coffee	Gender		Total
	Male	Female	
No	55	72	127
Yes	203	170	373
Total	258	242	500

Table 2.4 Male and yes to drinking coffee on Monday

Coffee	Gender		Total
	Male	Female	
No	55	72	127
Yes	203	170	373
Total	258	242	500

Table 2.5 Coffee consumers observed and expected on Monday

Coffee	Gender		Total
	Male	Female	
Observed who say 'no'	55	72	127
Expected numbers for 'no'	65.5	61.5	127.0
Observed who say 'yes'	203	170	373
Expected numbers for 'yes'	192.5	180.5	373.0
Total	258	242	500

Chi-square(1) = 4.688, p=0.030. Cramer's V=0.097 with p=0.030.

This gives the expected number of male coffee drinkers as 192.5 (38.5% of 500). This is shown shaded in Table 2.5 at the intersection of the row and column.

Table 2.5 contains the expected values for all the different outcomes. In the contingency table, Table 2.5, there is a difference between the expected values and the values we have observed during our data collection. You can see from the table that the difference is about 10 in every case. The question we need to ask is 'Is this difference enough to be significant or is it merely fluctuations in the data?'

Remember that this researcher collected data on three days of the week. Tables 2.6 and 2.7 show the expected and observed data for Wednesday and Friday. By looking at each of the days it can be decided on which day

SIGNIFICANCE AND CONTINGENCY TABLES

Table 2.6 Coffee consumers observed and expected on Wednesday

Coffee	Gender		Total
	Male	Female	
Observed who say 'no'	208	203	411
Expected numbers for 'no'	212.1	198.9	411.0
Observed who say 'yes'	50	39	89
Expected numbers for 'yes'	45.9	43.1	89.0
Total	258	242	500

Chi-square(1) = 0.909, p=0.340. Cramer's V=0.043 with p=0.340.

Table 2.7 Coffee consumers observed and expected on Friday

Coffee	Gender		Total
	Male	Female	
Observed who say 'no'	105	154	259
Expected numbers for 'no'	133.6	125.4	259.0
Observed who say 'yes'	153	88	241
Expected numbers for 'yes'	124.4	116.6	241.0
Total	258	242	500

Chi-square(1)= 26.316, p=0.001. Cramer's V=0.229 with p=0.001.

the difference between observed and expected values is greatest and hence most significant.

Tables 2.6 and 2.7 range from no differences in males and females tastes around different coffee choices to highly significant differences. These differences can been seen by looking at the numbers with Wednesday's results showing only small differences, less than 5 in cell values between expected and observed. Monday's results, as we have already said has differences of around 10. Then finally the Friday data has differences of around 20 in each cell between expected and observed. The 'by hand' calculations therefore provide some indication that Friday's coffee choices for men and women are more statistically different than Monday or Wednesday. Also Monday's coffee choices for men and women are more statistically different than Wednesday. Now you have got to know your data a bit better what you'd like to know is, are these difference statistically significant?

In statistical terms we can assess the relative significant of these three sets of data by using a Chi-square test. Running a Chi-square test produces the results reported under each table. The Chi-square test looks at the square of the differences in each of the cells to determine the level of significance.

■ ■ ■ ■ SIGNIFICANCE AND CONTINGENCY TABLES

A result of zero shows that there is no significant difference between the expected and observed values. As the resulting value from the Chi-square test increases then this implies greater differences.

Carrying out a Chi-square test for Monday gives a value of 4.688 with a p-value of 0.030, for Wednesday a Chi-square value of 0.909 and a p-value of 0.340 and finally for Friday a Chi-square value of 26.316 with a p-value of 0.001.

If we assume significant difference is measured by the p-value of 0.05 then the choices of coffee for males and females on a Monday and Friday are showing a significant difference between expected and observed observations. Monday's data shows significance with a p-value of 0.03 indicating that there is a greater likelihood that males are drinking Americano, latte and espresso than females. This test significance implies you would expect that 97% of the time of being confident with the result. Friday's data has a p-value of 0.001, giving the researcher 99.9% confidence in assuming that males are more likely to choose Americanos, lattes and espressos than females on a Friday.

The Chi-square test is said to be distribution free and is called a non-parametric test. A non-parametric test does not rely on assumptions being made about the population. Alternatively parametric tests involve the use of parameters such as the population mean, population proportion and variance. If we assume that the population is normally distributed then parameters will dictate that 95% of the population should lie in a range of values, 1.96 standard deviations above and below the mean value. In contrast non-parametric test such as the Chi-square test, considerations around whether the data fits a normal distribution are not necessary. If the reader is interested in finding out more about distributional issues these are explored in greater depth in Appendix 2.

This preliminary data exploration using contingency tables has shown three different levels of confidence. In the next section we will look further at Chi-square testing and explore levels of significance.

Issues around Chi-square tests

Chi-square tests are one of the most widely used significance tests, yet the user needs to apply these tests with caution. In the case of 2 by 2 contingency tables that we have explored the user should additionally check to see if the patterns being tested are in agreement with the results obtained. Many statisticians are critical of using these methods for larger than 2 by 2 tables. The increase in cells can sometimes result in false positive results. This kind of result is what is called a Type I error by statistician's, due to the fact that we are rejecting that there is no difference between the groups (Owen and Jones, 1982).

Another issue with a Chi-square test is its dependency on the size of the sample. The reason for this is that the more cells in your contingency table the more differences you are calculating and therefore inherently the larger your Chi-square value will become. In order to avoid issues around false

SIGNIFICANCE AND CONTINGENCY TABLES ▓ ▓ ▓ ■

results there are various checks you can perform. One of these tests is called Cramer's V and it is one of the most helpful measures to use as the number of cells increases in a contingency table.

A Cramer's V test can take values in the range from 0 to 1. A value of zero means that there is no association and a value of one implies perfect association. Cramer's V also gives an indication of the size of the effect of this association. In the coffee example considered in the section above the Cramer's V value of 0.229 for Friday's data represents a weak association to whether males are more likely to drink Americanos, lattes and espressos in coffee shops than females. This result is therefore suggesting that yes there is a significant difference in gender drinking habits but its effect size is relatively small. This result could be implied from Friday's contingency table, as the differences between observed and expected are not large. When assessing Cramer's V results the following interpretations should be applied:

0.00 up to but not including 0.10 – no association
0.10 up to but not including 0.30 – weak association
0.30 up to but not including 0.60 – moderate association
0.60 to 1.00 – strong association

Apart from using the Cramer's V to help interpret effect size it is common with discrete categorical data to use odds ratios. Odds ratios give a clear way of interpreting data in terms of likelihood ratios.

Odds ratios

Using the data on consumer's coffee-drinking habits on Wednesday we will explore in this final section of the chapter odds ratios. This section will demonstrate how odds ratios can be used with contingency tables, to find the likelihood of male coffee consumers being more likely to drink Americano, latte and espresso than females.

Taking the initial data from the Wednesday's consumer coffee-drinking habits we can calculate the following odds ratios. As in the previous example we are going to carry this out by hand to provide a greater understanding of where the numbers originate. There are three steps involved in calculating an odds ratio.

First the odds ratio of the number of males that drink certain types of coffee in relation to females who drink certain types of coffee:

= number males that drink/number of females who did
= 203/170 = 1.19

Second, the odds of the number of males that did not drink these types of coffee divided by the number of females who did not:

= number males that did not drink/number of females who did not
= 55/72 = 0.76

■ ■ ■ ■ SIGNIFICANCE AND CONTINGENCY TABLES

Third, we can calculate the odds ratio of males drinking certain types of coffee to drinking other types from the two figures generated above:

= 1.19/0.76
= 1.57

This result implies that male coffee consumers are 1.57 times more likely to drink Americano, latte and espresso than a female.

Next if we turn our attention to Friday's data, this has a higher Cramer's V (0.229) than Monday or Wednesday, suggesting a stronger statistical effect size than on the other two days. This would imply that we would expect a larger odds ratio associated with Friday than the one obtained for Wednesday.

Again there are three steps as for Wednesday's data. First, calculating the odds ratio for the number of males that drink Americano, latte and espresso to females who drank the same:

= number males/number of females
= 153/88 = 1.74

Second, the odds ratio for the number of males that did not drink Americano, latte and espresso divided by the number of females who also did not

= number males that did not/number of females who did not
= 105/154 = 0.68

Third, the odds ratio of males drinking Americano, latte and espresso to females using the two figures generated:

= 1.74/0.68
= 2.56

As anticipated the odds ratio is greater, implying that males are 2.56 times more likely to drink Americano, latte and espresso than females on a Friday.

In this chapter we looked at contingency tables and Chi-square tests when analysing associations between binary data. We also considered Cramer's V and its use as a check and a helpful measure for assessing the associations in a contingency table. Later in the book we will revisit contingency tables and odds ratios to explore in greater detail how they are useful in critically evaluating data before more rigorous analysis is performed. Contingency tables are presented in the chapters on logistic regression and discrete choice theory.

HOW TO REPORT CONTINGENCY TABLES

The data around coffee drinking presented under each of the day's data took the form:

Chi-square(1) = 26.316, p = 0.001. Cramer's V = 0.229 with p = 0.001.

Alternatively this can be written using the Chi-square symbol and p-value inequalities and thus a more concise and mathematical notation:

$\chi^2(1) = 26.316$, $p < 0.001$. Cramer's V = 0.229, $p < 0.001$

SIGNIFICANCE AND CONTINGENCY TABLES

Or

$P[\chi^2(1) = 26.316] < 0.001$. Cramer's V = 0.229, p<0.001

In this notation the '1' in the Chi-square bracket $\chi^2(1)$ is the degrees of freedom (df).

Calculating contingency tables with Stata and SPSS

For SPSS, select *Analyze – Descriptive Statistics – Crosstabs*. Then select the row and column variables to be analysed. The *cell* window gives options for cell statistics and the *statistics* window shows test statistics.

For Stata, select *Statistics – Summaries, tables and tests – Frequency tables – Two-way tables with measures of association*. In the drop down boxes the user needs to select the row and column variables. The window to the left side shows test statistics and the right side the cell statistics.

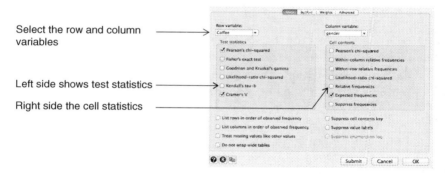

Figure 2.1 Stata two-way contingency table

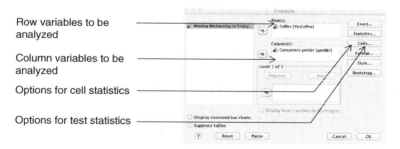

Figure 2.2 SPSS crosstabs contingency table

■ ■ ■ ■ SIGNIFICANCE AND CONTINGENCY TABLES

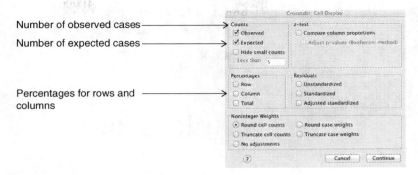

Figure 2.3 SPSS cell statistics

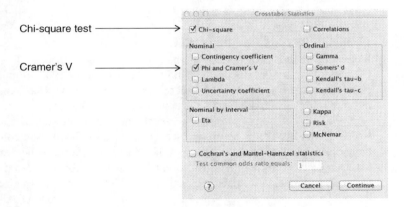

Figure 2.4 SPSS crosstabs statistics

CHAPTER 3

FACTOR ANALYSIS

Exploratory

In social science research it is often necessary to ascertain how a measured collection of factors have some common single variable affect. These are typically known as latent variables. A latent variable is inferred from observed variables in the data set.

One of the main ways to obtain rich data is by using a Likert scale. Interestingly the Likert scale is named after Rensis Likert a social psychologist who developed the 5-point Likert scale in 1932 to measure people's attitudes in behavioral research as part of his PhD. Data obtained through Likert scales are discrete, categorical and ordinal.

The number of responses for Likert scale questions can vary. The Likert scale is considered to be an ordinal scale as the person is asked to consider their answer to a question from one of the ordered categories. The distance between each response in the item for a Likert scale is not considered to be always equal. Each of the Likert questions is called an item. With a group of items measuring a construct(s) that cannot be directly measured. A five point Likert scale could be for example 5=strongly agree, 4=agree, 3=undecided, 2=disagree, 1=strongly disagree.

Factor analysis, both exploratory and confirmatory, allows you to identify groups or clusters of variables and understand the structure of these variables in questionnaires including Likert scales. Before we explore the detailed structures of such questionnaires using factor analysis let's consider a basic technique first.

A numerical addition of Likert scores in the questionnaire gives the researcher a rank order. This will help to give us an understanding of the data in a similar way to which we started exploring contingency tables in the last chapter.

When performing this calculation a researcher would use the numerical coded values to create the total. With positively worded items being scored directly and negatively worded items recorded in a reverse scale. To see what this means let's take the case of 5=strongly agree, 4=agree, 3=undecided, 2=disagree, 1=strongly disagree as shown in Table 3.1.

To illustrate how this would be performed we will use three questions from the happiness data study. In future chapters the whole of this study will be explored using a range of statistical techniques.

FACTOR ANALYSIS: EXPLORATORY

Table 3.1 Simplistic Likert scale scoring

	Strongly disagree (1)	Disagree (2)	Neutral (3)	Agree (4)	Strongly agree (5)
a) I feel that life is very rewarding.	☐	☐	☐	x	☐
b) I feel able to take anything on.	x	☐	☐	☐	☐
c) I feel that I am not especially in control of my life (R).	☐	☐	☐	x	☐

Note that the first two questions in Table 3.1 are positively worded and the third is negatively worded. If a person responded (a) 4; (b) 1; (c) 4 then their total score would be 4+1+2 = 7. Note that question (c) has been reversed scored from 4 to 2. When analysing Likert scale questions it can be difficult to interpret what the statistics are actually inferring about the responses. It is often advised that the median measure should be used for Likert scale data as opposed to calculating a mean value or as we have done here summing the total item scores.

Simplistic numerical addition of Likert scale questionnaires as we have just described does NOT reveal the underlying structure or themes within the data. This type of analysis would give you a rank order of the responses to this part of the questionnaire.

This chapter around factor analysis will enable you as a researcher to explore Likert scale data from a more sophisticated statistical standpoint and hence being able to unlock a greater wealth of information.

EXPLORATORY FACTOR ANALYSIS

Exploratory factor analysis (EFA) is the name given to a range of statistical techniques to evaluate the dimensionality of items in a questionnaire. The item responses could range from 'strongly disagree' to 'strongly agree'. Exploratory factor analysis explores and uncovers the smallest number of underlying constructs (called latent structures) in a questionnaire. Exploratory factor analysis is an 'exploratory' tool as no priori restrictions are put on the relationship found between the observed measures and the resulting latent variables. With confirmatory factor analysis the number of factors and their structure is specified in advance (see Chapter 5). This is the key difference between exploratory factor analysis and confirmatory factor analysis (CFA). Exploratory factor analysis is sometimes used as a precursor to confirmatory factor analysis. The estimates from exploratory factor analysis can be 'confirmed' in confirmatory factor analysis through detailed statistical evaluation (Dixon et al., 2016).

FACTOR ANALYSIS: EXPLORATORY ▪ ▪ ▪ ■

Factor extraction methods

Factor analysis is used to uncover the underlying constructs and identify associated items. The constructs can be thought of as themes contained in the questionnaire (Conway and Huffcutt, 2003). In this section we will explore how two types of exploratory factor analysis – principal factor (principal axis factoring in SPSS) and maximum likelihood – are used to identify latent factors created by a set of measured items.

Maximum likelihood (ML) is a method to find latent factors, which have the highest likelihood value of giving the best overall fit to the data. Its main advantage is that it allows for a detailed statistical evaluation of the factor solution. However maximum likelihood estimation requires the assumption of multivariate normality. Care needs to be taken when using maximum likelihood as it can produce improper solutions. An improper solution is when the factor model does not converge to give a final set of estimates or it produces an out of range estimate with indicators greater than 1.0.

Principal factor analysis (PF) has the advantage of having no distribution assumptions. If your data is markedly non-normal then principal factor analysis might be a preferred option. However, unlike a maximum likelihood estimation, principal factor analysis does not provide detailed statistical fit indices that are important if you are considering in the future performing confirmatory factor analysis.

DISCOVERING LATENT FACTORS

When carrying out factor analysis certain elements need to be considered in order to decide whether factor analysis is suited to your data. Being able to interpret the results given in the tables generated through statistical packages allows you to be confident that the analysis you are performing are providing meaningful results. The sections that follow take you through that interpretation to make and inform the decisions required.

Communality

There are a number of checks than can be made to see if variables should be included in the analysis. The first looks to see if variables share enough in common with each other. The total variance for individual items can be viewed as having two parts. One aspect being the amount of variance it shares with other items. This is called the common variance and the other aspect is its own unique variance. The proportion of common variance in an item is called communality.

To explore communality we will use the data that were developed by taking items from the Oxford happiness questionnaire (Argyle and Hills, 2002). Table 3.2 shows the ten items used in this data set taken from the original 29. Table 3.3 shows the five hundred responses provided to the questions around happiness. Looking at the figures it would seem that those responding to the questions are relatively happy, but not particularly healthy or in control of

FACTOR ANALYSIS: EXPLORATORY

Table 3.2 Happiness scale

	Strongly disagree (1)	Disagree (2)	Neutral (3)	Agree (4)	Strongly agree (5)
I am very happy.	☐	☐	☐	☐	☐
I laugh a lot.	☐	☐	☐	☐	☐
Life is good.	☐	☐	☐	☐	☐
I feel I have a great deal of energy.	☐	☐	☐	☐	☐
I am always committed and involved.	☐	☐	☐	☐	☐
I feel that life is very rewarding.	☐	☐	☐	☐	☐
I feel able to take anything on.	☐	☐	☐	☐	☐
I feel that I am not especially in control of my life.	☐	☐	☐	☐	☐
I don't feel particularly healthy.	☐	☐	☐	☐	☐
I don't have particularly happy memories.	☐	☐	☐	☐	☐

their own lives. This is not the whole story, so this is why we use factor analysis to gain a deeper understanding about what our data tells us.

In order to consider communality, initial and extraction values can be explored. These communality values are given in the range from zero to one. A value of zero means that a variable shares none of its variance with any of the other variables and a value of one means that all of the variance that is associated with the variable is common.

When performing exploratory factor analysis the communalities output is generated and provides information about the shared and proportional variance between items. The communalities table, Table 3.4, has two columns labelled 'initial' and 'extraction'. The initial communalities values indicate the amount of variance that is shared by the item and the others in the list. The extraction communalities values give the proportion of the variance that is explained by the extracted factors.

First check the values of the initial communalities to see if any of the items has a value that is much lower than the others. In this data set none of the values vary greatly. Since there is no great difference in the item scores there is no reason to suggest that any of the items should be removed from the analysis. After making these checks on the initial values you should next look at the column labelled 'extraction'. If you look for example at the item

FACTOR ANALYSIS: EXPLORATORY

Table 3.3 Responses to the happiness study

	Strongly disagree (1)	Disagree (2)	Neutral (3)	Agree (4)	Strongly agree (5)
I am very happy.	40	35	40	77	308
I laugh a lot.	29	37	62	88	284
Life is good.	32	31	38	93	306
I feel I have a great deal of energy.	40	39	61	80	280
I am always committed and involved.	79	65	74	85	197
I feel that life is very rewarding.	166	96	78	75	85
I feel able to take anything on.	81	82	116	107	114
I feel that I am not especially in control of my life.	38	54	107	118	183
I don't feel particularly healthy.	50	55	72	120	203
I don't have particularly happy memories.	126	96	120	81	77

Table 3.4 Communalities

Communalities

	Initial	Extraction
I am very happy.	.349	.518
I laugh a lot.	.315	.436
Life is good.	.279	.372
I feel I have a great deal of energy.	.268	.348
I am always committed and involved.	.146	.330
I feel that life is very rewarding.	.075	.172
I feel able to take anything on.	.071	.117
I feel that I am not especially in control of my life.	.130	.300
I don't feel particularly healthy.	.124	.210
I don't have particularly happy memories.	.089	.195

Extraction Method: Principal Axis Factoring.

'I am very happy', this has an extraction communality of 0.518. This means that 51.8% of the variance associated with this item is a shared (common) variance. All the extraction values are larger than the initial values. This then implies that there is more variance explained by each of the individual items.

FACTOR ANALYSIS: EXPLORATORY

Table 3.5 KMO and Bartlett's test

KMO and Bartlett's Test

Kaiser-Meyer-Olkin Measure of Sampling Adequacy		.759
Bartlett's Test of Sphericity	Approx. Chi-square	629.219
	df	45
	Sig.	.000

Tests suitability of factor analysis

Kaiser-Meyer-Olkin (KMO) is generally considered to be the best measure of sampling adequacy for carrying out factor analysis. Output tables can be generated in statistical packages providing you with the KMO measure of sampling adequacy. A value closer to 1 implies that the data set is most appropriate to be analysed using factor analysis giving factors that are robust and useful. A KMO value of 0.5 is considered to be mediocre (and the minimum to carry out factor analysis), values between 0.7 and 0.8 as good, between 0.8 and 0.9 very good and between 0.9 and 1.0 excellent (Kaiser, 1970; Hutcheson and Sofroniou, 1999).

Table 3.5 provides a KMO of 0.759 for the happiness data set, which would imply a good suitability of the data for structure detection. The Bartlett Test of Sphericity is usually given when performing factor analysis to verify whether items correlate. If the test produces a significant result ($p<0.05$) then factor analysis is appropriate because relationships between variables have been detected. The assumption of this test is that the data are normally distributed and if this is not true for your data then the Bartlett results should be used with caution.

Looking at the communality, KMO and Bartlett results factor analysis would be an appropriate statistical technique to use with the happiness data.

How many factors to include

It is not always obvious how many latent variables (factors) should be retained. It can vary due to the particular constructs expected in the research or the level of required simplicity required from the data reduction. As with our data it would not be sensible to reduce the ten items into nine latent variables as this would clearly not achieve our goal of using factor analysis to simplify the problem. Experience plays a part here and you will learn with practice to decide on what is the optimal number of latent variables in different situations. Yet saying this there are guidelines to follow and criteria you can use to help you make an informed decision.

The statistical software gives the table in Table 3.6 showing how much variation is accounted for by each factor. These have the technical name of eigenvalues and are calculated as the sum of all the squared factor loadings

FACTOR ANALYSIS: EXPLORATORY

Table 3.6 Total variance explained

Factor	Total	Initial eigenvalues % of variance	Cumulative %
1	2.608	26.076	26.076
2	1.429	14.290	40.366
3	1.075	10.750	51.116
4	.941	9.411	60.527
5	.814	8.136	68.662
6	.755	7.551	76.213
7	.689	6.891	83.104
8	.636	6.355	89.460
9	.563	5.630	95.089
10	.491	4.911	100.000

for each factor. Eigen in German means 'own' or 'belonging to'. In terms of our context with eigenvalues and eigenvectors this relates to the value and the vector that belong to that particular matrix. If you would like more information concerning factor analysis, eigenvalues and eigenvectors then please see Appendix 3. As with all the information in the appendices this is not necessary to understand and perform the statistical techniques.

As we have ten items in our Happiness questionnaire there are ten eigenvalues in Table 3.6. The eigenvalues for each factor give the variance explained by it. Therefore factor 1 in Table 3.6 explains 26.076% of the total variance. In the table it is clear that the first few eigenvalues explain the large proportion of the variance, with smaller and smaller percentages for subsequent factors.

The default setting in the software for SPSS and Stata is to retain eigenvalues greater than one as those smaller than one explain less variance this is called the Kaiser criterion. It is also good if total percentage of variance explained by the factors with eigenvalues greater than one is larger than 50%. You can see in our particular example this is 51.116%

However as suggested in the introduction to this section the researcher needs to be aware that a factor with an eigenvalue of 1.075 (factor 3 in Table 3.6) is very similar to an eigenvalue of 0.941 (factor 4 in Table 3.6). When selecting a cut-off value use your research questionnaire rationale and decisions around why you are undertaking factor analysis to check that the correct number of latent factors are taken into consideration. Yet as a rule of thumb the Kaiser criterion is a sensible starting point (Kaiser, 1970; Jolliffe, 1986; Stevens, 1992).

To support you in making your decision in the number of factors you retain, it is also useful to look at the scree plot. The scree plot shown in

■■■■ FACTOR ANALYSIS: EXPLORATORY

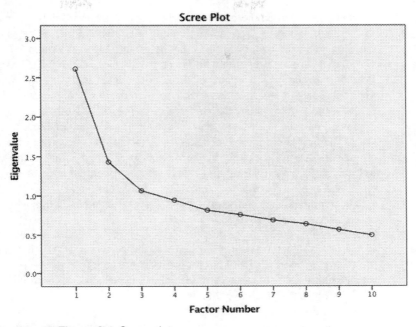

■ **Figure 3.1** Scree plot

Figure 3.1 shows the relative sizes of the eigenvalues for our happiness data. With the scree diagram you are looking to see where the graph loses its steepness. What we mean by steepness in this context is if you look at the left hand side of the graph the line is clearly descending quickly, but at some point around eigenvalue three and four there is a flatting out and a clear change in direction after eigenvalue three.

We will assume that in our particular example we are going to move forward with our three latent variables, as the tests detail above suggest that these offer the best possible solution.

The next section will consider the output that factor analysis gives in relation to the latent factor groupings of the items themes.

Rotation methods

Rotation of factors in factor analysis is an important mathematical procedure in order to help to produce a solution that clarifies its interpretation. The system is rotated until there is a maximized solution of the sum of the variances of the squared loadings. This mathematical procedure called rotation preserves the relationship between individual variables. With our happiness study an oblique rotation technique is more appropriate as we are looking for correlations within factors. The oblique rotation technique called Promax should be used as it allows for the inter-woven correlated structures between items.

FACTOR ANALYSIS: EXPLORATORY

Table 3.7 is called the pattern matrix giving the factor loading for each of the items. These values can be thought of equivalent to the correlations between items and factors, with factors between 1 and -1. In Table 3.7 'I am very happy' has a correlation with factor 1 with a loading of 0.744. As with Pearson correlation the square of these coefficients obtains a measure of the importance of a particular variable to a factor. Hence in this case $0.744^2 = 0.554$ and so we can say as with r^2 values that 55.4% of the variance is explained by this latent factor and 44.6% ($1-0.744^2$) unexplained. In other words the first latent factor accounts for 55.4% of the variance of the item 'I am very happy'. Looking at the next item 'I laugh a lot' in the same first factor, then by squaring this value you can obtain the level of variance explained as 42.25% ($0.650^2 = 0.4225$) by this latent factor.

The happiness data shown in Table 3.7 has three latent factors which we could offer having titles as follows:

- 'happy' (factor 1) with four items; 'I am very happy'; 'I laugh a lot'; 'Life is good'; 'I feel I have a great deal of energy';
- 'positive' (factor 2) with three items; 'I am always committed and involved'; 'I feel that life is very rewarding'; 'I feel able to take anything on';
- 'unhappy' (factor 3) with three items; 'I am not particularly optimistic about the future'; 'I don't have particularly happy memories'; 'I don't feel particularly healthy'.

Table 3.7 Pattern matrix

	Factor 1	Factor 2	Factor 3
I am very happy.	.744		
I laugh a lot.	.650		
Life is good.	.576		
I feel I have a great deal of energy.	.545		
I am always committed and involved.	.317	.473	
I feel that life is very rewarding.		.414	
I feel able to take anything on.		.301	
I feel that I am not especially in control of my life.			.503
I don't feel particularly healthy.			.357
I don't have particularly happy memories.			.334

SPSS output table with extraction method: principal axis factoring. Rotation method: Promax with Kaiser normalization. Only loadings of magnitude above 0.30 are shown

Stata command: factor <variables>, ipf and postestimation of rotate, promax oblique kaiser factors(3) blanks(0.27) gives a similar three factor output.

■ ■ ■ ■ FACTOR ANALYSIS: EXPLORATORY

Exploratory factor analysis produces a solution with the best simple structure maximizing factor loadings close to one and minimizing those close to zero. Loadings greater than or equal to 0.3 are said to be salient, relating meaningfully to a primary or secondary factor (Brown, 2006). According to Guadagnoli and Velicer (1988) a factor with ten item loadings greater than 0.4 is stable for a sample size greater than 150, with Field (2000) suggesting that retained factors should have at least three items with a loading greater than 0.4.

Before we move to look at how we can use exploratory factor analysis as a technique in data reduction let us consider the other factor extraction method that we discussed at the start of this chapter – maximum likelihood (ML).

Maximum likelihood

Research shows that maximum likelihood is robust for small kurtosis values (Chou and Bentler, 1995). As discussed in Chapter 1 skewness and kurtosis values of zero are said to be perfectly normal. Deviations of less than ±1 from zero are considered very good. Values lying outside of this range between ±1 and ±2 considered acceptable (Field, 2000; Trochim and Donnelly, 2006; Muijs, 2010; Gravetter and Wallnau, 2014). Maximum likelihood has been shown to be a very well behaved estimator for non-normal data so long as there are no extreme outliers (Curran et al., 1996). Using these conditions on normality we can check our happiness data. Table 3.8 shows descriptive statistics including the

■ **Table 3.8** Skewness and Kurtosis statistics

	Mean	Std. Deviation	Skewness	Kurtosis
I am very happy.	4.16	1.294	−1.378	.562
I laugh a lot.	4.12	1.224	−1.242	.391
Life is good.	4.22	1.211	−1.509	1.123
I feel I have a great deal of energy.	4.04	1.310	−1.147	.021
I am always committed and involved.	3.51	1.500	−.493	−1.231
I feel that life is very rewarding.	2.63	1.490	.348	−1.321
I feel able to take anything on.	3.18	1.382	−.179	−1.187
I feel that I am not especially in control of my life.	3.71	1.270	−.652	−.650
I don't feel particularly healthy.	3.74	1.352	−.770	−.671
I don't have particularly happy memories.	2.77	1.390	.189	−1.192

FACTOR ANALYSIS: EXPLORATORY

values for skewness and *excess* kurtosis, which mainly fall into the very good and acceptable regions.

This analysis shows that we can have confidence to apply the maximum likelihood extraction when performing exploratory factor analysis. Table 3.9 shows the pattern matrix. Notice that the extraction produces the same three latent factors as found previously using principal axis factoring. The principal axis factoring factors from the first factor analysis are shown in brackets. As well as producing the same latent factors, it can be seen that maximum likelihood extraction method individual item scores are very similar to principal axis factoring. The relative error being small for all items (1-2%), with only the one item 'I feel that I am not especially in control of my life' having a larger relative error of 7%

Table 3.9 Comparison of extraction methods

Pattern Matrix

	Factor 1	Factor 2	Factor 3
I am very happy.	0.753 (0.744)		
I laugh a lot.	0.646 (0.650)		
Life is good.	0.585 (0.576)		
I feel I have a great deal of energy.	0.545 (0.545)		
I feel that I am not especially in control of my life.		0.536 (0.503)	
I don't feel particularly healthy.		0.363 (0.357)	
I don't have particularly happy memories.		0.318 (0.334)	
I am always committed and involved.	0.303 (0.317)		0.466 (0.473)
I feel that life is very rewarding.			0.433 (0.414)
I feel able to take anything on.			0.295 (0.301)

SPSS output in the table with extraction method maximum likelihood. In brackets extraction method is principal axis factoring. Rotation method: Promax with Kaiser normalization.

Stata command: factor <variables>, ml factors(3) blanks(0.29) and postestimation command: rotate, promax oblique kaiser factors(3) detail blanks(0.29) gives a similar three factor output.

■ ■ ■ ■ **FACTOR ANALYSIS: EXPLORATORY**

FACTOR ANALYSIS FOR DATA REDUCTION

Factor analysis can also be used as a data reduction technique. This next section will look at an example of how data reduction can be used with socio-economic factors. This data reduction into a smaller number of more manageable factors allows for greater levels of interpretation.

Principal components analysis (PCA)

The factor extraction technique that is used for data reduction is called principal components analysis. Both exploratory factor analysis and principal components analysis methods are similar as they are both used to examine correlations and covariance's between sets of items. The two methods are often confused due to this similarity.

Principal components analysis accounts for the variance in the observed measures rather than explain the correlations amongst them as with maximum likelihood and principal factor analysis. Principal components analysis reduces a larger set of measured items into a smaller number of composite variables. These composite variables can then be used in subsequent analysis, without any consideration of prior constructs of the underlying structure. As with maximum likelihood and principal factor analysis, principal components analysis takes a purely exploratory approach.

A difference with principal components analysis is that it requires orthogonal rotation technique such as Varimax as the items under investigation are assumed to be unrelated to each other. If this is not the case with your data reduction, and the items are related, then you should as we have seen earlier in the chapter use an oblique rotation such as Promax.

In the following study we will illustrate the use of principal components analysis for data reduction of socio-economic variables. The sample is of 500 households from poor informal settlements in the Global South. The questionnaire in Table 3.10 shows the possible family possessions of these households.

■ **Table 3.10** Socio-economic data

	Yes	No
The family have a generator	☐	☐
The family own a car or jeep	☐	☐
The family have a computer	☐	☐
The family have a gas stove	☐	☐
The family own land	☐	☐
The family have electricity	☐	☐
The family have a television	☐	☐
The family own a radio	☐	☐
The family own a cell/mobile	☐	☐

FACTOR ANALYSIS: EXPLORATORY

Table 3.11 Frequencies for socio-economic data

	Yes	No
The family have a generator	64	436
The family own a car or jeep	169	331
The family have a computer	152	348
The family have a gas stove	146	354
The family own land	159	341
The family have electricity	439	61
The family have a television	433	67
The family own a radio	427	73
The family own a cell/mobile	471	29

Table 3.12 Eigenvalues: socio-economic data

	Initial eigenvalues		
Factor	Total	% of variance	Cumulative %
1	2.281	25.340	25.340
2	1.366	15.175	40.515
3	1.081	12.012	52.527
4	.980	10.887	63.414
5	.824	9.154	72.567
6	.734	8.154	80.721
7	.693	7.696	88.417
8	.643	7.140	95.557
9	.400	4.443	100.000

The questionnaire contains the following responses shown in Table 3.11. It can be seen from this table that there is a clear split with these poor households. A number of the households have electrical devices such as mobile phone, television and radio, with less respondents saying that they have a computer, car, own land or have an electrical generator.

When principal components analysis data reduction is performed it suggests that there could be a three factor solution. This can be seen in Table 3.12 as three of the eigenvalues are greater than one, having values of 2.281, 1.366 and 1.081.

This three factor solution offers the following common themes:

- Factor one is the most affluent households possessing cars, generator, gas stove and computers.

■ ■ ■ ■ FACTOR ANALYSIS: EXPLORATORY

■ Factor 2 being a fairly common factor with television and electricity. As we have seen in the descriptive statistics that 433 have a television and 439 have electricity out of 500.
■ Factor 3, is mobile phone, radio and land. We have seen from the descriptive data that most families have a mobile phone (471 of the 500 households).

This data reduction suggests a scale of the most affluent households to the least being factor 1 to factor 3 respectively.

It can be seen that one of the eigenvalues is close to 1.0 with a value of 1.081 (factor 3 in Table 3.12). In this situation it is always worth checking to see if a lower solution gives a better set of real life factors. Running principal components analysis specifying a fixed number of factors as two yields the results shown in Table 3.14.

Looking at these two latent factors it is possible to define differences between latent factors 1 and 2. This two factor solution seems to generate more common themes than the initial three factor solution obtained by simply allowing the Kaiser criterion of all eigenvalues greater than 1.0 to be factors. Factor 1 suggests a more affluent household who can afford extras in a Global South context such as computer, car and generator. A generator supply for electricity in most Global South countries tends to imply a wealthier household owing to publically supplied electricity having erratic provision, with daily cases of power cuts.

■ **Table 3.13** Three factor rotated PCA solution

Rotated Component Matrix

	Component 1	Component 2	Component 3
The family own a car or jeep	.673		
The family have a generator	.671		
The family have a computer	.655		
The family have a gas stove	.627		
The family have a television		.865	
The family have electricity		.826	
The family own a cell/mobile			.793
The family own a radio			.539
The family own land	.359		.425

SPSS extraction method is principal component analysis. Rotation Method: Varimax with Kaiser Normalization.

Stata command principle component factor: factor <variables>, pcf and postestimation command: rotate, kaiser factors(3)

FACTOR ANALYSIS: EXPLORATORY

Table 3.14 Two factor rotated PCA solution

Rotated Component Matrix

	Component 1	Component 2
The family have a generator	.680	
The family own a car or jeep	.672	
The family have a computer	.654	
The family have a gas stove	.564	
The family own land	.436	
The family have electricity		.855
The family have a television		.818
The family own a radio		.366
The family own a cell/mobile		.362

Extraction Method: Principal Component Analysis. Rotation Method: Varimax with Kaiser Normalization. In Stata use principal-component factor. Stata command principle component factor: factor <variables>, pcf and postestimation command: rotate, kaiser factors(2)

Clearly we can argue the pros and cons of both of these outputs. The decision around which of these you would choose to use for your research as the wealth factors would be based on your understanding of the data and/or your literature review relating to the context you are working in.

CALCULATING AND USING LATENT FACTORS IN FUTURE ANALYSIS

A linear regression example

In later chapters we look at how factor analysis can be used to explore links between variables. To illustrate this with an example we will look to see how the happiness latent factors are affected by socio-economic backgrounds using the data we have created in the examples in this chapter.

In the happiness data one of the latent factors was having a positive attitude to life. The three items in this latent factor are 'I am always committed and involved', 'I feel that life is very rewarding' and 'I feel able to take anything on'. As you can see these suggest a very positive outlook to life. Using this as the dependent variable we can ask the following research question:

Does your socio-economic background affect your commitment attitudes to life?

FACTOR ANALYSIS: EXPLORATORY

Table 3.15 Linear regression for positive happiness

Coefficients

Model		Unstandardized Coefficients		Standardized Coefficients	t	Sig.
		B	Std. Error	Beta		
	(Constant)	1.988E-5	.030		.001	.999
	Wealth 1 richer	.071	.030	.106	2.379	.018
	Wealth 2 poorer	−.005	.030	−.008	−.183	.855

Dependent Variable: Positive happiness

Table 3.15, a linear regression table (regression will be covered in greater detail later in the book), suggests due to the positive significance B-value of 0.071 and associated p-value of 0.018 that if you come from a more affluent household then you have a greater likelihood of having a positive attitude to life.

Calculating the appropriate latent factor score

Having discovered the factor scores for the latent variables it is possible to interpret these results relative to the different individuals who have answered the questionnaire. To demonstrate how this can be done we shall use the three factor scores relating to a 'positive attitude to life' from the happiness questionnaire in the early part of this chapter.

We can write down an equation for this latent factor where the numbers are factor loadings given in Table 3.16 and can be thought of as weightings for the various variables:

Positive = 0.473 x Committed + 0.414 x Rewarding + 0.301 x Anything

From this we can calculate the latent factor scores for each person. If for example a person had given answers to these three items as 2, 4, and 3 in the questionnaire this would result in a factor score of 3.505 for that particular individual. The calculation to obtain this value is:

Positive = 0.473 x (2) + 0.414 x (4) + 0.301 x (3)
= 0.946 + 1.656 + 0.903 = 3.505

Table 3.16 Factor scores: positive attitude to life

Item	Variable name	Factor loading
I am always committed and involved.	Committed	0.473
I feel that life is very rewarding.	Rewarding	0.414
I feel able to take anything on.	Anything	0.301

FACTOR ANALYSIS: EXPLORATORY

This value can be computed by SPSS and Stata, for all the participants in the survey giving the latent variable that can be used in further analysis.

The way we calculate the factor score of 3.505 is called a coarse factor score and created by a non-refined method. This illustrates how to derive a simplistic weighted value of the raw score.

Statistical packages offer the user a range of alternative more sophisticated methods to evaluate the latent factors with greater internal consistency. These are called refined methods. There are three main refined methods used in factor score extraction, Regression, Bartlett and Anderson-Rubin. All three have advantages and the method of choice depends on how the extracted factors are going to be used.

The Regression method (Thurstone, 1935) modifies the factor loadings to compensate for the initial correlations between the variables. In most cases the regression method is the most frequently used method to estimate refined factor scores. With this method the factor scores have a mean of zero. The resulting factor scores correlate not only with the items in the latent factor but also with the items in the other latent factors. These factor scores are standardised to reflect a Z-score metric with the values ranging from -3 to +3 (Brown, 2006).

The Bartlett method, in contrast to the regression method produces factor scores that are only correlated with items within that latent factor. One advantage of Barlett factor scores is that they are most likely to give 'true' factor scores as they are produced using maximum likelihood estimates (Hershberger, 2005).

The third method used to extract factor scores is the Anderson-Rubin. With this method the factor scores are uncorrelated and are standardised to have a mean of zero and standard deviation of one. Then these are often standardised using a T-score which is a shifted Z-score scaled to have a mean of 50 and standard deviation of 10, using a data transformation such as trunc(50 + 10*Fac1_1 + 0.5). If you wish to create factor scores that are uncorrelated for data reduction then the use of Anderson-Rubin method is often preferred (Harman, 1976; Grice, 2001; Tabachnick and Fidell, 2001; Carifio and Perla, 2008; Di Stefano et al., 2009)

MISSING VALUES

Factors score values will only be calculated for items that contain no missing values. If there are any missing item values no factor scores will be produced pertaining to that person's questionnaire category. It is possible to avoid these missing data issues by using one of the many imputation techniques. In an ideal world data imputation would always be avoided but for a multitude of reasons this is not always the case. In Chapter 1 we gave more detail on the various options that are available to deal with missing values.

■ ■ ■ ■ **FACTOR ANALYSIS: EXPLORATORY**

HOW TO REPORT FACTOR ANALYSIS

As we have seen in this chapter it is important to report the Kaiser-Meyer-Olkin measure, the Bartlett Test of Sphericity, a Scree plot and the percentage of variance explained by the eigenvalue factors included. The report should also include factor weightings in the relevant matrix with the extraction and rotation method used. When using factor score the extraction method should be given, i.e. Regression, Bartlett or Anderson-Rubin method.

Calculating factor analysis with Stata and SPSS

For SPSS, select *Analyze – Dimension Reduction – Factor* to open a dialog box that allows variables and options to be selected. First select the variables to be used in factor analysis and drop these into the variable box. Then on the right hand side of this window select *Descriptives* and tick KMO. Next select the *Extraction* window to obtain options for factor method – Principal components, Maximum likelihood, or Principal axis factoring. In this window you can also select Scree plot and the number of factors to extract. The third dialog box is *Rotation* to select the appropriate rotation, either orthogonal Varimax or oblique Promax. The fourth window *Scores* allows you to calculate and save latent score factors by ticking the *Save as variables* box and then selecting the appropriate method. The final window *Options* gives display format with options *Sorted by size* and *Suppress small coefficients*. It is usual to set the *Absolute value below:* as 0.3

For Stata, select *Statistics – multivariate analysis – Factor and principal component analysis* to open the dialog box. In the menu (Model) select the variables (items) that are required for your particular factor analysis. In 'model2' identify the method to be used principal factor, maximum likelihood or principle-component factor. To select the appropriate rotation, either orthogonal Varimax or oblique Promax then select *Statistics – multivariate analysis – Factor and principal component – Postestimation – rotate loadings*. To generate a Scree plot use the same commands as this, changing only the final option to 'scree plot of eigenvalues', *Statistics – multivariate analysis – Factor and principal component – Postestimation – Scree plot of eigenvalues*. In the '*Statistics – multivariate analysis – postestimation reports and statistics*' section you can select the estat tools such as KMO.

To calculate and save latent score factors type in the command line 'predict' and your variable names for these factor scores. The default setting is the Regression Method. Hence if you have two factors you would type *predict var1 var2* or if you wished to use the Bartlett method then you would type *predict var1 var2, bartlett*.

FACTOR ANALYSIS: EXPLORATORY ▓ ▓ ▓ ■

Identify the method to be used - principal factor, maximum likelihood or iterated principle component factor

Decide on the maximum number of factors

Set the minimum value for eigenvalues. Default is one

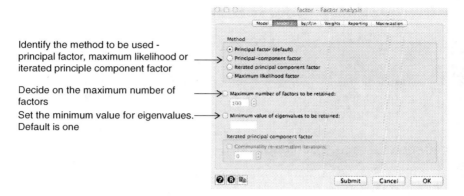

Figure 3.2 Stata factor analysis: select model

Select for orthogonal Varimax

Select for oblique Promax

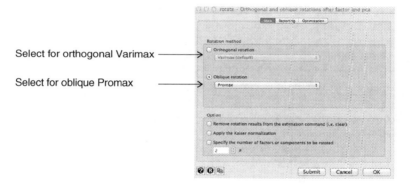

Figure 3.3 Stata Varimax or Promax rotation

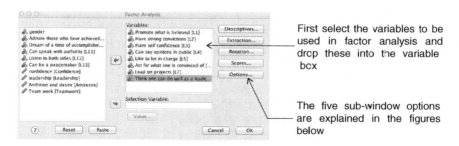

First select the variables to be used in factor analysis and drop these into the variable box

The five sub-window options are explained in the figures below

Figure 3.4 SPSS factor analysis

48

▪▪▪■ FACTOR ANALYSIS: EXPLORATORY

Methods of factor extraction – Principal components, Maximum likelihood, Principal axis factoring

Select Scree plot

If required you can select the number of factors to be extracted

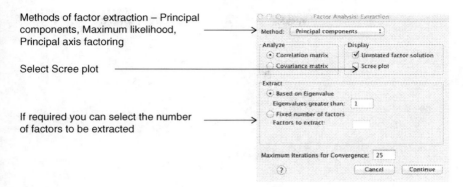

Figure 3.5 SPSS extraction window

Select the appropriate rotation, either orthogonal Varimax or oblique Promax

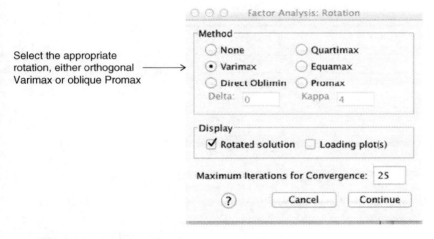

Figure 3.6 SPSS rotation window

To calculate a new variable for each of the factor scores in the data

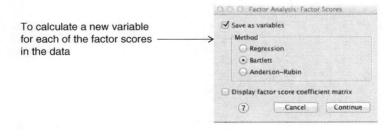

Figure 3.7 SPSS factor scores

FACTOR ANALYSIS: EXPLORATORY

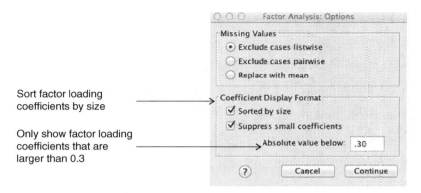

Sort factor loading coefficients by size

Only show factor loading coefficients that are larger than 0.3

Figure 3.8 SPSS options window

CHAPTER 4
CORRELATION AND LINEAR REGRESSION

In this chapter several statistical techniques and processes will be explored to consider relationships that exist between variables. Firstly we will consider the three main statistical techniques that can be used to investigate correlations – Pearson, Spearman and Kendal. Visual representations allow for greater understanding about what correlation actually means. Therefore the chapter starts by interpreting scatterplot diagrams as they assist in the understanding of what the output from a Pearson Correlation Coefficient represents. The chapter will then move on to analysing ordinal data with the use of Spearman rho and Kendal tau correlation techniques. These statistical correlation procedures will then be used to explore a study of parental involvement in education. Factor analysis in conjunction with correlation techniques is used to explore the association between themes in the study.

In the second part of this chapter we will continue this exploration of statistical relationships between variables looking at linear regression. Regression enables you to estimate the value of one variable (dependent variable) given what is known about another variable (independent variable). We will start the section taking forward the ideas presented on correlations and look at obtaining a line of best fit on a scatter diagram. The section then explores multivariate linear regression where a number of independent variables can influence a dependent variable and illustrate how to interpret and report findings from SPSS and Stata outputs. Concluding sections in this chapter explore variable selection methods and appropriate sample sizes for regression models.

SCATTER DIAGRAM

In the first instance, one way of obtaining a sense of an association between two variables is to draw a scatterplot. A scatterplot looks at general trends in the data. SPSS and Stata provide the tools to plot these diagrams to compare visually the relationships between variables.

Many examples can be given to show how scatterplot graphs can be helpful when exploring associations. Whether in science, social science or health, looking to see whether associations exist or not can help in our desire to search for the truth around what does or does not affect daily living.

CORRELATION AND LINEAR REGRESSION

Examples could include a reflection on whether the number of sales of a produce is associated with advertising costs or the advertising campaign. Once data have been collected over a number of years, they can be used in order to forecast behaviour. Looking for positive, negative or no association then reveals the way forward for the investigator.

A positive relationship implies as one variable increases the other increases. With the advertising example above, we would expect that a good advertising campaign, with increased advertising costs would generate greater volume of sales.

Scatterplots can also be used to find relationships between variables that have been hypothesised. Figure 4.1 shows that reading scores increase with reading age. That is there is a positive relationship in education between reading age and reading score. This could be expected but as a researcher you need evidence to support your hypothesis. A scatterplot can be the first stage in your analysis of data when you are looking for trends and patterns.

Figure 4.2 demonstrates negative correlations in data. In this particular case as a person's level of happiness decreases their level of helpfulness increases. As one variable increases the other decreases. This is an example of a negative correlation.

Other examples of negative correlation could be the more goods you buy the less money you have in your bank account and the more you exercise the lower your body weight.

The two cases illustrated in Figures 4.1 and 4.2 show clear relationships, this is not always the case. In some situations no clear correlation is observable as shown in Figure 4.3.

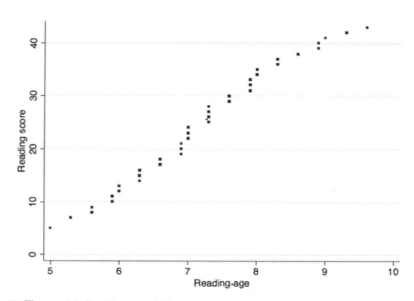

Figure 4.1 Positive correlation

CORRELATION AND LINEAR REGRESSION

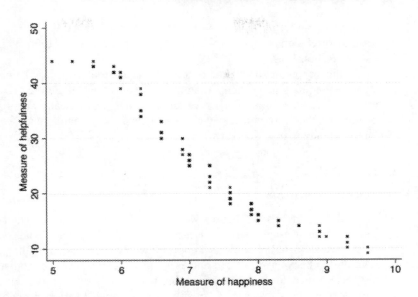

Figure 4.2 Negative correlation

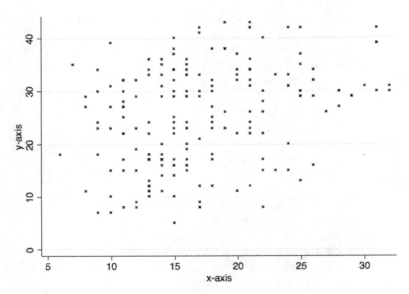

Figure 4.3 No clear correlation

A note of caution needs to be stated before venturing more deeply into correlation. Even when a very strong correlation is obtained between variables it cannot be assumed that there is a cause and effect relationship. This correlation analysis merely tells us that between these two sets of data there is a relationship between the pairs of numbers, showing positive,

CORRELATION AND LINEAR REGRESSION

negative or no trend. It is up to the researcher to critically evaluate this result. Correlation analysis provides a starting point in order to investigate causal relationships.

Confident predictions around the significance of the correlation of variables requires more than a diagram. Statistical tests therefore are able to assess whether correlations between variables are statically significant or not. We therefore consider the use of Pearson Correlation and how to interpret outputs from statistical packages.

CORRELATION

Pearson correlation

In the first part of this chapter we looked at how scatterplot diagrams can be used to graphically illustrate associations between variables. In addition to a visual check it is important to measure the strength of the relationship between the two variables using a statistical test. The statistical test determines the relative strength or weakness of the relationship and whether the correlation is positive or negative. Pearson correlation coefficient measures the strength of a linear relationship between continuous variables.

The Pearson correlation gives an r-value that lies between −1 and +1, with a value of +1 indicating a perfect positive correlation and −1 a perfect negative correlation. A value of zero indicates no correlation. The measure of importance of these is termed as an effect size. The strength of the effect and the associated r-values are as follows:

> Weak: −0.1 to +0.1
> Modest: In the interval −0.1 to −0.3 or +0.1 to +0.3
> Moderate: In the interval −0.3 to −0.5 or +0.3 to +0.5
> Strong: In the interval −0.5 to −0.8 or +0.5 to +0.8
> Very Strong: In the interval −0.8 to −1.0 or +0.8 to +1.0

The Pearson correlation coefficient (the r-value) is calculated by summing all the differences between each individual item value with the mean of all the values. Dividing this by the standard deviation of the variables allows for standardisation. This is a sophisticated statistical method of calculating the average distance of all the points on our scatterplot from an assumed best fit straight line through these points.

Figure 4.4 shows a set of seven points with an estimated line drawn as close to as many of the points as possible so as to minimize the error. In Appendix 4 there is more technical information on how this calculation can be made by hand. Fortunately SPSS and Stata are capable of doing these calculations for us quickly. This takes away the requirement of calculation but interpreting the outputs from SPSS and Stata is crucial in order to gain a clear understanding of statistically significant associations.

■ ■ ■ ■ **CORRELATION AND LINEAR REGRESSION**

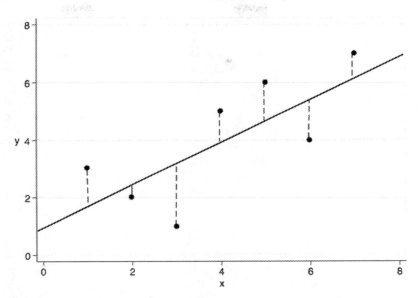

■ **Figure 4.4** Estimated linear relationship

By squaring the r-value we calculate what is called a coefficient of determination. The r^2 value provides a measure of how much of the variation can be accounted for due to the variables under consideration and how much is due to other factors. For example, obtaining an r-value of 0.745, with associated r^2-value of 0.555, indicates that 55.5% of the variation can be explained by the correlation. This leaves less than 44.5% to be explained by other factors. If the r-value was lower, say for example a value of 0.367 then the coefficient of determination would be r^2=0.135 implying that only 13.5% of the variation is explained. These two examples would be classified as the first result of 0.745 being around three times as significant as the second result of 0.367.

Factor analysis was the topic focus in Chapter 3 and this next part of the chapter links exploratory factor analysis with Pearson Correlation. This allows us to explore how to analyse Likert scale questionnaires using latent factor scores. The following study shows how Likert scale questionnaire items can be converted using factor analysis into single latent scores and then analysed using correlation.

Correlation using latent factor scores

Much research has shown there to be a significant association between student outcomes and parental involvement. According to Hoover-Dempsey and Sandler (1995, 1997, 2005) there are three major sources of motivation for parents to become involved in their child's education. The

CORRELATION AND LINEAR REGRESSION

parental involvement process is made up of three main sources. First, is the motivational beliefs of the parents that their role and self-efficacy can be important for helping their children to be successful at school. The second part of the model relates to how parents can be involved with their children's schooling. The final aspect of the model is around time and ability, and how the parents' beliefs in their own skills and knowledge can affect outcomes. The study of 500 parents considers whether the three main sources of parental involvement are associated with each other and if so how.

The 25 questions used in this study are taken from the work of Hoover-Dempsey and Sandler's model as set out in Walker et al. (2005). All the measures are given on a four-point Likert scale, with 1 as strongly disagree, 2 disagree, 3 agree, and 4 strongly agree. The following procedure in this section is the one that Hoover-Dempsey and Sandler have used in their research.

First, principal components analysis will be used as a data reduction technique to create latent factor themes of Likert scale items. This will reduce the 25 original Likert scale questions into nine variables. Then the Pearson correlation technique will be applied to the nine variables created using principal component analysis to find the relative associations between these themes. In the model suggested by Hoover-Dempsey and Sandler these factor item groups will have correlated inter-woven structure. The Promax oblique rotation method will be applied to capture these groupings with the Bartlett method being used to create latent output scores. The Bartlett method is used for factor scores as the correlated items are within particular latent variable themes. The groups of latent factors fall into three categories:

1) Psychological motivators – with two themed groups – Role activity beliefs and Parental self-efficacy;
2) Invitations to involvement – with three themed groups – General school invitations, Specific teacher invitations, and Specific child invitations;
3) Life context – with two themed groups – Skills and knowledge and Time and energy.

The next part of this chapter considers each of these categories in turn.

Psychological motivators

The first theme in the psychological motivators category is the parent's motivational beliefs and how parents feel they should play an active role in their children's education. These are shown in the two single constructs (Tables 4.1 and 4.2). Within each of these constructs are a group of three items. These three items are combined into single latent factors. In the factor relating to the role activity beliefs of the parent, it can be seen in Table 4.1 that the single item question 'Communicate with my child's teacher

■ ■ ■ ■ **CORRELATION AND LINEAR REGRESSION**

■ **Table 4.1** Role activity beliefs

	Factor
Communicate with my child's teacher regularly (School)	.806
Talk with my child about the school day (Home)	.780
Volunteer at the school (School)	.527

SPSS output in the table with extraction method principal component analysis. Rotation method Promax. Kaiser-Meyer-Olkin 0.558. Bartlett's Test of Sphericity(3)=119.241, p<0.001. 51.206% of variance explained.

Stata command for principle component factor: factor rab1 rab2 rab3, pcf factors(1) and postestimation command: rotate, promax oblique kaiser factors(1)

■ **Table 4.2** Parents self-efficacy

	Factor
I feel successful about my efforts to help my child learn	.871
I know how to help my child to do well in school (Home)	.828
I do know if I'm getting through to my child	.613

SPSS output in the table with extraction method principal component analysis. Rotation method Promax. Kaiser-Meyer-Olkin 0.579. Bartlett's Test of Sphericity(3)=293.723, p<0.001. 60.691% of variance explained

Stata command principle component factor: factor pse1 pse2 pse3, pcf factors(1) and postestimation command: rotate, promax oblique kaiser factors(1)

regularly' has the highest factor weighting with λ equal to 0.806. All of the loadings in the factors 'role activity beliefs' and 'parents' self-efficacy' are greater than 0.3 and so are said to be salient and relate meaningfully to these factors. Regarding the parents' self-efficacy factor there are three items in this factor concerning the parents' ability to make a difference to their children's education through their involvement. The item 'I feel successful about my efforts to help my child learn' has the highest factor weighting of 0.871. The latent construct for parents' self-efficacy can therefore be said to explain 75.9% (0.871^2) of the variation in this item with only 24.1% ($1-0.871^2$) left unexplained.

Invitations to involvement

Invitations to involvement is the second theme and focuses on parents' feelings regarding involvement in school generally, covering a wide range of opportunities for parental involvement as set out in Tables 4.3–4.5. The

CORRELATION AND LINEAR REGRESSION

Table 4.3 General school invitations

	Factor
I feel welcome at the school (School)	.880
The school lets me know about special school events and meetings (School)	.811
The teachers at the school keep me informed about my child's progress in school (School)	.686

SPSS output in the table with extraction method principal component analysis. Rotation method Promax. Kaiser-Meyer-Olkin 0.596. Bartlett's. Test of Sphericity(3)=337.216, $p<0.001$. 63.436% of variance explained.

Stata command principle component factor: factor gsi1 gsi2 gsi3, pcf factors(1) and postestimation command: rotate, promax oblique kaiser factors(1)

Table 4.4 Specific teacher invitations

	Factor
My child's teacher asked me to talk with my child about the school day (Home)	.918
My child's teacher asked me or expected me to help my daughter with her homework (Home)	.861
My child's teacher asked me to attend a special event at school (School)	.790
My child's teacher asked me to help out at the school (School)	.657

SPSS output in the table with extraction method principal component analysis. Rotation method Promax. Kaiser-Meyer-Olkin 0.693. Bartlett's Test of Sphericity(6)=996.267, $p<0.001$. 66.008% of variance explained.

Stata command principle component factor: factor sti1 sti2 sti3 sti4, pcf factors(1) and postestimation command: rotate, promax oblique kaiser factors(1)

three themes contain three and four items. All of the factor loadings are greater than 0.3 and so relate meaningfully to the themes.

The general school invitations theme is divided into three items. The first two items relate to parents feeling welcome at school ($\lambda=0.880$ and $\lambda=0.811$) and the other item is regarding the parents being informed about their children's progress ($\lambda=0.686$).

The second theme has a group of items that are associated with the teacher inviting parental involvement.[1]

■ ■ ■ ■ CORRELATION AND LINEAR REGRESSION

Table 4.5 Specific child invitations

	Factor
My child asked me about her homework (Home)	.731
I know how to supervise my child's homework (Home)	815
My child asked me to explain things about her homework (Home)	801

SPSS output in the table with extraction method principal component analysis. Rotation method Promax. Kaiser-Meyer-Olkin 0.653. Bartlett's Test of Sphericity(3)=247.637, p<0.001. 61.337% of variance explained

Stata command principle component factor: factor ci1 ci2 ci3, pcf factors(1) and postestimation command: rotate, promax oblique kaiser factors(1)

The last factor group can be classified as interactions between the child and parent solely, in relation to the child's homework and the support that the parent gives.

Life context

The final life context category contains two themes. The first is related to skills and knowledge and the second is around parents' perception of the demands put on their time. Concerning the first theme, a parent may not feel that they have the background skills to help their child due to their own school history and education journey. All of the items in the skills and knowledge factor are nearly equally weighted (0.972, 0.964 and 0.960) implying that these items play almost an equal role in the construction of this latent factor.

This has not been seen with the other educational constructs. For example, regarding the theme, role activity beliefs, the weightings for the first two items are similar with 0.806, 0.780 but the third is 0.527. When calculating the explained variances for these items this difference becomes

Table 4.6 Skills and knowledge

	Factor
I know enough about subjects to help my child with homework	.972
To be able to look for more information about subjects if required	.964
To believe that she can learn new things	.960

SPSS output in the table with extraction method principal component analysis. Rotation method Promax. Kaiser-Meyer-Olkin 0.776. Bartlett's Test of Sphericity(3)=1772.763, p<0.001. 93.166% of variance explained.

Stata command principle component factor: factor sk1 sk2 sk3, pcf factors(1) and postestimation command: rotate, promax oblique kaiser factors(1)

CORRELATION AND LINEAR REGRESSION

Table 4.7 Time and energy

	Factor
I have enough time and energy to help out at my child's school (School)	.872
I have enough time and energy to help my child with homework (Home)	.838
I have enough time and energy to attend special events at school (School)	.823
I have enough time and energy to communicate effectively with my child's teacher (School)	.792
I have enough time and energy to supervise my daughter's homework (Home)	.622

SPSS output in the table with extraction method principal component analysis. Rotation method Promax. Kaiser-Meyer-Olkin 0.797. Bartlett's Test of Sphericity(10)=1233.163, p<0.001 .63.879% of variance explained

Stata command principle component factor: factor te1 te2 te3 te3 te5, pcf factors(1) and postestimation command: rotate, promax oblique kaiser factors(1)

clearer with the first two being 65% (0.806^2) and 61% (0.780^2) and the final item only explaining 28% (0.527^2) of the variation. There is nothing wrong with this as all the weightings are above accepted limits (0.3). This just tells us that the make-up of the latent construct factor for role activity beliefs has a low weighting on the 'volunteer at school' question. It could be implied from this that the parents in this data set feel that communicating with their child's teacher and talking to their child about their day at school hold more importance for them than volunteering at school.

The final theme in this category is time and energy. There are five items that relate to the perception that parents have when they are thinking about involvement with school, teachers and the child.

Home and school based items

The analysis of this study thus far has formed seven themed groups of reduced factors. In addition to these themed groups Hoover-Dempsey and Sandler also created two additional groups from the original 25 questions in their research. These items are related to either involvement behaviours for parents around 'home-based' or 'school-based' questions. All the home-based items are given in Table 4.8. They include statements such as 'I know how to supervise my child's homework' and 'I have enough time and energy to supervise my daughter's homework' ($\lambda=0.722$ and $\lambda=0.478$ respectively).

School-based involvement items included questions that are related to parents' involvement with teachers and school, for example 'I have enough

■■■■ CORRELATION AND LINEAR REGRESSION

Table 4.8 Home based items

	Factor
I have enough time and energy to help my child with homework (Home) TE2	.887
My child asked me about her homework (Home) CI1	.810
I know how to help my child to do well in school (Home) PSE2	.810
I know how to supervise my child's homework (Home) CI2	.722
I know how to explain things to my child about their homework (Home) CI3	.612
My child's teacher asked me to talk with my child about the school day (Home) STI 1	.568
My child's teacher asked me or expected me to help my daughter with her homework (Home) STI2	.545
I have enough time and energy to supervise my daughter's homework (Home) TE5	.478

SPSS output in the table with extraction method principal component analysis. Rotation method Promax. with Kaiser Normalization. 48.054% of variance explained.

Stata command principle component factor: factor te2 ci1 pse2 ci2 ci3 sti1 sti2 te5, pcf factors(1) and postestimation command: rotate, promax oblique kaiser factors(1)

Table 4.9 School based items

	Factor
I have enough time and energy to help out at my child's school (School) TE1	.831
I have enough time and energy to communicate effectively with my child's teacher (School) TE4	.803
I have enough time and energy to attend special events at school (School) TE3	.784
The school lets me know about special school events and meetings (School) GSI2	.739
My child's teacher asked me to attend a special event at school (School) STI3	.559
My child's teacher asked me to help out at the school (School) STI4	.553
Communicate with my child's teacher regularly (School) RAB1	.519
The teachers at the school keep me informed about my child's progress in school (School) GSI3	.455

SPSS output in the table with extraction method principal component analysis. Rotation method Promax. Kaiser-Meyer-Olkin 0.761. Bartlett's Test of Sphericity(28)=1441.990, $p<0.001$. 44.897% of variance explained

Stata command principle component factor: factor te1 te4 te3 gsi2 sti3 sti4 rab1 gsi3, pcf factors(1) and postestimation command: rotate, promax oblique kaiser factors(1)

CORRELATION AND LINEAR REGRESSION ▪ ▪ ▪ ▪

time and energy to help out at my child's school' and 'Communicate with my child's teacher regularly' ($\lambda=0.831$ and $\lambda=0.519$ respectively).

Pearson correlation and association between themes

The nine themes that have been constructed are termed latent constructs and are used by Hoover-Dempsey and Sandler to see if correlations exist between these nine variables. Table 4.10 shows the results for this data set with stars indicating if the Pearson correlation is significant.

Table 4.10 shows that all of the correlations are positive and that most are significant. Only four of the variables are not significant. All of these variables relate to the factor 'skills and knowledge'. There are two variables that are said to have a very strong correlation with values in the interval from +0.8 to +1.0. One of these is the positive correlation between 'home-based involvement' with 'specific child invitations'. This particular correlation has an r-value of 0.908.

The r-values in the range 0.5 to 0.8 are strong significant correlations and in the table there are fifteen of these. The latent construct 'time and energy' features here in this class with a correlation of 0.582 with 'general school invitations'.

Seven correlations are in the range 0.3 to 0.5 suggesting moderate correlations. The remaining eight correlations are in the modest category with r-values ranging from 0.1 to 0.3. Overall this data shows that there are clear correlations in parent's attitudes around their child's schooling. Hoover-Dempsey and Sandler published similar findings to these shown in Table 4.10 in their research.

When to use Pearson correlation

Pearson's correlation coefficient is not appropriate to use when we are looking to find correlations between variables with data that has outliers, ordinal scales and non-linear relationships. This is due to the fact that Pearson's correlation coefficient can be sensitive to outliers, with even just a few extreme data points, leading to wide variations in r-values. When your data is not continuous, such as ordinal data in a Likert scale then we cannot use Pearson's coefficient. We could, as we have seen in Chapter 2, use the Chi-square test in this situation, as it is a robust measure as long as there are not too many categories.

The final important condition to bear in mind when deciding to use an alternative statistical correlation test is that of non-linearity. This is sometimes found when the data that you are analysing has unequal gaps due to the discrete choices on offer in the item scales. Willingness to pay options often have this kind of structure. An illustration of such a willingness to pay scale is one that is measured in six discrete units such as $1, $5, $10, $20, $50 and $100. Gaps between these values are $4 ($5-$1), $5 ($10-$5), $10 ($20-$10), $30 ($50-$20), $50 ($100-$50). The gaps are $4, $5, $10, $30,

Table 4.10 Pearson correlations

Variable	1	2	3	4	5	6	7	8	9
Psychological motivators									
1. Role activity beliefs	1	–	–	–	–				
2. Parental self-efficacy	0.176**	1	–	–	–				
Invitations of involvement									
3. General school invitations	0.245**	0.723**	1	–	–				
4. Specific teacher invitations	0.273**	0.472**	0.587**	1	–				
5. Specific child invitations	0.346**	0.625**	0.493**	0.289**	1				
Life context									
6. Skills and knowledge	0.063	0.009	0.076	0.082	0.163**	1			
7. Time and energy	0.487**	0.467**	0.582**	0.428**	0.737**	0.144**	1		
Involvement behaviours									
8. Home-based	0.332**	0.795**	0.690**	0.555**	0.908**	0.120**	0.771**	1	
9. School-based	0.601**	0.500**	0.703**	0.664**	0.625**	0.150**	0.901**	0.718**	1

**significant at the 0.01 level, * significant at the 0.05 level

CORRELATION AND LINEAR REGRESSION

and $50 and as these are not a constant value they are said to be non-linear. In a linear sequence such as $4, $6, $8, $10, $12, all the differences have constant difference of $2.

When the conditions such as these described occur then the requirements for using Pearson's correlation coefficient are not met. It is then necessary to use a non-parametric statistic such as Spearman's rho and Kendall's tau. In the next two sections we will look at each of these statistical tests in turn.

SPEARMAN'S RANK CORRELATION COEFFICIENT (SPEARMAN'S RHO)

Spearman's rho can be used with ordinal, non-linear or continuous data that describes a monotonic relationship. A monotonic relationship is defined to be one in which as one variable increases the other either increases or decreases. As seen earlier in this chapter this is another way of saying a positive or negative correlation. As with the Pearson correlation coefficient a rho value (ρ) of +1 is a positive correlation and ρ-value of −1 is a negative correlation.

The way Spearman's rho calculates this coefficient is to create a ranking order for each of the two variables under consideration. The statistical test then measures the difference between these two ranks for each of the survey respondents. Details on how this test is calculated are set out in Appendix 4.

Let us apply the Spearman's rho correlation to two Likert scale items from the parent's survey we looked at earlier in this chapter based on the work of Hoover-Dempsey and Sandler. We can use SPSS or Stata to calculate the Spearman's rho for two of the questions from the school and home categories. The questions 'communicate with my child's teacher regularly (School)' and 'talk with my child about the school day (Home)' show that there is a positive correlation $\rho = 0.434$ with significance of $p < 0.01$. Note that when Pearson's correlation test was used to calculate the correlation for these same two questions it gave a value of 0.418, with a significance of $p<0.01$. Both of these statistical techniques are very robust to variations in data types as the results will usually show little difference.

The limitation with using Spearman's rho correlation is you need to be able to demonstrate that the rankings are equidistant. If your Likert scale questionnaire ranks are not equidistant then the statistical test called Kendall's Tau can be used instead of Spearman's rho. This is because Kendall's Tau does not include the restriction around the assumption of equidistance between consecutive ranks.

KENDALL'S TAU CORRELATION (τ)

The statistical procedure is very similar to Spearman's rho in that Kendall's tau assigns ranks for the two variables under investigation. The statistical test differs slightly from Spearman's rho by ordering one of the variables in rank order and using this as an anchor column. This anchor column is then compared against the other variable known as a reference column.

■ ■ ■ ■   **CORRELATION AND LINEAR REGRESSION**

Deviations from the monotonic association, i.e. perfectly positive or negative are termed the amount of rank disarray. The amount of rank disarray is given as the number of cases in the reference column differing from the anchor column as a percentage. The Kendall's tau value produced via this test gives a result in the same range as Spearman's rho, with Kendall's tau (τ) of -1 indicating completely negative correlation and $\tau=+1$ complete positive correlation. As the value of Kendall's tau approaches zero this indicates complete rank disarray with a great number of the pairs of ranked values not following a monotonic pattern.

Looking at the same Likert scale questions 'communicate with my child's teacher regularly (School)' and 'talk with my child about the school day (Home)' as we did previously gives $\tau = 0.410$, $p<0.01$. Again a similar result to that obtained previously, showing the strength of these statistical techniques to deal with a range of data types.

Note that Kendall's tau-b is a slightly different statistical test that is offered in statistical packages as it corrects for cases when there are tied ranks. In Appendix 4 you can find greater mathematical detail on how both Spearman's rho and Kendall's tau statistical techniques are calculated.

CORRELATIONS BETWEEN TWO VARIABLES OF DIFFERENT SCALES

The three different correlation techniques described so far in this chapter can be used with continuous (Pearson) and ordinal (Spearman and Kendall) data. If you wish to find associations between two variables with different scales then Kendall's tau is recommended. Analysing the correlation between age and the Likert question 'I have enough time and energy to supervise my daughter's homework (Home)' gives the result that as the child gets older the parent feels that they have *less time* and energy to spend helping with homework. We know that the result implies '*less time*' as the Kendall's tau for this is negative with a value of $\tau = -0.109$, and significant with $p<0.05$ having an exact p-value of 0.014

HOW TO REPORT CORRELATIONS

As we have seen in this chapter it is important to report whether the correlation is positive or negative. The report should also include the type of correlation you have used and the level of significance given by the result. Hence the statement:

> shows that there is a positive correlation, Spearman's rho value of 0.434 with a significance of $p < 0.01$

This can be given in a more condensed form if required:

> *positive correlation* $\rho = 0.434$, $p < 0.01$

CORRELATION AND LINEAR REGRESSION

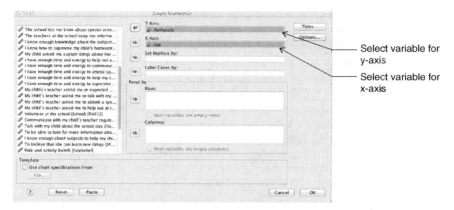

Figure 4.5 SPSS scatterplot

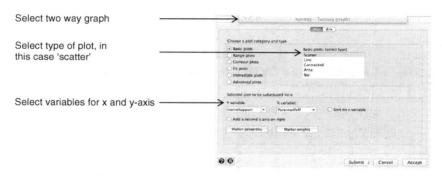

Figure 4.6 Stata scatterplot

Scatterplots with Stata and SPSS

In SPSS select *Graphs – Legacy Dialogs – Scatter/Dot*. Select one of the scatterplot options and then insert variables in x- and y-axis boxes.

In Stata select Graphics – *Two way Graph – Create – Scatter*. In the drop down windows select the correct variables for the scatterplot.

CALCULATING CORRELATION WITH STATA AND SPSS

In SPSS select *Analyze – Correlate – Bivariate*. From this select the required correlation, either Pearson, Spearman or Kendall, depending on the scale of the variables to be correlated. Using Pearson with continuous variables and Spearman or Kendall with ordinal, non-linear or continuous data that describe a monotonic relationship. Next click the arrow to move the marked items to the variable box to be correlated. Then click OK to carry out the calculation.

■ ■ ■ ■ CORRELATION AND LINEAR REGRESSION

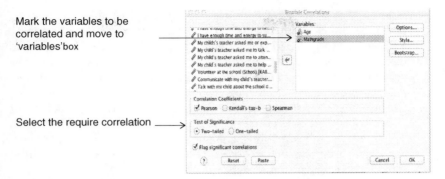

Mark the variables to be correlated and move to 'variables' box

Select the require correlation

■ **Figure 4.7** SPSS correlation

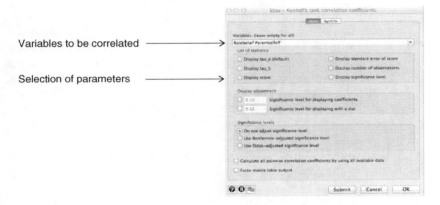

Variables to be correlated

Selection of parameters

■ **Figure 4.8** Stata correlation

In Stata, for Pearson correlation select Statistics – *Summaries, tables and tests – Summary and descriptive statistics – Correlations and covariances*. This is just for Pearson and to perform Spearman or Kendall correlations you need to select *Statistics – Summaries, tables and tests – Nonparametric tests of hypotheses*. Next choose which correlation you wish to use either Spearman or Kendall.

LINEAR REGRESSION

Linear regression looks to fit the 'best' straight-line relationship for a set of points. This is a similar statistical procedure to the one discussed earlier in this section on bivariate correlation. Linear regression is a more powerful statistical technique as it allows us to assess how a group of variables can influence a single variable. This technique is called multivariate linear regression.

In this section we will start by looking at a two variable case, modelling the relationship between the dependent and the independent variable. This

CORRELATION AND LINEAR REGRESSION ▪▪▪▪

is linear regression. We then move onto the more complex multivariate linear regression where a number of independent variables may influence a dependent variable. To help explore this technique we will continue to use the study on parental motivation (Green et al., 2007). The study will be used to illustrate how to interpret and report findings from SPSS and Stata outputs. The chapter then continues exploring purposeful variable selection, which is a method to help when making significant variable choices for regression models. The chapter concludes with a short discussion around appropriate sample sizes for regression models. If you would like more mathematical information on linear regression and associated statistical tests this is contained in Appendix 5.

Linear regression using latent factor scores

Once Likert scale questions have been transformed into latent factors using exploratory factor analysis, then they can be used in regression analysis. This allows for a detailed exploration of Likert scale questionnaires using linear regression. To illustrate this we will explore aspects of parents' home-based and school-based involvement. Starting with a two variable example with the dependent variable being 'home support' and the independent variable 'child invitations' we then build on this to consider multivariate linear regression. Using these two variables in linear regression gives the output shown in Table 4.11.

Let's interpret the linear regression output set out in Table 4.11. It is important to remember that linear regression with two variables is visually

▪ **Table 4.11** Linear regression

Coefficients

Model	Unstandardized Coefficients B	Std. Error	Standardized Coefficients Beta	t	Sig.	95.0% Confidence Interval for B Lower Bound	Upper Bound
Constant	−4.714E-15	.019		.000	1.000	−.037	.037
Child invitations requests for parental help at home	.908	.019	.908	48.388	.000	.871	.945

SPSS Linear regression: Dependent Variable: Home support. Tolerance=1, VIF=1

Stata linear regression command: regress Home CI

■ ■ ■ ■ CORRELATION AND LINEAR REGRESSION

a two dimensional straight line. The equation for this line can be obtained from our output and can be written as follows using the B-values:

Home support = 0.908×Child invitations −4.714E−15

The value of 0.908 is the slope coefficient of the line. In this case its approximately one. If you look at the graph in Table 4.9 for every one you move to the right in the x direction (child invitation) you move one up in the y direction (home support) along the line. This is called the gradient of a line. The other value in the equation, -4.714×10^{-15} gives the intercept on the y-axis. You can see on the graph in Figure 4.9 that the line nearly goes through the point (0,0).

This line suggests that parents' home based involvement is significantly dependent on child invitations. The p-value is less than 0.001 and the beta coefficient indicates for every 0.908 standard deviations in home support this will result in one standard deviation change in child invitations. Once you have a model that you feel confident with it is necessary to check significance to confirm that the model is a better representation than the initial base model with no independent variables. The F-test statistic is a ratio that calculates the significant change in the value of the R^2 when additional independent variables are added to the base model. If the t is significant then this suggests that the independent variables added, play an important part in the model. This model has a significant p-value with an F-test of $P[F(1, 498) \geq 2341.393] < 0.001$ and

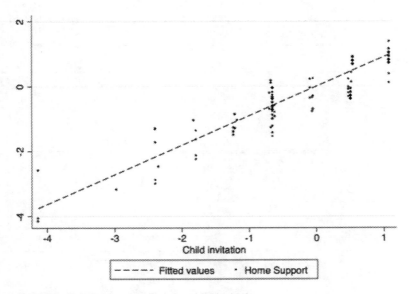

■ **Figure 4.9** Regression line for child invitations

CORRELATION AND LINEAR REGRESSION

$r^2=0.824$, showing that the independent variable is important. You can see from Figure 4.9 that the points are scattered fairly close to the regression line. The 95% confidence limits for the B–value of 0.908 are between 0.871 and 0.945. These upper and lower bound values for 95% confidence are close to the B-value as the standard error is small. These values can be calculated by hand as follows:

$$0.908 - 1.96 \times 0.019 = 0.871$$

$$0.908 + 1.96 \times 0.019 = 0.945$$

Next we will add a single additional variable, 'teacher invitations', and see how this affects the model. This model has two independent variables 'child invitations' as before and now the additional variable 'teacher invitations'. Notice that the weighting on 'child invitations' is still high and a dominant part of the model. Both independent variables can be seen to be significant from Table 4.12. The model's equation can be written as follows using the B-values set out in the table:

Home support = $0.816 \times$ Child invitations
$+ 0.320 \times$ Teacher invitations $- 4.665 \times 10^{-15}$

There is no improvement in the F-test as the value has not reduced (2341.393 to 2789.356) showing that the one variable model is a better fit. By calculating the R^2 it can be seen that the amount of variance left unexplained has reduced from 18% (1–0.824) to 8% (1–0.918).

Table 4.12 Home support regression

Coefficients

Model		Unstandardized Coefficients B	Std. Error	Standardized Coefficients Beta	t	Sig.
1	Constant	–4.665E–15	.013		.000	1.000
	Child invitations requests for parental help at home	.816	.013	.816	60.891	.000
	Teacher invitations	.320	.013	.320	23.846	.000

SPSS Linear regression: Dependent Variable: Home support. P[F(2, 497) ≥2789.356] <0.001, adjusted R^2=0.918 Tolerance=0.917, VIF=1.091

Stata linear regression command: regress Home CI STI

■ ■ ■ ■ **CORRELATION AND LINEAR REGRESSION**

MULTICOLLINEARITY

A possible issue that sometimes occurs with multiple regression analysis is that of multicollinearity. This occurs when independent variables in the model are highly correlated. The result of multicollinearity is that some variables may become redundant. A good literature review can often help to inform survey design prior to data collection and may help to avoid major multicollinearity issues around highly correlated variables.

Typical ways of measuring for multicollinearity include variance inflation factors (VIF) and tolerance statistics (Meyers, 1990; Bowerman and O'Connell, 1990; Hair et al., 2006; Sheather, 2009). Variance inflation factors with values close to one imply that no multicollinearity exists and if the VIF is greater than 10 then there is multicollinearity.

A tolerance statistic measures the amount of variance unexplained by other factors. A value close to one indicates that none of the other independent variables explain the variance in that particular variable. A value close to zero indicates nearly all the variance is explained and hence there are tolerance problems.

A simple complimentary way to detect multicollinearity is by calculating the correlations between variables as we saw earlier in this chapter. If you have variables that are close to being perfectly correlated then there is likely to be mutlicolineariy. When you have independent variables that are highly correlated, i.e. close to one, it is a good policy to remove one of these variables or to combine variables to create a new variable. A possible method of combining variables is as we have seen in Chapter 3 through factor analysis. If multicolinearity is detected then the variable with the highest VIF of the correlating variables should be removed. Once one variable has been removed then others with high VIF can be removed until the VIF of all the variables reaches an acceptable level. Care also needs to be taken with your sample size as small samples can often yield multicolinearity.

MULTIVARIATE LINEAR REGRESSION

We are now ready to extend our regression technique to a multivariate linear regression model with seven independent variables. The equation for this multiple regression can be written as follows using the B values from Table 4.13:

Home support = $0.599 \times$ Child invitations +
$0.205 \times$ Teacher invitations
$+0.134 \times$ Time and energy $+ 0.250 \times$ Parental Self-efficacy
$+0.028 \times$ General school invitations
$-0.046 \times$ Role and activity beliefs
$-0.015 \times$ Skills and knowledge
-4.115×10^{-16}

Table 4.13 shows the results for multivariate linear regression. This next part of the chapter sets out how to interpret and report the findings using the figures in the table. In addition to the unstandardised coefficients (B)

CORRELATION AND LINEAR REGRESSION ▓ ▓ ▓ ■

Table 4.13 Home support multivariate regression

Coefficients

Model	Unstandardized Coefficients B	SE	Standardized Coefficients Beta	t	Sig.
Constant	−4.115E−16	.009		.000	1.000
Role and activity beliefs	−.046	.010	−.046	−4.490	.000
Parental self-efficacy	.250	.015	.250	16.243	.000
General school invitations	.028	.015	.028	1.846	.066
Teacher invitations	.205	.011	.205	17.998	.000
Child invitations requests for parental help at home	.599	.016	.599	37.891	.000
Skills and knowledge	−.015	.009	−.015	−1.686	.092
Time and energy	.134	.016	.134	8.406	.000

SPSS Linear regression: Dependent Variable: Home support P[F(7, 492) ≥1746.911] <0.001, Adjusted R^2=0.961. 'Time and energy' Tolerance=0.312, VIF=3.209

Stata linear regression command: regress Home CI STI TE PSE GSI RAB SK

and robust standard errors (SE) Table 4.13 shows standardised beta values (Beta), which indicate the number of standard deviations that a dependent variable will change as a result of one standard deviation change in the independent variable. So for example as 'home support' is our dependent variable, if the independent variable 'child invitations' changes by one standard deviation, then 'home support' will change by 0.599 standard deviations (1.0×0.599). Note that in this particular example as all of these variables were created by factor analysis their standard deviations are 1.0 and hence B and Beta-values are the same. There are five statistically significant independent variables with one being negative as shown in the 'Sig column'. The role and activity beliefs of the parent have a negative impact on home support (B=−0.046, p<0.001). If the parent has greater self-efficacy (B=0.250, p<0.001) and more time and energy (B=0.134, p<0.001) to spend on their child then home support will be greater. If the teacher (B=0.205, p<0.001) or the child asks (B=0.599, p<0.001) for support at home the parent is more likely to offer home support than if the invitation is not made. We can see that by using home support as our dependent variable this has helped us to gain a greater understanding and awareness of parents' home based involvement. The constructs account for a significant amount of the variance, P[F(7, 492) ≥1746.911] <0.001, adjusted R^2=0.961. The F-value shows that this model is a significant improvement from the base model and only 3.9% of the variance is left unexplained (1−0.961).

Table 4.14 School support multivariate regression

Coefficients

Model	Unstandardized Coefficients B	SE	Standardized Coefficients Beta	t	Sig.	95.0% Confidence Interval for B Lower Bound	Upper Bound	Collinearity Statistics Tolerance	VIF
(Constant)	-5.820E-16	.010		.000	1.000	-.020	.020		
Child invitations	-.048	.018	-.048	-2.678	.008	-.084	-.013	.314	3.181
Teacher invitations	.266	.013	.266	20.490	.000	.240	.291	.609	1.643
Role and activity beliefs	.195	.012	.195	16.621	.000	.172	.218	.746	1.340
Parental self-efficacy	-.077	.018	-.077	-4.371	.000	-.111	-.042	.333	3.007
General school invitations	.203	.017	.203	11.732	.000	.169	.237	.341	2.936
Skills and Knowledge	.016	.010	.016	1.538	.125	-.004	.036	.948	1.055
Time and energy	.643	.018	.643	35.516	.000	.608	.679	.312	3.209

SPSS Linear regression: Dependent Variable: School support P[F(7, 492) ≥1328.772] <0.001, adjusted R^2=0.949

Stata linear regression command: regress School CI STI TE PSE GSI RAB SK

CORRELATION AND LINEAR REGRESSION

Before we move on let us run the multivariate linear regression again, but this time with the dependent variable being 'school support'. Looking at the data in Table 4.14 we can see that of the seven variables six are significant, with only 'skills and knowledge' (p=0.125) being not statistically significant. As with the 'home support' model set out above the F-value is significant and R^2-value is high.

Looking at the coefficients given by the B value and taking into account whether the variable is statistically significant, then concerning 'parental self-efficacy', there is a negative relationship with 'school support' (B=−0.077, p<0.001). As parental self-efficacy increases then this will decrease the likelihood for the need of school support.

This part of the chapter has considered how to interpret the regression output that will be provided using statistical packages. The next section looks at how decisions can be made around retaining or not retaining variables in the model.

Variable selection for models

When carrying out regression it is easy to fall into the trap of entering into the model everything that you have collected and inputted into SPSS or Stata. This can often be done without considering carefully why and what you are looking to discover through the data. So sit back before you start selecting everything and think:

What does your literature review suggest will be significant?
What is your hypothesis?
What are your research questions around this hypothesis?

In many cases there are a number of variables that you could choose to include in the regression model. The goal of a researcher is to select those variables that construct the 'best' model. It is sensible to have a plan for selecting variables and a method for assessing the quality of the final model achieved. There is no one correct method for doing this and the method(s) you use will vary depending on a number of factors. The reason for variable selection could be due, in part, to past literature and findings. Think about the springboard you are using for your own research and what have the findings in the past determined to be significant around your research question. The research literature will often suggest certain empirical models and these will have informed your own research design. The model you have decided to use as a researcher could have been heavily influenced due to time constraints or survey collection limitations. All these factors will impact on the final structure and you as a researcher will balance, reflect and in the end state limitations of your study in relation to these.

Two methods for statistical selection that can be performed using statistical software are stepwise and purposeful. Stepwise procedures can inform the researcher very quickly about the 'best' significant model and

■ ■ ■ ■ CORRELATION AND LINEAR REGRESSION

are a useful tool in the total process of variable selection. The disadvantage of the stepwise method is that the whole procedure is performed without the researcher being allowed to make any judgments informed by their literature review at any intermediate stage in the process of variable selection. In the next section we suggest an approach to variable inclusion based purely on statistical considerations. This approach can be used wholly or in part to help a researcher to make final decisions on variables that are included in the final analysis.

Purposeful selection of variables

In this section we consider purposeful data selection as a possible technique to help the researcher have a clearer understanding of the variables in their data set that have a significant affect and should be retained in the model (Bursac et al., 2008; Hosmer et al., 2013). The method builds a statistical model based on the data you have collected without being influenced by any other factors.

The first step in purposeful selection begins with the uni-variable analysis of each of the independent variables in relation to the dependent variable. It is important at this stage, as we have suggested in Chapter 2, to make use of contingency tables. This will help the researcher to become familiar with their data set. During this initial stage, variables that have a p-value less than 0.25 should be kept for future use. This criteria around a significance of 0.25 comes from Bendel and Afifi (1977) and Mickey and Greenland (1989) who show that if you initially retain variables that only satisfy the p-value to equal 0.05 then some important variables will be discounted too early in the decision-making process.

Once the initial variable selection has been made in the first stage the model can be tested for any variables with p-values outside of a significant range. At this point the researcher needs to make a decision about which level of significance they are happy to retain for further investigation.

The new smaller model's quality of fit can then be compared with the initial larger model. At this stage particular attention should be paid to any variables whose coefficients have greatly altered. A value that has greater than 20% absolute variation is considered significant and requires further investigation. The following example shows how the calculation would be carried out for a particular variable. If in your first model the coefficient B-values for a particular variable was 1.80 and it changed in the new model to a B-value of 1.40, then the variation can be calculated as:

$$(1.80 - 1.40)/1.40 = 0.286.$$

The percentage change is 28.6% implying that one of the variables taken out of the first model was important. The removed variable may not have been statistically significant but it was having an effect on the other variables and so should be retained. Removed variable(s) need to be added

CORRELATION AND LINEAR REGRESSION

back into the new model and the cycle described above repeated. To make these stages easier it is best to remove only one or two variables at a time. Once you have a model that you feel confident with it is necessary to check significance to confirm that the model is a better representation than the initial base model. The F-test can be used to check to see if the independent variables added to the model play a significant role.

Once you have obtained the basic model then more complex interactions can be investigated if it is felt that certain variables may have product interactions. Decisions for this need to be made not only at a statistical level but also related to whether it makes sense for these variables to interact in this way. To clarify this discussion we will look at an example involving the relationship between weight and age. Three models involving weight and age variables are illustrated in Table 4.15. As well as having variables of weight and age separately you can also check to see if there are any interactions involving multiple variables. In our example we include in Model 3 the variable – Weight*Age. This type of interaction variable implies that the effect of the individual variables, weight and age in this example, are not linearly dependent and there is some higher order interaction. In the example shown in Table 4.15 it can be seen that it would have been incorrect to stop at Model 2. When we add interaction term 'Weight*Age' in Model 3 all of the independent variables are still significant. The value of $p<0.001$ gives considerable evidence of statistical interaction between the two covariates of weight and age.

The interaction variables should be assessed for statistical significance as previously outlined above. At this stage of the purposeful section procedure the main individual variables should not be removed. These variables are the main part of the model and the interaction terms should be seen as adding to this. If an interaction term is to be included then the individual

Table 4.15 Purposeful selection

Model	Variable	Coeff.	SE	t	P	95% CI	
1	Weight	−1.353	0.471	−2.873	0.004	−2.278	−0.428
	Constant	79.392	5.062	15.683	0.000	69.446	89.338
2	Weight	−0.941	0.457	−2.059	0.040	−1.838	−0.043
	Age	0.324	0.050	6.497	0.000	0.226	0.422
	Constant	67.259	5.210	12.910	0.000	57.023	77.495
3	Weight	−0.921	0.451	−0.087	0.042	−1.807	−0.034
	Age	0.259	0.052	4.977	0.000	0.157	0.362
	Weight*Age	1.169	0.311	3.762	0.000	0.157	0.362
	Constant	62.843	5.284	11.892	0.000	52.460	73.226

■ ■ ■ ■ CORRELATION AND LINEAR REGRESSION

variable terms should also be retained. This allows for clarity around how the variables relate to the dependent variable.

LINEAR REGRESSION SAMPLE SIZE CONDITIONS

Green (1991) suggests for linear regression a minimum sample size 50 + 8n where n is the number of variables. With 10 independent variables you would require a minimum sample of 50 + 8×10 = 130. Appendix 6 contains more information on sample size.

As well as the number of independent variables you may also wish to consider the relative effect size and the sample required for this. Cohen (1988) suggests that r=0.1 is a small effect size, r=0.3 is medium effect and r=0.5 is a large effect. These r-values explain 1%, 9% and 25% of the total variance respectively. Care needs to be taken not to use these values as absolutes as there is debate concerning what constitutes 'small', 'medium' and 'large' effect sizes. Therefore, it is best to use these as markers to help form judgments (Sedlmeier and Gigerenzer, 1989; Schagen and Elliot, 2004; Thompson, 2007; Zientek et al., 2010). Miles and Shevlin (2001) suggest for a large effect size then a sample of 80 is sufficient for up to 20 independent variables. A medium effect size requires a sample of over 200 for up to 20 variables and a small effect size requires a sample of over 600 with up to 6 independent variables.

HOW TO REPORT LINEAR REGRESSION

As we have seen in this chapter it is important to report B-values, standard errors and standardised beta values, include the significance of the B-values. If these significance values are reported in tabular form then it is usual to indicate the level with multiple asterisks, such as * $p<0.1$, ** $p<0.05$, and *** $p<0.01$. It is also usual to give an F-value and R^2-value to validate the significance of the overall model and the amount of variance left unexplained. A concise notation for the F-value has been seen in this

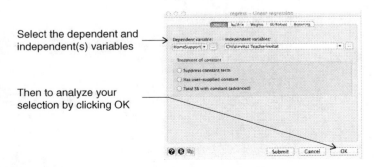

■ **Figure 4.10** Stata linear regression

CORRELATION AND LINEAR REGRESSION

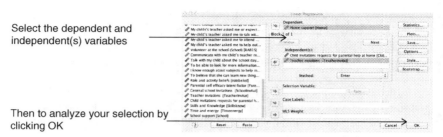

Select the dependent and independent(s) variables

Then to analyze your selection by clicking OK

Figure 4.11 SPSS linear regression

chapter takes the form of P[F(7, 492) ≥1836.505] <0.001, for example. Where in this example the notational positioning of the values is given by '7' degrees of freedom, '492' residual degrees of freedom, '1836.505' the F-value and '0.001' p-value significance.

Calculating linear regression with Stata and SPSS

In SPSS to open the linear regression window by selecting *Analyze - Regression – linear*. Then select the dependent and independent variables you require. Then to analyse your selection click OK.

Linear regression in Stata select *Statistics – linear models and related – linear regression*. Then enter the dependent variable in dependent variable field and independent variables in the independent variable field. Then you can click OK or submit to analyse your selection.

NOTES

1   These 'invitation' questions come from the work of Epstein and Salinas (1993)

CHAPTER 5

FACTOR ANALYSIS

Confirmatory

In Chapter 3 we looked at exploratory factor analysis and investigated techniques to find groups of items that have a common latent structure. We investigated how exploratory factor analysis (EFA) determines the hidden underlying structure in a set of items in a questionnaire. Chapter 4 applied this exploratory concept to explore correlations. Firstly a factor analysis data reduction technique was used to create latent factor themes of the Hoover-Dempsey and Sandler Likert scale questionnaire. Once these latent factors were obtained then Pearson correlation was used to find any association between these themes. This chapter takes forward the ideas from Chapters 3 and 4 to considers how we can confirm these latent structures using statistics. Confirmatory factor analysis (CFA) assesses the hypothesised structure of items in grouped constructs and quantifies the quality of the fit.

Confirmatory factor analysis is useful in assessing a prior belief or an empirical models structure of items. It can also be used in conjunction with exploratory factor analysis to confirm the fit of an exploratory structure. The difference between exploratory factor analysis and confirmatory factor analysis is that for confirmatory the researcher needs to have a good prior understanding of how the variable items in the model are thought to inter-relate and the connections between these items. Hence in confirmatory factor analysis the researcher specifies the pattern of how the items and latent factors are related in advance as well as any covariance that may exist between these. This pre-specified model structure is then evaluated through rigorous statistical procedures.

Confirmatory factor analysis is a subset of a much wider class of modelling called structural equation modelling (SEM). Structural equation modelling allows for a set of linear equations to be constructed and evaluated. A range of disciplines such as psychology, economics, medicine, psychiatry and social science use structural equation modelling.

The software to perform confirmatory factor analysis is available in Stata and is located in the strand of utilities called structural equation modelling. There are other packages which cover the techniques involved in structural equation modelling. If you do not have access to Stata then you can use LISREL, EQS, Mplus, Amos, R and SAS. It is worth noting that Amos is an added SPSS module and belongs to the IBM SPSS software collection.

FACTOR ANALYSIS: CONFIRMATORY

It is specially designed for structural equation modelling, path analysis and confirmatory factor analysis.

CONSTRUCTING FIRST ORDER CFA MODELS

To illustrate how confirmatory factor analysis can be used to test the validity of the structure of a model we will use the happiness study that was first explored in Chapter 3. There are four items in the happiness survey that form the first latent factor. A latent variable is not directly observed but inferred from directly observed variables. In this case the latent variable is made up of four questions that together have a single dimensional theme around being happy. Forming this one latent factor from four items is a similar concept to having an overall factor score in exploratory factor analysis.

The four observed items are 'I am very happy', 'I laugh a lot', 'life is good' and 'I feel I have a great deal of energy' with variable names vhappy, Laugh, Goodlife and Energy respectively. It can be seen from the exploratory factor analysis table (Table 5.1) that all of these factors have strong weightings ranging from 0.545 to 0.744 suggesting that they will form a good single factor.

Table 5.1 Exploratory factor structure for happiness study

Pattern Matrix

	Factor 1	Factor 2	Factor 3
I am very happy (vhappy)	.744		
I laugh a lot (Laugh)	.650		
Life is good (Goodlife)	.576		
I feel I have a great deal of energy (Energy)	.545		
I am always committed and involved	.317	.473	
I feel that life is very rewarding		.414	
I feel able to take anything on		.301	
I feel that I am not especially in control of my life			.503
I don't feel particularly healthy			.357
I don't have particularly happy memories			.334

SPSS output table with extraction method: principal axis factoring. Rotation method: Promax with Kaiser normalization. Only loadings of magnitude above 0.30 are shown.

Stata command: factor <variables> and postestimation of rotate, promax oblique kaiser factors(3) blanks(0.27) gives a similar three factor output.

■ ■ ■ ■ **FACTOR ANALYSIS: CONFIRMATORY**

Drawing the model

Figure 5.1 shows the model for these four items. The oval shape is used in confirmatory factor analysis models to indicate a latent variable. The observed variables are given by the rectangles. These observed variables can be thought of as similar to the items making up one factor in exploratory factor analysis. The smaller circles are the error terms (ε) made up of the unique error to that variable and the associated random error.

Interpreting model output

Once you have built your SEM diagram then clicking the 'Estimate' icon will produce the diagram in Figure 5.1. As we have seen with exploratory factor analysis in Chapter 3 it is common to report results as standardised solutions and all statistical packages give the option to do this. The diagram in Figure 5.1 shows a standardised solution for this confirmatory factor analysis model.

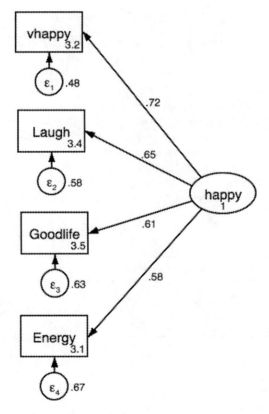

■ **Figure 5.1** CFA for happiness items

FACTOR ANALYSIS: CONFIRMATORY

The latent factor is standardised to have a mean of zero and standard deviation of one. This is the number written in the latent variable oval. The numbers given in the item rectangles are the standardised mean values for these observed variables. The diagram can be thought of as a visual representation of these four equations:

$$vhappy = \lambda_1 \times happy + \varepsilon_1$$
$$Laugh = \lambda_2 \times happy + \varepsilon_2$$
$$Goodlife = \lambda_3 \times happy + \varepsilon_3$$
$$Energy = \lambda_4 \times happy + \varepsilon_4$$

Adding the numbers from the diagram results in the following equations:

$$vhappy = 0.72 \times happy + 0.48$$
$$Laugh = 0.65 \times happy + 0.58$$
$$Goodlife = 0.61 \times happy + 0.63$$
$$Energy = 0.58 \times happy + 0.67$$

Factor loadings (λ) can be interpreted as standardised regression coefficients. For example this implies looking at Figure 5.1 that a one standard deviation increase in the happiness latent factor is associated with a 0.65 standardised score increase in 'I laugh a lot'. This factor loading can also be interpreted as a correlation between the latent factor and the item. As explained in previous chapters, squaring the standardised factor loading, gives an indication of the proportion of the variance in that item that is explained by the latent factor. By calculating one minus the square of the factor loading we will obtain the proportion of the variance in the item that is not explained by the latent factor. Notice that this result is the value of the error (ε) term. Table 5.2 shows how this calculation can be performed for the four items.

Table 5.2 Proportion of variance explained calculations

Item	Factor loading (λ)	Proportion of variance explained. (Square of factor loading)	Proportion of variance not explained
vhappy	0.72	$0.72^2 = 0.52$	$1 - 0.72^2 = 0.48$
Laugh	0.65	$0.65^2 = 0.42$	$1 - 0.65^2 = 0.58$
Goodlife	0.61	$0.61^2 = 0.37$	$1 - 0.61^2 = 0.63$
Energy	0.58	$0.58^2 = 0.33$	$1 - 0.58^2 = 0.67$

■ ■ ■ ■ **FACTOR ANALYSIS: CONFIRMATORY**

Expanding the model

The next three questions in the happiness study relate to a person's positive and committed outlook. These three questions are 'I am always committed and involved', 'I feel that life is very rewarding' and 'I feel able to take on anything'. Using these three questions we can build on this confirmatory factor analysis happiness model as shown in Figure 5.2. Note that as is suggested by the exploratory factor analysis result, in Table 5.1, the item 'I am always committed and involved' has weights of 0.317 and 0.473 in the exploratory factor analysis with factor one and two respectively. We add this cross loading to the confirmatory factor analysis to allow for the convergence of the model as shown in Figure 5.2.

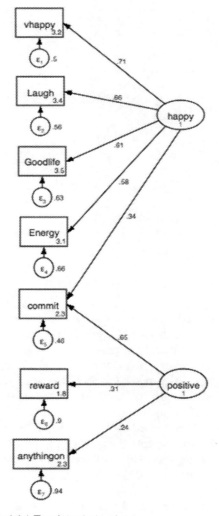

■ **Figure 5.2** Model 1 Two latent structure

FACTOR ANALYSIS: CONFIRMATORY

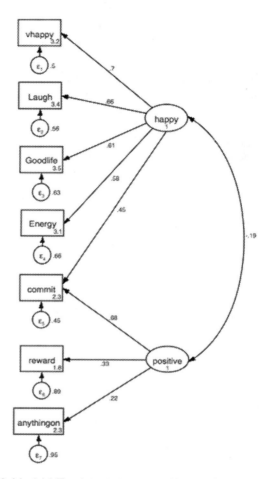

Figure 5.3 Model 2 Two latent structure with covariance

Continuing to expand on this happiness model we can add an additional correlation between the latent factors. This correlation is shown in Figure 5.3 as a 'double headed arrow' between the two latent variables 'happy' and 'positive'. This demonstrates that there is only a weak negative correlation of −0.19 between these two latent factors in this model.

The first order model fit can then be estimated using the post estimation tools for SEM. A range of fit and comparison-based indices, including Chi-square, can be used to determine a models fit to the data (Bentler, 1990; Steiger, 1990; Browne and Cudeck, 1993; Brown, 2006). The fit indices include Root Mean Square Error of Approximation (RMSEA), Standardised Root Mean Square Residual (S-RMR), Coefficient of Determination (CD), Tucker-Lewis Index (TLI) and Comparative Fit Index (CFI). Hu and Bentler (1999) suggest various cut offs for these fit indices. To minimise Type I and Type II errors we should use these in combination with S-RMR

FACTOR ANALYSIS: CONFIRMATORY

Table 5.3 Table of fit indices

	X^2	df	RMSEA	S-RMR	CD	TLI	CFI
Model 1: Happy and positive with cross loading	17.489	13	0.026	0.032	0.875	0.984	0.990
Model 2: Happy, positive with cross loading and correlated latent variables	15.511	12	0.024	0.027	0.879	0.987	0.992
Model 3: Uni-dimensional model	50.640	14	0.072	0.049	0.749	0.881	0.921

or the RMSEA. In general good models should have an S-RMR <0.08 or the RMSEA <0.06. The fit index values for CD, TLI and CFI should be >0.8 for an acceptable fit, greater than 0.9 for a good fit, and greater than 0.95 representing an excellent fit. Information regarding RMSEA, S_RMR, CD, TLI and CFI for Model 1 and Model 2 are given below. It can be seen with RMSEA, S-RMR both less than 0.06 and CD greater than 0.8 and TLI and CFI greater than 0.95 that the goodness of fit for both models is good to excellent.

When all items are connected to one latent factor this is known as a uni-dimensional model. Table 5.3 shows the uni-dimensional model (Model 3) does not provide such a good fit as the other two models. This implies that the construct of happiness, as built from our data, is multi-dimensional. The research supports this multi-dimensional construct model of happiness and so CFA is useful here as a way to confirm this (Furnham and Brewin, 1990; Argyle and Hills, 2002; Mason, 2015).

We will now look in greater detail at how to interpret the Chi-square and degrees of freedom for each of the three models. Degrees of freedom (df) refers to the number of items that we can arbitrarily assign values to after fixing the Chi-square (x^2) value. Before we explore this in greater detail let us first look at how these degrees of freedom are determined.

Chi-square and degrees of freedom

Three happiness models are now considered in turn in order to illustrate how the value of degrees of freedom is obtained.

- Model 1 – happy and positive with cross loading: has 15 parameters, is made up of eight factor loading (λ_1 to λ_8) and seven variances (ε_1 to ε_7). The observed correlation matrix has 7 variances, plus 21 correlations, a total of 28 terms. Consequently the postulated model has 28−15=13

FACTOR ANALYSIS: CONFIRMATORY

degrees of freedom (df), which is the difference between the input matrix and the number of parameters.

- Model 2 – happy and positive with cross loading and correlated latent variables: happy and positive has 16 parameters. The extra parameter is due to the correlated latent variable. Eight factor loading (λ_1 to λ_8) and seven variances (ε_1 to ε_7) and one correlation between happy and positive. The observed correlation matrix has 7 variances, plus 21 correlations, a total of 28 terms. Consequently the postulated model has 28−16=12 degrees of freedom. The equations below show how this model is formed.

$$Vhappy = \lambda_1 \times happy + \varepsilon_1$$
$$Laugh = \lambda_2 \times happy + \varepsilon_2$$
$$Goodlife = \lambda_3 \times happy + \varepsilon_3$$
$$Energy = \lambda_4 \times happy + \varepsilon_4$$
$$commit = \lambda_5 \times happy + \varepsilon_5$$
$$commit = \lambda_6 \times positive + \varepsilon_5$$
$$reward = \lambda_7 \times positive + \varepsilon_6$$
$$anythingon = \lambda_8 \times positive + \varepsilon_7$$
$$COV(happy, positive)$$

- Model 3 is the uni-dimensional model which only has one latent variable and 14 parameters, seven factor loading (λ_1 to λ_7) and seven variances (ε_1 to ε_7). The observed correlation matrix has 7 variances and 21 correlations, a total of 28 terms. Consequently the postulated model has 28−14=14 degrees of freedom.

The fit indices for Model 1 and Model 2 show that the goodness of fit is good to excellent. We therefore need to investigate using Chi-square and the degrees of freedom if one of the models is the better fit.

Firstly looking at Model 1 and 2 the respective Chi-square values are 17.489 and 15.511. The difference between these is 1.978. The difference in the degrees of freedom in these models is 1. Therefore we can calculate a p-value to see if there is any statistically significant difference between these two models. Using Microsoft Excel we can calculate the p-value by typing into any cell =CHIDIST(1.978, 1). This gives a p-value of 0.1596, which is greater than 0.05 and so we accept our null hypothesis that there is no significant difference between the two models. Therefore in this particular case both Model 1 and 2 are equally good representations. This can also been seen from how the fit indices are very similar for both models.

Now if we compare Model 2 with the uni-dimensional (Model 3) using the Chi-square and degrees of freedom, Excel gives an extremely small

■ ■ ■ ■ **FACTOR ANALYSIS: CONFIRMATORY**

p-value for =CHIDIST(35.129, 2) that is p<0.001. We would reject the null hypothesis that there is no difference between the models. That implies then that there is a statistically significant difference between Model 2 and Model 3. Model 2 with the better fit indices would be the model to choose in this case. This result again supports us in suggesting that the construct of happiness is multi-dimensional. In the next section we shall explore more complex SEM models and illustrate with examples how these can be used to gain a greater understanding of data sets.

MORE COMPLEX CFA MODELS

In this section we will firstly investigate the Roets rating scale for leadership and then continue with the parental involvement study that featured in Chapter 4. The Roets rating scale is a self-reporting assessment questionnaire, which is intended to measure leadership qualities, including leadership, confidence, ambition, desire and teamwork (Roets, 1997). Before building a SEM model we will generate factor scores to explore the correlation relationships of these variables. This same process was carried out with the parental motivation study, as this is a useful first step when analyzing data providing an understanding of structures and interrelations between variables.

There are 26 items in the original Roets questionnaire that looks at leadership characteristics. The scale was developed by Roets to help identify people who may benefit from leadership skills training programmes. This study only considers 13 of the original 26 items. Using principal axis factoring with Promax on these thirteen items from the Roets questionnaire we generate the four latent factor structure shown in Table 5.4.

In this particular example of the Roets leadership questionnaire we are using a binary scale. A response is scored '0' if the person feels that this is 'not very often like me' and '1' if the person feels that this is 'quite often like me'. In Table 5.4 factor analysis reveals that there is a clear four factor latent structure.

Factor 1 – Confidence (C1, C2, C3, C4)
Factor 2 – Leadership (L1, L2, L3, L4)
Factor 3 – Ambition and desire (A1, A2, A3)
Factor 4 – Teamwork (T1, T2)

Table 5.5 shows that five of the six correlations are positively significant. The strongest correlations are between confidence and leadership (r=0.644) with r^2=0.415. This means that 41.5% of the variations can be explained by the correlation and 58.5% (100% − 41.5%) is explained by other factors. The next strongest correlation is between confidence and teamwork (r= 0.624). The only correlation that is not significant is between 'ambition and desire' and 'teamwork' (r=0.034). This correlation has a weak measure of importance with a value very close to zero.

■ **Table 5.4** Pattern matrix for Roets leadership study

Pattern Matrix

	Factor			
	1	2	3	4
Have strong convictions (C1)	.672			
Have self confidence (C2)	.660			
Promote what is believed (C3)	.637			
Can say opinions in public (C4)	.626			
Act for what one is convinced of (L1)		.788		
Like to be in charge (L2)		.629		
Think one can do well as a leader (L3)		.549		
Lead on projects (L4)		.548		
Dream of a time of accomplishment (A1)			.915	
Admire those who have achieved (A2)			.586	
Can speak with authority (A3)			.577	
Can be a peacemaker (T1)				.753
Listen to both sides (T2)				.595

SPSS output table with extraction method: principal axis factoring. Rotation method: Promax with Kaiser Normalization.

Stata command: factor c1 c2 c3 c4 l1 l2 l3 l4 a1 a2 a3 t1 t2, ipf factors(4) and post-estimation rotate, promax oblique kaiser factors(4).

C=Confidence; L=Leadership; A=Ambition and desire; T=Team work. Only loadings of magnitude above 0.3 are shown. Variation explained = 60.949% KMO=0.790 Chi-square(78)=1497.645, $p<0.001$.

■ **Table 5.5** Pearson correlations for Roets leadership study

Correlations

	1	2	3	4
1. Confidence				
2. Leadership	0.644**			
3. Ambition and desire	0.127**	0.257**		
4. Team work	0.624**	0.520**	0.034	

**Correlation is significant at the 0.01 level (2-tailed).

■ ■ ■ ■ FACTOR ANALYSIS: CONFIRMATORY

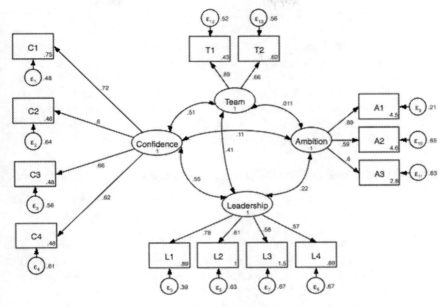

Figure 5.4 Complex CFA structure for Roets leadership study

The covariate analysis correlation can be used as a way of refining SEM models. Figure 5.4 shows a SEM diagram illustrating the power of this technique to reveal interrelated complex structures. In the diagram we can see that the correlation between 'confidence' and 'ambition' (r=0.11, p=0.056), and 'ambition' and 'team' (r=0.01, p=0.860) are both small with ambition and team not significant. Removing the correlation between ambition and team as this is not significant from Model 1 gives Model 2 (see Table 5.6). It can be noted that both models give an extremely good fit. This study illustrates the level that can be achieved when exploring the structures and relationships within questionnaires.

Table 5.6 Fit indices for Roets leadership study

	x^2	df	RMSEA	S-RMR	CD	TLI	CFI
Model 1: Roets	55.315	59	0.000	0.025	0.994	1.003	1.000
Model 2: Roets	55.347	60	0.000	0.025	0.994	1.004	1.000
Uni-dimensional model	637.121	65	0.133	0.100	0.803	0.523	0.602

Note that the TLI is non-normed and hence it can have values greater than 1.

FACTOR ANALYSIS: CONFIRMATORY

Looking at the uni-dimensional model where all 13 items are connected to one latent factor, as in the previous study on happiness the model is not a good fit. As suggested in the literature around Roets, our study indicates that leadership is multi-dimensional. It is always good when writing up your CFA to show the range of possible models and their goodness of fit indices.

The statistics for this study in Stata will not only generate the fit index measures, but also values for r^2. Generating the statistics for Model 2 will provide you with an r^2 value of 0.803. This implies that only 19.97% (1−0.803) of the variation is not explained using this model.

UNCOVERING STRUCTURES IN QUESTIONNAIRES

In this next section we will continue to look at the benefits of SEM and confirmatory factor analysis as a way of uncovering structures in questionnaires. If you are working your way through this book you will remember the parental involvement study that featured in Chapter 4. We will now use the same data from that study to create models of best fit as well as to explore relationships and structures. According to Hoover-Dempsey and Sandler (1995, 1997, 2005) there are three latent constructs, with seven items in their model and these are:

1) Psychological motivators – Role activity beliefs and Parental self-efficacy;
2) Invitations to involvement – General school invitations and Specific teacher invitations, and Specific child invitations;
3) Life context – Skills and knowledge and Time and energy.

The first construct relates to how parents perceive their role and self efficacy as being important to their child's success at school. The second construct relates to how parents can become involved with their children's schooling. The final aspect of the model is around time and ability, and how the parent's beliefs in their own skills and knowledge can affect outcomes. The three latent variables 'psychological motivators', 'invitations to involvement' and 'life context' have not been measured. The values of these latent variables can be determined using the seven items in the model. In the last chapter we created seven factor scores using PCA data reduction and the Bartlett method. We will investigate the first model of parental involvement using the PCA data. Using these PCA factor scores we can create the CFA diagram shown in Figure 5.5.

Figure 5.5 shows the model for parental involvement. The oval shapes are the latent variables, three in this case representing our three constructs. The observed variable items are given in rectangles. The smaller circles are the error terms made up of the unique error to that variable and the random error associated with that variable.

Having created the three latent constructs and their respective items, double-headed correlation connections can be added between the relevant

FACTOR ANALYSIS: CONFIRMATORY

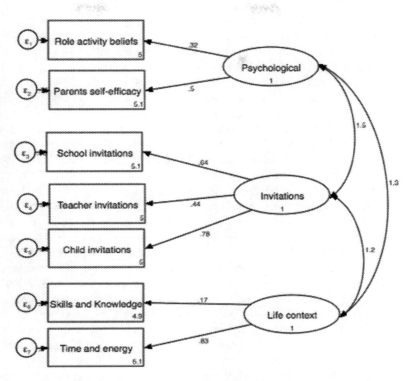

Figure 5.5 Simple factor structure for parental involvement study

latent variables. In Figure 5.5 we have added three such correlations to link the three latent constructs. Clicking the 'Estimate' icon in Stata will produce the diagram in Figure 5.5. As in previous examples the model fit can then be estimated using the 'postestimation tools for SEM'. A range of fit and comparison-based indices, including Chi-square, can be used to determine the models fit to the data (Bentler, 1990; Steiger, 1990; Browne and Cudeck, 1993; Brown, 2006).

Table 5.7 shows that the model is not a good fit. The RMSEA should be less than 0.06 and the fit index values for CD, TLI and CFI should all be

Table 5.7 Fit indices for parental involvement study

	x^2	df	RMSEA	S-RMR	CD	TLI	CFI
Model	293.713	11	0.227	0.081	0.545	0.648	0.815
Uni-dimensional model	383.010	14	0.230	0.094	0.934	0.638	0.759

FACTOR ANALYSIS: CONFIRMATORY

greater than 0.8. The uni-dimensional model is also not a good fit. However, to determine which is the 'better' fit we can use the following calculations. First calculate the difference between the two model's Chi-square (χ^2) value, that is 383.010−293.713 = 89.297. The difference between the df is 3. Using Excel we then calculate '=CHIDIST(89.297, 3)' which gives a very small value. This means that p<0.001. We therefore reject the null hypothesis that there is no difference between the two models as the test reveals that there is a statistically significant difference. There being a difference in the models we would choose the uni-dimensional model as it is the one with the slightly better fit indices. Therefore there is a lack of latent structure in our data and further investigation is required.

First we can investigate the coefficients for each of the individual items. Figure 5.5 shows these coefficients on the single arrows emanating from the latent factors to the observed variables. Stata offers the option to obtain greater detail concerning these coefficients and these values are shown in Table 5.8. These coefficients can be thought of as equivalent to the factor loadings given in exploratory factor analysis. Any factors that are small are an indication that this item should not be included in the model. In this example all of the values are above 0.3, apart from 'skills and knowledge'. Second we can explore the correlations between factors. As seen in the diagram these are sufficiently larger than zero (1.2, 1.3, and 1.5) and the Stata output shows that these have p-value significance of less than 0.001.

Third we can test for the overall goodness of fit. The overall model R^2-value is 0.545, which is good. When we look at the R^2 values for each of the individual variables most of these are fairly low and offer an indication of the models lack of fit. Note in Table 5.9 only 'child invitation' and 'time and energy' have R^2 values greater than 0.6. There is also a very low value for 'skills and knowledge' of 0.0294 being nearly zero implying that this item is not related to the latent variable.

Table 5.8 Coefficient for parental involvement study

	Coefficient	Standard error	95% confidence interval	
Role belief	0.3199	0.0526	0.2168	0.4230
Parent self efficacy	0.5026	0.0629	0.3791	0.6261
School invitation	0.6429	0.0282	0.5877	0.6981
Teacher invitation	0.4384	0.0376	0.3646	0.5122
Child invitation	0.7798	0.0197	0.7411	0.8185
Skills and knowledge	0.1716	0.0454	0.0825	0.2607
Time and energy	0.8347	0.0691	0.6991	0.9702

All significance p<0.001

FACTOR ANALYSIS: CONFIRMATORY

Table 5.9 R^2 values for parental involvement

	R-squared value
Role belief	0.1023
Parent self-efficacy	0.2526
School invitation	0.4133
Teacher invitation	0.1922
Child invitation	0.6081
Skills and knowledge	0.0294
Time and energy	0.6967

When looking in detail at the correlations, Table 5.10 confirms the fact that some of these items are not correlated. Again we see that 'skills and knowledge' is only correlated with one of the six items and the correlation with 'parental self-efficacy' (0.009) is close to zero. This implies that these two items are completely unrelated and orthogonal to each other.

From the above investigation we see that the model has some issues. As the PCA reduced data model causes concern we can explore the original data to investigate if a better model could be produced. At this stage as a researcher we may want to go back to the original individual item data.

Going back to the original data we see that all the measures for the individual question items are given on a 4 point Likert-scale (1 as strongly disagree, 2 disagree, 3 agree and 4 strongly agree). The diagram in Figure 5.6 shows a second order SEM model, giving the latent structure of the Likert scale questions in relation to the overall structure. Figure 5.6 reveals the complex structures that can be uncovered when you use SEM to explore questionnaires. The 21 item categories form six latent factors that separate into two distinct groupings. These structures form at the first order into two groups of three latent factors. On the left we see the three invitation groups of items – school invitations (GSI 1–3), teacher invitations (STI 1–4), child invitations (CI 1–3). On the right the three resulting latent groups are – skills and knowledge (SK 1–3), time and energy (TE 1–5) and role beliefs (RAB 1–3).

At the second order level there is a latent factor that links these six first order latent factors. We have labelled this on the diagram as parental involvement. Emanating from this second order latent factor are direct regression paths (single headed arrows) and correlation connectors (double headed paths). This complex structure model shows why our first simple model was not sufficient in capturing the detail. The power of confirmatory factor analysis is its ability to reveal this kind of complex latent structure. In this particular example we see first and second order factors in a model, revealing a highly interwoven themed structure created from a single simple Likert scale questionnaire.

Table 5.10 Correlations for parental involvement study

Variable	1	2	3	4	5	6	7	8	9
Psychological motivators									
1. Role activity beliefs	1	–	–	–	–				
2. Parental self-efficacy	0.176**	1	–	–	–				
Invitations of involvement									
3. General school invitations	0.245**	0.723**	1	–	–				
4. Specific teacher invitations	0.273**	0.472**	0.587**	1	–				
5. Specific child invitations	0.346**	0.625**	0.493**	0.289**	1				
Life context									
6. Skills and knowledge	0.063	0.009	0.076	0.082	0.163**	1			
7. Time and energy	0.487**	0.167**	0.582**	0.428**	0.737**	0.144**	1		
Involvement behaviours									
8. Home-based	0.332**	0.795**	0.690**	0.555**	0.908**	0.120**	0.771**	1	
9. School-based	0.601**	0.500**	0.703**	0.664**	0.625**	0.150**	0.901**	0.718**	1

**significant at the 0.01 level, * significant at the 0.05 level

■ ■ ■ ■ **FACTOR ANALYSIS: CONFIRMATORY**

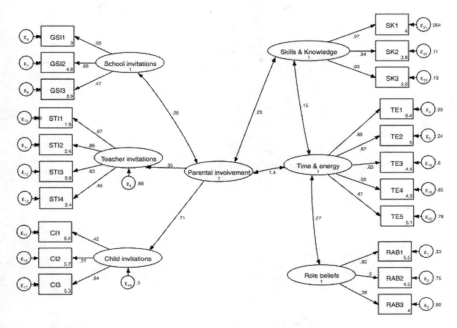

■ **Figure 5.6** Higher order CFA model for parental involvement study

LONGITUDINAL MEASUREMENT INVARIANCE

Longitudinal measurement invariance is a technique used to assess the equality of a construct measurement over time. It determines whether the change is a true change in the construct or if it is due to structure and/or measurement. Figure 5.7 shows an evaluation of an intervention with the same four item questions being asked before (A1 to A4) and after (B1 to B4) the intervention.

The model is hypothesised to be structurally the same at both assessment points in time and hence invariant. If the factor structure is found to be equivalent then other tests on the data can be performed confident in the knowledge that it is a true change and not one brought about by structural issues. In this particular example we estimate and run the model to assess the quality of the fit.

It can be seen that the model is a good fit from the data in Table 5.11 and hence this implies that this model is structurally invariant. This therefore establishes, with this longitudinal data, that we are satisfied that the same factor structure is present at both of the testing occasions. We can proceed with the longitudinal analysis confident that any differences are due to the change in the construct (Golembiewski et al., 1976; Chan, 1998; Brown, 2006). To test for significant differences in the latent factors due to the intervention we can use an ANOVA or MANOVA if we wish to control

FACTOR ANALYSIS: CONFIRMATORY ■ ■ ■ ■

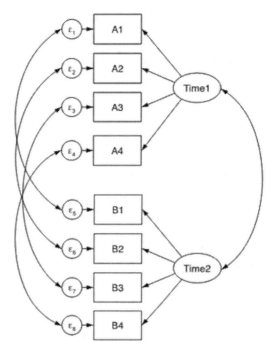

■ **Figure 5.7** Longitudinal measurement invariance

■ **Table 5.11** Fit indices for longitudinal measurement invariance

			Fit Index			
	χ^2	df	RMSEA	S-RMR	CD	TLI	CFI
Model	424.799	28	0.030	0.026	0.837	0.969	0.983

for covariates, such as socio-economic factors. If we wish to compare the change in individual Likert scale items then Kilmogorov-Smirnov test can be used as a non-parametric test (see Appendix 2).

HOW TO REPORT CONFIRMATORY FACTOR ANALYSIS

It has been highlighted in this chapter that it is important to report the fit indices when carrying out confirmatory factor analysis. The fit indices include Root Mean Square Error of Approximation (RMSEA), Standardised Root Mean Square Residual (S-RMR), Coefficient of Determination (CD), Tucker-Lewis Index (TLI) and Comparative Fit Index (CFI). To minimise

■ ■ ■ ■ **FACTOR ANALYSIS: CONFIRMATORY**

Type I and Type II errors you should use these fit indices in combination with S-RMR or the RMSEA. In general good models should have an S-RMR <0.08 or the RMSEA <0.06. The fit index values for CD, TLI and CFI should be >0.8 for an acceptable fit, >0.9 good fit and >0.95 representing an excellent fit. The report should also include Chi-square comparisons between evaluated CFA uni-dimensional and multi-dimensional models. Additional mathematical detail on how to report CFA is contained in Appendix 7.

Calculating confirmatory factor analysis with Stata and SPSS (Amos)

The software to perform confirmatory factor analysis (CFA) is available in Stata and is called Structural Equation Modeling (SEM). In SPSS Amos is an added SPSS module and belongs to the IBM SPSS software collection. Amos is specially designed for structural equation modelling, paths analysis and confirmatory factor analysis. The confirmatory factor analysis drawing board is similar in both of these packages and allows you to create a visual representation of the model to be tested.

For Stata, select Statistics – *SEM (Structural equation modeling)* – *Model building and estimation* to open the dialog box.

In the SEM builder select the variables (items) for each latent factor using the tool *add measurement component (M)* that are required for your particular confirmatory factor analysis. Repeat using the *add measurement component (M)* tool to all the latent factors. Next add in any covariance between these latent factors using the *add covariance (c)* doubled headed arrows. If second order terms are present use the *add latent variable (L)* oval to select these, making any links to other terms with covariance or path arrows. Stata has options to add/amend name 'labels' for the variables and alter the size and orientations of the boxes. Once the model is drawn select 'estimate' from the tool bar to run the model.

Goodness of fit statistics RMSEA, S_RMR, CD, TLI and CFI that have been illustrated in the above studies for the model can be found selecting Statistics – *SEM (Structural equation modeling)* – *Goodness of fit* – *Overall goodness of fit*. In the 'Statistics to be displayed' select 'All of the above' from the drop down box. If as in exploratory factor analysis, you wish to save the factor scores for the latent variables these can be obtained by selecting *SEM (Structural equation modeling)* – *Predictions* – *Factor score*.

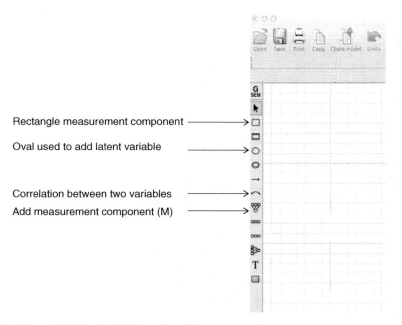

Figure 5.8 Stata drawing palette icons

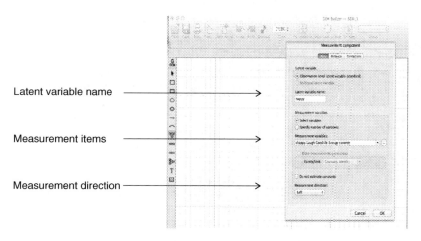

Figure 5.9 Stata defining the factor structure

Once the model is drawn select 'estimate' from the tool bar to run the model.

To find the overall goodness of fit, in the 'Statistics to be displayed' drop down box select 'All of the above'.

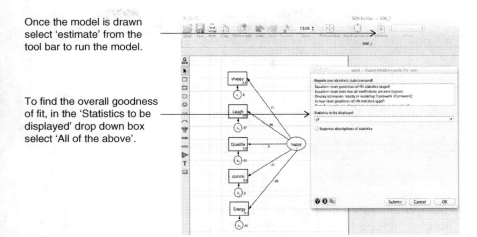

Figure 5.10 Stata goodness of fit

Goodness of fit statistics RMSEA, S_RMR, CD

Comparative fit index (CFI)
Tucker-Lewis index (TLI)

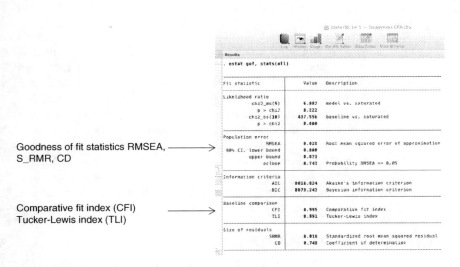

Figure 5.11 Stata goodness of fit statistics

CHAPTER 6

REGRESSION

Logistic

This chapter explores logistic regression which is the technique to use when the outcome variable is discrete taking two or more possible values. There are differences in the form of the logistic model and its assumptions, but the techniques used in both linear and logistic regression have many similarities. In this chapter we will use contingency tables to help support and illustrate logistic regression. Additional technical detail on the mathematics that underlies logistic regression can be found in Appendix 8.

The chapter starts by illustrating how to interpret and report simple outputs from SPSS and Stata for dichotomous, polychotomous and continuous independent variables. Using data sets, techniques such as reference cell and negative question coding are explored to consider how Likert scale data can be analysed. Next the section explores multivariable analysis, as up to this point in the chapter we have been mainly concerning ourselves with cases of a single independent variable in the fitted model. These more complex multivariable models are used to provide an understanding and an interpretation of SPSS and Stata outputs. In the final section of the chapter a range of additional examples are provided to illustrate how to perform and report multinomial logistic regression with three dependent variable categories.

SIMPLE LOGISTIC REGRESSION

The first study considered in this chapter is one around student's aspirations to attend university (coded 1 if the student has aspirations to go to university and zero if they do not). It is used to illustrate, case by case, how we calculate simple logistic regression when the independent variable is either dichotomous, polychotomous or continuous.

The research literature suggests that aspirations are a progressive developmental process that builds from childhood into adulthood. Studies have found that gender, academic attainment, self-efficacy and student interests significantly influence aspirations (Pottorff et al., 1996; Trusty et al., 2000; Chenoweth, 2003; Strand and Winston, 2008). As well as personal factors, research into aspirations suggests that teachers and school environment can encourage students to help to cultivate aspirations

■ ■ ■ ■ **REGRESSION**

(Khoo and Ainley, 2005; Archer et al., 2014). Positive peer support and friends having high aspirations have also been shown to influence student aspirations (Strand and Winston, 2008; David-Kacso et al., 2014).

Dichotomous independent variables

Our first example is where the independent variable in the logistic regression is dichotomous. The dichotomous variable that we will use from the aspirations study in this section is gender. This has been coded one for girls and zero for boys. The contingency table (Table 6.1) sets out the data concerning the education aspirations for boys and girls and whether they wish to attend or not attend university.

Following the same procedure, used in Chapter 2, we can calculate the odds ratio from this contingency table as follows:

Odds of the number of girls that have aspirations to go to university, to girls who do not

= number of girls who have aspiration to go to university/number not
= 239/72 = 3.319

Odds of the number of boys that have aspirations to go to university, to boys who do not

= number boys/number of boys who do not
= 126/63 = 2.0

Odds ratio of girls to boys of having aspirations to go to university

= 3.319/2.0
= 1.66

This calculation implies that in our data girls are 1.66 times more likely to have aspirations to go to university. In this case as Cramer's V of 0.111 is low there is only a weak association. If you prefer not to calculate the odds

Table 6.1 Contingency table: education aspirations

		Education aspiration		
		Non-university (0)	University(1)	Total
	Boy (0)	63	126	189
	Girl (1)	72	239	311
Total		135	365	500

Chi-square(1) = 6.184, p=0.001. Cramer's V=0.111 with p=0.013.

REGRESSION

Table 6.2 Logistic regression: education aspiration

Uni aspire	Odds ratio or EXP(B)	Std Err	Z	P	95% con. Interval on odds ratio (EXP(B)	
Gender	1.660	0.3397	2.48	0.013	1.1113	2.4787
Constant	2	0.3086	4.49	0.000	1.4780	2.7062

SPSS logistic regression: Dependent variable: Education Aspiration $P[\chi^2(1)>6.09] \leq 0.05$
Cox and Snell $R^2 = 0.012$ and Nagelkerke $R^2 = 0.018$

Stata logistic regression command: logistic univaspire gender

ratio by hand, that is that girls are 1.66 times more likely to have aspirations to go to university than boys, you are able to obtain this by running logistic regression in SPSS or Stata. Table 6.2 shows this result and the fact that it is statistically significant with a p-value of 0.013 (p<0.05). The odds ratio can also be written as EXP(B) (we will explain why this is the case later in the book).

Table 6.2 shows that the output when performing logistic regression in SPSS or Stata provides the same odds ratio value as calculated from our contingency table. When we have only one independent variable calculating odds ratios by hand is fairly simple. It will become clear as we progress through the chapter that as we add more independent variables to a model, calculations by hand become more complex.

In the gender and education aspirations case the odds ratio was greater than one implying that *there is an increase in the likelihood* of this event occurring. If the odds ratio is less than one then this implies that *there is a decrease in the likelihood* of the event occurring. Hence, if in our example above the resulting odds ratio had been 0.5 we would say *there is a decrease in the likelihood of girls having aspirations to go to university as opposed to boys by a factor of 0.5*.

In this section we have dealt with a dichotomous case. In other words, a dependent variable with only two possible values, sometimes called a binary variable. In our case this binary variable took a value of one for a girl and zero for a boy. If the independent variable has a number of distinct values as opposed to only two, then you need to deal with this in a slightly different way and this is illustrated in the next section.

Polychotomous independent variables

There are a number of ways you can approach polychotomous independent variables and the method chosen largely depends on the objective of the analysis (Dodd et al., 1995). To understand why this is the case we will continue to explore children's aspirations around university attendance. First, let us consider the case of a four point Likert scale question 'I work hard at school' to investigate if this item has an impact on children's aspirations. The data for each Likert scale value is shown in Table 6.3.

■ ■ ■ ■ REGRESSION

Table 6.3 Contingency table: work hard at school

		Education aspiration			
		non_university(0)	University(1)	Total	Odds ratio
I work hard at school (Workhard)	Least like me (1)	8	10	18	1
	A little like me (2)	23	23	46	0.8
	Very much like me (3)	44	96	140	1.745
	Most like me (4)	60	236	296	3.147
Total		135	365	500	

Chi-square(3)=22.02, p<0.001. Cramer's V=0.216 with p<0.001.

The final column of Table 6.3 sets out the odds ratios for the categories as compared to the base category 'least like me (1)'. The base category is made up of those children who responded 'least' to the question 'I work hard at school' (Workhard). The odds ratios in the table can be calculated by hand similarly to before as follows:

OR(Little, Least) = (23/10)/(23/8) = (23×8)/(10×23) = 0.8
OR(very much, least) = (96/10)/(44/8) = (96×8)/(10×44) = 1.745
OR(Most, least) = (236/10)/(60/8) =(236×8)/(10×60)= 3.147

In the following section we will illustrate how these odds ratios can be calculated using a technique called reference cell coding. This is required when using SPSS and Stata as they do not generate automatically odds ratio figures and you will need to use the reference cell coding technique to do so.

Reference cell coding

You will need to create three new columns in your data to allow for the polychotmous independent variable to be transformed into binary variables for each of the category choices. These estimates can also be obtained from logistic regression by setting the base as 0 and each of the other categories as 1 depending on the Likert scale response. This is termed 'reference cell coding'. Note that all reference (base) categories are set to zero in Table 6.4. A single variable is assigned a value one in each of the categories.

Table 6.5 can be generated using Stata or SPSS now that you have your 'new' dichotomous variables. Running a logistic regression with education aspiration as your dependent variable and including the new reference cell coded variables (Workhard1, Workhard2 and Workhard3) we can see this produces the same odds ratios obtained in Table 6.3.

REGRESSION

Table 6.4 Reference cell coding: work hard at school

	Workhard1	Workhard2	Workhard3
Least like me	0	0	0
Very little like me	1	0	0
Much like me	0	1	0
Most like me	0	0	1

Table 6.5 Logistic regression: work hard at school

	B	S.E.	Sig.	Exp(B)
Workhard1	−.2231	.5585	.690	.8
Workhard2	.5570	.5080	.273	1.7454
Workhard3	1.146	.4958	.021	3.1466
Constant	.2231	.4743	.638	1.25

SPSS logistic regression: Dependent variable: Education Aspiration $P[\chi^2(3) > 22.02] \leq 0.0001$
Cox and Snell $R^2 = 0.043$ and Nagelkerke $R^2 = 0.063$

Stata logistic regression command: logistic univaspire workhard1 workhard2 workhard3

Note that in this case only 'Workhard3' is significant at the p<0.05 (5% level) with a p-value of 0.021. The result show that only students who responded that it was 'most like me' to the survey question 'I work hard at school' are 3.1466 times more likely to have aspirations to go to university than those who said it was 'least like me' (base case). Now that the technique is becoming familiar we can continue with this reference cell coding process and analyse other items in the questionnaire.

To start let's look at the question that asked children to rank again under the headings 'least like me', 'a little like me', 'very much like me' and 'most like me' the answer to the question 'my friends think doing well at school is important'. Just as in the case above new reference cell coded variables (Doingwell1, Doingwell2, Doingwell3) will be inserted into the SPSS and Stata worksheet. The base case will be 'least like me' with a 1 given to each in turn to the other categories.

When running logistic regression a table will be generated again with education aspiration being the dependent variable (see Table 6.6). The data in Table 6.6 show that only the final factor, the 'most like me' category is close to being significant at the 5% level with a p-value of 0.059. That is children who responded that it is was most like them, that their friends think doing well at school is important, were 3.042 times more likely to have aspirations to go to university.

■ ■ ■ ■ **REGRESSION**

Table 6.6 Logistic regression: doing well at school

	B	S.E.	df	Sig.	Exp(B)
Doingwell1	1.099	.816	1	.178	3.000
Doingwell2	.659	.620	1	.287	1.933
Doingwell3	1.113	.589	1	.059	3.042
Constant	.000	.577	1	1.000	1.000

SPSS logistic regression: Dependent variable: Education Aspiration Cox and Snell R^2 = 0.012 and Nagelkerke R^2=0.017. $P[\chi^2(3)>6.038]\leq 0.11$

Stata logistic regression command: logistic univaspire doingwell1 doingwell2 doingwell3

The 'most like me' category questions for both 'work hard' and 'doing well' have been shown to be the most significant so far in our analysis. Before moving on to consider other types of simple logistic regression we will investigate the model containing these two variables. Table 6.7 shows that the 'doing well' variable is not significant in this model with a p-value of 0.246.

The likelihood ratio test is used to evaluate the fit of the model in a similar way to the F-test in linear regression. The likelihood ratio test is calculated by the difference in the base model (only containing constant term) to the model including the variables Workhard3 and Doingwell3. The test is obtained in this case by calculating the difference between the –2log likelihood values of 37.372 and 19.571 in the model fit output. By multiplying this log likelihood value by minus two creates a Chi-square distribution that can be used for testing. The Chi-square value in this case is 17.802 (37.372–19.571). The reduction in this value tells us that the model is a better predictor than the constant model. Chi-square and log likelihood values are output given as model fit information in both SPSS and Stata. This information can be written in a concise form as $P[\chi^2(2)>17.80]\leq 0.0001$.

Table 6.7 Logistic regression: work hard and doing well at school

Variables in the Equation

	B	S.E.	df	Sig.	Exp(B)
Doingwell3	.275	.237	1	.246	1.316
Workhard3	.773	.210	1	.000	2.168
Constant	0.365	.209	1	.082	1.440

Dependent variable: Education Aspiration Cox and Snell R^2 = 0.035 and Nagelkerke R^2=0.051 $P[\chi^2(2)>17.80]\leq 0.0001$

Stata logistic regression command: logistic univaspire doingwell3 workhard3

REGRESSION

The Chi-square test is highly significant in this case, showing that the model is a significant improvement on the base model and so at this stage is worth keeping for further investigation.

Another useful fit measure as we have seen with multiple linear regression is the R^2-value. In logistic regression this is called a Pseudo R^2–value and is analogous to the R^2-value and can be calculated using tests such as the Cox and Snell or Nagelkerke. Results for these tests have been given under each of the tables. These values are typically lower when compared to linear regression R^2-values. Hosmer et al. (2013) have suggested an alternative R^2 measure that is calculated by simply dividing the -2log likelihood model value by the original base value. For our example above this would be $R^2 = 19.571/37.372 = 0.523$. This is called the Hosmer and Lemeshow R^2-value. It is often useful to use these R^2 measures to discriminate between two outcome groups and not as a measure for an individual model. The appendix offers greater information on goodness of fit measures and their relative benefits. There is also more technical information on log likelihood statistics and its analogous F-test used in linear regression in Appendix 8.

Negatively worded questions

Before discussing the continuous independent variable case, we will illustrate how to analyse questions that are phrased in a negative fashion. This technique of using negatively worded questions in surveys is a way of ensuring that the respondent is actively thinking and considering their answers. To understand why this is a useful technique we can consider the case when all the questions in your survey are positively phrased. In a case such as this a person may just tick all the same responses i.e. 'strongly agree'. One way to avoid this kind of non-thinking response is to interspace your questionnaire with some 'reversed' phrased questions. In the aspirations questionnaire there is a question that is phrased in this reversed fashion 'family members do not think that school is very important'. In our survey on aspirations let us see how the group of students responded to this negatively worded question. The contingency table (Table 6.8) shows 219 students out of the 365 who have aspirations to go to university report that this is 'least like me'. In other words, they are saying that if they have aspirations to go to university then their family members **do think** that school is very important.

In cases such as this we can reverse the coding so that the base case becomes 'most like me'. This can be done by recoding the variable to have 'most like me' as the base. Reverse coding in this way allows the item under consideration to be changed to reflect the positive response (see Table 6.9).

Table 6.10 shows the results from logistic regression. The data show that those students who responded that it was 'least like them' (Schoolimport3) that their family do not think school is important is significant ($p<0.0001$). They are 2.781 times more likely to have aspirations to go to university than those who said it was 'most like me' to have parents who did not think school was important.

Table 6.8 Contingency table: family attitudes to school

*Family members **do not think** that school is very important. Education aspiration (non uni =0)*

		non_university	university	Total
Family members/carers do not think that school is very important	least	60	219	279
	a little	15	50	65
	very much	28	54	82
	most	32	42	74
Total		135	365	500

Dependent variable: Education Aspiration Chi-square(3)=16.812, p<0.001. Cramer's V=0.183 with p<0.001.

Table 6.9 Reverse coding: school is important

	Schoolimport1	*Schoolimport2*	*Schoolimport3*
Least like me	0	0	1
Very little like me	0	1	0
Much like me	1	0	0
Most like me	0	0	0

Table 6.10 Logistic regression: school is important

Variables in the equation

	B	S.E.	df	Sig.	Exp(B)
Schoolimport1	.385	.331	1	.244	1.469
Schoolimport2	.932	.376	1	.013	2.540
Schoolimport3	1.023	.276	1	.000	2.781
Constant	.272	.235	1	.246	1.312

SPSS logistic regression: Dependent variable: Education Aspiration Cox and Snell R^2 = 0.032 and Nagelkerke R^2=0.046. P[χ^2(3)>16.032]≤0.001

Stata logistic regression command: logistic univaspire schoolimport1 schoolimport2 schoolimport3

REGRESSION ■ ■ ■ ■

We can also see from Table 6.10 that those students who reported that it was 'very little like me' were also significant (p=0.013). These students being 2.540 times more likely to have aspirations to go to university than those who had parents who did not feel school was very important.

We will use what we have learnt through this initial investigation around the data set later on in the chapter when considering multivariable models. First in the next part of the chapter we will look at continuous independent variables and how we interpret the output that is given when carrying out logistic regression.

Continuous independent variable

The previous sections have dealt with dichotomous and polychotomous cases, where the independent variable has either two possible values or a number of distinct values. In this section we will consider a continuous independent variable case. Once again the student aspiration survey provides us with data but this time we are considering a continuous independent variable of English test scores. The result of running logistic regression with English test scores is shown in Table 6.11. This output shows that English test scores are highly significant (p<0.001) related to children's aspirations to attend university. The estimate for the B-value is 0.06, with an odds ratio of 1.061.

It should be noted that the output for the odds ratio for a continuous variable is given in the same format as in the previous examples for dichotomous and polychotomous cases. By this we mean that the estimate is related to a probability change between 0 and 1. When considering continuous variables a change of 1 may not be of interest to the researcher. More often you will be interested in a change by a certain amount, such as by a specific score, for example 10 or 50, or by a change in one standard deviation (SD). Let us take these different possible cases one at a time and explore what this means when we are working with continuous independent variables in logistic regression.

First, consider the case when the change is by a certain amount. The estimate for an increase in the English test scores by 10 marks, with the B-value of 0.06, gives an odds ratio of OR(10) = EXP(10×0.06) = 1.822. This shows that for every increase in the students' test score by 10 marks

■ **Table 6.11** Linear regression: continuous independent variable

	B	S.E.	df	Sig.	Exp(B)
English	.060	.009	1	.000	1.061
Constant	−1.890	.415	1	.000	.151

Dependent variable: Education Aspiration Cox and Snell R^2 = 0.108 and Nagelkerke R^2 =0.157. $P[\chi^2(1) > 57.213] \leq 0.0001$

the odds that a student has aspirations to go to university increases by 1.822 times. There is a caveat to this statement in that an increase in marks from 30 to 40 may be very different to an increase from 80 to 90 marks, as the English test scores may not follow a linear distribution.

Second, and maybe a more common interpretation for a continuous independent variable, is that the odds ratio can be written in terms of standard deviations (SD). The odds ratio would be given by OR(SD)= EXP(SD×coeff.). When calculating the standard deviation for this set of English test scores we see that it is 14.19. Using this figure we can calculate the odds ratio thus: OR(14.19)=EXP(14.19×0.06) = 2.34. This is the estimated odds ratio for an increase of one standard deviation (SD), where 1 SD is said to be a meaningful change in the continuous variable. From this information we can report the results as follows:

> Students with higher English test scores are more likely to have aspirations to attend university. Increasing this English test score characteristic by 1 SD increases the likelihood of a student having aspirations to attend university by a factor of 2.34 ($p < 0.001$).

Or in an alterative form:

> The English test score indicator suggests that students are 2.34 ($p < 0.001$) times more likely to have aspirations to go to university than not for every 1 SD increase in this English test score.

The next part shows you how to visually present data around test scores and educational aspirations for boys and girls.

Estimating marginal effects

The command 'margins' in Stata is a useful way of estimating marginal effects. A marginal effect is defined as changes in responses for a change in a covariate. In Figure 6.1 we illustrate this technique by estimating the predictive margins for boys and girls at various English test score results from 40 through 90 using the multivariable model just analysed. The graph in Figure 6.1 shows a greater likelihood for girls to have university educational aspirations regardless of English test score results, but this gap does reduce as test scores improve. Additional detail on how to perform margins in Stata is given in Appendix 9.

Estimating models with only single independent variables is not common as usually there are associations that variables have with a range of other variables in a model. To get a comprehensive picture of data in a study it is therefore usual to use multivariable analysis. Next, we will illustrate multivariable analysis using the data from previous sections in this chapter to create a model that includes gender and English.

REGRESSION ▨ ▨ ▨ ■

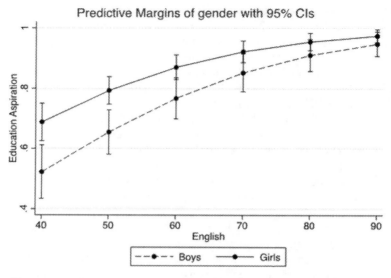

▨ **Figure 6.1** Margin plot: university aspirations

MULTIVARIABLE ANALYSIS

Table 6.12 shows three logistic regression models. The first model contains only one dichotomous variable (gender) which is significant (p=0.013) and $P[\chi^2(1)>6.09]\leq0.05$. The pseudo R^2-values for Cox and Snell = 0.012 and Nagelkerke =0.018 show the amount of variance in the dependent variable (education aspiration) which is explained by the model.

In Model 2 the continuous variable English test score has been added to Model 1 resulting in gender and English both being significant (p<0.01). The probability reduces to $P[\chi^2(2)>64.69]\leq0.0001$ indicating an improved model. Cox and Snell R^2 = 0.121 and Nagelkerke R^2=0.176 both increase. Model 2 is a better fit than Model 1.

It has been shown previously in this chapter that only 'workhard3' was significant and so we add this variable to Model 3. The results for Model 3 are shown in Table 6.12. Using the change in the likelihood ratio test to calculate the difference in the base model to the final Model 3 yields a p-value of $P[\chi^2(3)>77.297]\leq0.0001$ which is highly significant.

Note also for this third model that our pseudo R^2-values are also greater than in the previous two models with Cox and Snell R^2=0.144 and Nagelkerke R^2=0.210. This demonstrates that Model 3 is a significant improvement on the base model. This procedure for assessing the significance of the model is similar to the F-test in linear regression. The Chi-square (χ^2) value is given in Stata and SPSS outputs as standard.

When we include other variables that have been independently found to be significant this results in a more complex multivariable logistic

Table 6.12 Multivariate logistic regression

Model	Variable	Coeff B	Std Err	Sig	Exp(B)
1	Gender	0.506	0.204	0.013	1.659
	Constant	0.693	0.154	0.000	2
2	English	.060	.009	0.000	1.062
	Gender	.602	.220	0.006	1.825
	Constant	−2.287	.447	0.000	0.102
3	gender	.716	.229	0.002	2.047
	English	.058	.009	0.000	1.059
	Workhard3	.825	.225	0.000	2.282
	Constant	−2.692	.475	0.000	0.068

Dependent variable: Education Aspiration

Table 6.13 Logistic regression with multiple independent variables

	B	S.E.	Sig.	Exp(B)
Gender	.685	.233	.003	1.983
English	.058	.009	.000	1.060
Workhard3	.783	.232	.001	2.187
Doingwell3	.062	.270	.818	1.064
Schoolimport2	.930	.370	.012	2.535
Schoolimport3	.394	.251	.116	1.483
Constant	−3.056	.515	.000	.047

SPSS logistic regression: Dependent variable: Education Aspiration $P[\chi^2(6)>84.559]\leq 0.0001$, Cox and Snell $R^2 = 0.157$ and Nagelkerke $R^2=0.228$

Stata logistic regression command: logistic univaspire gender english workhard3 doingwell3 schoolimport2 schoolimport3

regression model, which is shown in Table 6.13. There are four significant variables with $p<0.05$.

Continuous approximations to ordinal variables

It is advisable when dealing with Likert scale independent variables in logistic regression to use the reference cell technique, which has been demonstrated previously, although alternative methods of calculation are possible. In this section we will illustrate one of these different techniques, using the dataset on university aspirations. The technique assumes that a

REGRESSION

continuous approximation can be made to the ordinal variable rather than using reference cell coding.

Looking at the same calculation we performed in the last section on university aspirations it can be seen from Table 6.14 that we obtain very similar results to those in Table 6.13. The variables Gender, English and Workhard are all significant (p<0.01). The variable 'Doingwell' is not significant (p=0.922). The only variable that falls on the boundary is 'Schoolimport' as it is nearly significant at the 10% level. This is not surprising for if we look at Table 6.13 we see that 'Schoolimport2' is significant (p=0.012) and 'Schoolimport3' (p=0.116) is not. These results would imply that the variable requires further investigation. Note also that this variable has a negative B-value as it is a negatively worded question.

When the variable 'Doingwell' is removed from the model the following solution is obtained as shown in Table 6.15. The variable 'Schoolimport'

Table 6.14 Model 1 continuous approximations to ordinal variables

	B	S.E.	Sig.	Exp(B)
Gender	.681	.230	.003	1.976
English	.056	.009	.000	1.058
Workhard	.527	.132	.000	1.694
Doingwell	−.016	.166	.922	0.984
Schoolimport	−.159	.098	.106	.853
Constant	−3.544	.920	.000	.028

SPSS logistic regression: Dependent variable: Education Aspiration $P[\chi^2(5)>85.31]\leq 0.0001$, Cox and Snell $R^2 = 0.157$ and Nagelkerke $R^2=0.228$.

Stata logistic regression command: logistic univaspire gender english workhard doingwell schoolimport

Table 6.15 Model 2 continuous approximations to ordinal variables

	B	S.E.	Sig.	Exp(B)
Gender	.681	.230	.003	1.976
English	.056	.009	.000	1.058
Workhard	.526	.132	.000	1.692
Schoolimport	−.157	.095	.100	.855
Constant	−3.600	.722	.000	.027

SPSS logistic regression: Dependent variable: Education Aspiration $P[\chi^2(4)>85.30]\leq 0.0001$, Cox and Snell $R^2=0.157$ and Nagelkerke $R^2=0.228$

Stata logistic regression command: logistic univaspire gender english workhard schoolimport

■ ■ ■ ■ **REGRESSION**

Table 6.16 Odds ratio calculations

	B	SD	BxSD	EXP(BxSD)
English	0.056	14.189	0.795	2.214
Workhard	0.526	0.651	0.342	1.408
Schoolimport	−0.157	1.143	−0.179	0.836

Dependent variable: Education Aspiration

becomes significant ($p < 0.10$) with B = −0.157 indicating, as expected, that lower values on the Likert scale imply a greater likelihood of aspirations to go to university.

We are assuming these are continuous independent variables and can therefore calculate the odds ratio using EXP(SD×coeff.) as described earlier in this chapter. The results of these calculations are shown in Table 6.16 which gives the estimated odds ratio for an increase of 1 SD where one standard deviation is a meaningful change in the continuous variable. We can report the result related to working hard at school as:

> Students reporting higher scores on the Likert scale for 'My friends think doing well at school is important' are more likely to have aspirations to attend university. Increasing this score characteristic by 1 SD increases the likelihood of a student having aspirations to attend university by a factor of 1.408 ($p < 0.001$).

Care needs to be taken when reporting a reverse question, such as 'Family members do not think that school is very important'. Lower values on the Likert scale are correlated with 'less likely' to aspire to go to university. Reporting can be carried out thus:

> Students who state that 'Family members do not think that school is very important' are less likely to have aspirations to attend university. Increasing this outcome by 1 SD decreases the likelihood of a student having aspirations to attend university by a factor of 0.836 ($p < 0.05$).

Multinomial logistic regression

So far we have explored logistic regression with a binary dependent variable. When using multinomial logistic regression we can have a dependent variable that is expressed through a number of levels. To illustrate how logistic regression can be used in such situations, the mood questionnaire will be explored together with the hunger scale (see Chapter 1 if you have forgotten what these scales are). The dependent variable 'hunger scale' has three categories. We will use this variable to explain how to carry out multinomial logistic regression and extend beyond the binary case.

REGRESSION ▪ ▪ ▪ ▪

The study will be used to investigate how eating breakfast affects children's moods. Breakfast is one of most important meals of the day, however an American study has shown there to be an increasing trend for children not to have breakfast (Siega-Riz et al., 1998). Other studies in America have reported that around 50% of young children aged 6 to 11 years do not eat breakfast before going to school. Eating breakfast has been shown to have a significant impact on young children's cognitive function and in the long term decreasing the risk of being overweight in later life (Cromer et al., 1990; Kanarek, 1997; Dwyer et al., 2001; Mahoney et al., 2005; Pearson et al., 2009).

In this study the Visual Analogue Scale (VAS) hunger scale is from zero to ten, with zero denoting extreme hunger and ten representing being full. This is our dependent variable for this multinomial logistic regression and provides a measure for the participant's hunger and fullness. Participants in the study indicated the point on the line that they thought was most appropriate to them at that moment in time when the question was asked. For each participant the question was always asked at the same time of day.

First, we can define the dependent variable in the model by using bands defined by the standard deviation. Table 6.17 shows the range of responses from the children in this data set, with a mean of 5.1 and SD of 3.5. These

Table 6.17 Hunger scale

0-very hungry, 10-full

Scale	Frequency	Percent	Valid Percent	Cumulative Percent
0	69	13.8	13.8	13.8
1	32	6.4	6.4	20.2
2	42	8.4	8.4	28.6
3	36	7.2	7.2	35.8
4	32	6.4	6.4	42.2
5	83	16.6	16.6	58.8
6	45	9.0	9.0	67.8
7	22	4.4	4.4	72.2
8	12	2.4	2.4	74.6
9	9	1.8	1.8	76.4
10	118	23.6	23.6	100.0
Total	500	100.0	100.0	

Mean = 5.1 SD = 3.5

■ ■ ■ ■ **REGRESSION**

responses can be grouped into three approximate bands using roughly plus and minus one standard deviation about the mean. The first band (base = 0) is made up of children who scored 0, 1 and 2 (less than one SD) and totals 28.6% of the respondents. This band we now call *Hungry*. The second band (1) is children who marked a score of 3, 4, 5, 6, or 7. This band contains 43.6% of the respondents and is denoted as *Fine*. The final band (2) contains children that scored their hunger level between 8 and 10, containing 27.8%. This band is titled *Full*. These bands are shaded in Table 6.17. These three bands are used in the analysis for the categories of the dependent variable in the multinomial logistic regression.

The mood questionnaire provides us with our eight independent variables. Originally Thayer (1989) used four components – energy, tiredness, tension and calmness. For our purpose each of these moods will have two adjectives to describe them as follows:

Energy: energetic and enthusiastic;
Tiredness: tired and drowsy;
Tension: worried and stressed;
Calmness: calm and quiet.

When asked to rate their hunger on the hunger scale, questions were also answered about mood. The mood scale is a three point Likert scale made up of 'I do not feel like this' 'Undecided' and 'I feel like this'. The contingency table (Table 6.18) gives an understanding of the part played by variables involved in this model. For example, if we take the mood 'energetic' under the component of Energy, the contingency table shows the 500 children's responses.

Previously in this chapter we have looked at a dependent variable with only two categories (aspirations to attend university). As there are now three dependent variable categories (hunger scale) in this model then this results in a larger number of odds ratio values. To calculate these odds ratios, comparisons need to be made at each category level referenced to the base. To illustrate how these can be calculated by hand we will use the item

■ **Table 6.18** Contingency table: hunger scale and energetic mood

Energetic	0 Hungry	1 Fine	2 Full	Total
I do not feel like this (1)	31	60	5	96
Undecided (2)	59	63	66	188
I feel like this (3)	53	95	68	216
Total	143	218	139	500

Chi-square(4) = 36.763, $p < 0.0001$. Cramer's $V = 0.192$ with $p < 0.0001$.

REGRESSION

energetic mood given in Table 6.18. Using 'I do not feel like this' as the base category gives the four odds ratios as follows:

$$\widehat{OR}_2 \text{ (hunger scale (1), hunger scale (0))} = (63/60)/(59/31)$$
$$= (63 \times 31)/(60 \times 59) = 0.552$$
$$\widehat{OR}_2 \text{ (hunger scale (2), hunger scale (0))} = (66/5)/(59/31)$$
$$= (66 \times 31)/(5 \times 59) = 6.936$$
$$\widehat{OR}_3 \text{ (hunger scale (1), hunger scale (0))} = (95/60)/(53/31)$$
$$= (95 \times 31)/(53 \times 60) = 0.926$$
$$\widehat{OR}_3 \text{ (hunger scale (2), hunger scale (0))} = (68/5)/(53/31)$$
$$= (68 \times 31)/(53 \times 5) = 7.954$$

The results of fitting the multinomial logistic regression model to the data using SPSS or Stata is given in Table 6.19. This output is the same as we obtained from the by hand calculation using the contingency table shown in Table 6.18.

The total model significance of the variable 'energetic' is given by the change in the log-likelihood relative to the constant model. This is given as 44.916, with a highly significant p-value of $P[\chi^2(4) > 44.916] \leq 0.0001$. The pseudo R^2 values of Cox and Snell $R^2 = 0.086$ and Nagelkerke $R^2 = 0.097$ should also be quoted when reporting results. These values seem low, but this is typical for logistic regression. Hosmer et al. (2013, p.185) say that this is sometimes a problem when reporting these values to those who are used to seeing larger R^2 values in linear regression.

Table 6.19 Multinomial logistic regression: energetic mood

Hunger scale		B	Std. Error	Sig.	Exp(B)	95% Confidence Interval for Exp(B) Lower Bound	Upper Bound
1 (Fine)	Intercept	.660	.221	.003			
	[Energetic=3]	−.077	.280	.784	.926	.535	1.603
	[Energetic=2]	−.595	.286	.038	.552	.315	.966
2 (Full)	Intercept	−1.825	.482	.000			
	[Energetic=3]	2.074	.516	.000	7.955	2.896	21.852
	[Energetic=2]	1.937	.514	.000	6.936	2.532	18.999

SPSS multinomial logistic regression dependent variable: Hunger scale. Firstly, transform independent factor 'energetic' variable so that 1 becomes 3, 2 becomes 2 and 3 becomes 1, using the routine *Transform – Recode into Different Variable*. $P[\chi^2(4) > 44.916] \leq 0.0001$ Cox and Snell $R^2 = 0.086$ and Nagelkerke $R^2 = 0.097$

Stata multinomial logistic regression command: mlogit hungryscale i. energetic, baseoutcome(0) rrr

■ ■ ■ ■ **REGRESSION**

It can be concluded from the multinomial logistic regression model that 'energetic' is significant in relation to 'hunger'. Children from the upper band (full), report a greater likelihood that 'energetic' was a mood associated with them. The significance is p<0.001 with an odds ratio of 7.955 times more likely to have energetic moods as opposed to those reporting this is not the way they feel. The estimated 95% standard errors of the coefficients for the odds ratio 7.955 have a lower bound of 2.896 and an upper bound of 21.852. These bound values also illustrate why the p-value is so significant, as even the lower bound value is approximately three times the likelihood of children who are full having an energetic mood.

COMPLEX MULTINOMIAL MODELS

We have seen in the previous section of this chapter how to undertake multinomial logistic regression when we have a three category dependent variable. In this section we will illustrate how this can be extended to a full multinomial model with a number of independent variables.

First, we will analyse a full model. Then the variables in this model will be reduced and analysed in dichotomous form. Finally, purposeful selection is used to reduce the model down to just a few significant variables. There are alternative schools of thought around reducing the number of variables in a model. One reason for this is the concern that non-significant results can be relevant. Hence care needs to be taken and each particular data set viewed on its own individual merit (Hosmer et al., 1997).

There is a range of alternative methods that can be used to build a model. In this particular example we will firstly check to see which of the items in the model may have significance. We will do this through an exploratory examination using a continuous approximation to the ordinal variables. The continuous approximation method is one that we have already explored earlier in this chapter. This technique gives an 'initial feel' for which variables could be important. We can then explore these variables in greater detail using reference cell coding and purposeful selection.

Table 6.20 shows that most of the 'mood' items are significant. Four of these – energetic, enthusiastic, drowsy and worried are significant at p<0.05. The moods 'quiet' (p=0.06) and 'stressed' (p=0.113) are outside of the 5% level of significance. The moods 'tired' and 'laidback' fall outside of the significant levels and it would seem from this exploratory analysis that these items have little significance in this particular data set.

If we explore each of the covariates in turn there is a greater level of significance associated with the Likert scale response 'I feel like that' (3) in relation to 'I do not feel like that' (1) and the 'undecided' (2) response. From the initial exploration of the mood items, we can form a dichotomous covariate with 1 as 'definitely feel like that' and 0 as both 'unsure and not'. Pooling categories like this is a technique that is used in complex logistic regression models to allow significant factors to emerge.[1] Let's proceed now to carry out a multinomial logistic regression to explore how a child's

REGRESSION

Table 6.20 Model 1 multinomial logistic regression: hunger scale

Parameter Estimates

Hunger scale		B	Std. Error	Sig.	Exp(B)	95% CI Lower Bound	95% CI Upper Bound
1 (Fine)	Intercept	1.160	.848	.171			
	Energetic	.087	.153	.569	1.091	.809	1.472
	Enthusiastic	.171	.140	.225	1.186	.901	1.562
	Drowsy	−.436	.184	.018	.647	.451	.927
	Tired	.128	.178	.473	1.136	.801	1.611
	Stressed	.247	.138	.074	1.280	.976	1.678
	Worried	−.335	.130	.010	.715	.554	.923
	Quiet	−.291	.161	.070	.747	.545	1.024
	Calm	.078	.168	.644	1.081	.777	1.503
2 (Full)	Intercept	−2.573	1.019	.012			
	Energetic	.671	.180	.000	1.956	1.375	2.783
	Enthusiastic	.360	.159	.024	1.433	1.049	1.958
	Drowsy	−.499	.212	.018	.607	.401	.919
	Tired	.080	.200	.688	1.084	.733	1.602
	Stressed	.325	.160	.041	1.385	1.013	1.893
	Worried	−.383	.148	.010	.682	.510	.911
	Quiet	.303	.177	.087	1.354	.957	1.916
	Calm	.285	.197	.148	1.330	.904	1.957

SPSS multinomial logistic regression dependent variable: Hunger scale and independent variables covariates. $P[\chi^2(16)>57.267] \leq 0.0001$ Cox and Snell $R^2 = 0.108$ and Nagelkerke $R^2 = 0.122$

Stata multinomial logistic regression command: mlogit hungryscale energetic enthusiastic tired drowsy worried stressed calm quiet, baseoutcome(0)

hunger is associated with the mood adjectives now the responses have been transformed into dichotomous values. Table 6.21 shows the results from the regression that now uses the pooled category for the mood items. This now allows for purposeful selection to be carried out in order to reduce the model to contain only those variable that are significant.

Let us now look at reducing the model. First let's start by taking out some of the non-significant variables and check for any change in the coefficients of the B-values. By removing 'tired' and 'quiet' we see there is no change greater than 20% of the absolute variation. Remember from previously, in

■ ■ ■ ■ **REGRESSION**

▨ **Table 6.21** Model 2 multinomial logistic regression: hunger scale

Hunger scale		B	Std. Error	Sig.	Exp(B)	95% Confidence Interval for Exp(B) Lower Bound	95% Confidence Interval for Exp(B) Upper Bound
1	Intercept	.288	.311	.383			
	Energ1	.338	.230	.140	1.403	.894	2.200
	Enthus1	.169	.236	.474	1.184	.745	1.881
	Drowsy1	−.515	.226	.023	.598	.384	.931
	Tired1	.483	.438	.270	1.621	.687	3.822
	Stress1	.330	.227	.146	1.391	.891	2.171
	Worried1	−.524	.235	.026	.592	.374	.938
	Quiet1	−.299	.303	.324	.742	.410	1.343
	Calm1	.328	.292	.261	1.388	.784	2.458
2	Intercept	−.689	.389	.076			
	Energ1	.622	.256	.015	1.862	1.128	3.074
	Enthus1	.352	.261	.178	1.422	.852	2.373
	Drowsy1	−.608	.253	.016	.545	.332	.894
	Tired1	.301	.482	.533	1.351	.525	3.473
	Stress1	.674	.257	.009	1.963	1.187	3.247
	Worried1	−.867	.273	.001	.420	.246	.717
	Quiet1	.324	.312	.299	1.383	.750	2.551
	Calm1	.544	.332	.101	1.723	.899	3.302

SPSS multinomial logistic regression dependent variable: Hunger scale. First, pooling categories and then transform independent factors so that 1 becomes 0 and 0 becomes 1, using the routine *Transform – Recode into Different Variable*

$P[\chi^2(16) > 37.085] \leq 0.01$ Cox and Snell $R^2 = 0.071$ and Nagelkerke $R^2 = 0.081$

Stata multinomial logistic regression command: mlogit hungryscale energ1 enthus1 drowsy1 tired1 stress1 worried1 quiet1 calm1, baseoutcome(0) rrr

Chapter 4, that with purposeful data selection you need to check for variables whose coefficients have altered by more than a 20% absolute variation. A 20% absolute variation implies that these items may have an effect on other variables still in the model and further investigate is required. Removing these moods results in a variation of 3.8% ((0.352−0.366)/0.366 = −0.038) of the mood 'enthusiastic'. This is an absolute change of 3.8%, which is not significant. We will continue and remove these variables from the model along with other non-significant variables.

REGRESSION

Table 6.22 Model 3 reduced multinomial logistic regression: hunger scale

hungryscale		B	Std. Error	Sig.	Exp(B)	95% Confidence Interval for Exp(B) Lower Bound	Upper Bound
1	Intercept	.685	.195	.000			
	Energ1	.364	.225	.106	1.439	.926	2.236
	Drow1	−.454	.221	.039	.635	.412	.978
	worr1	−.434	.225	.054	.648	.417	1.007
2	Intercept	.261	.214	.222			
	Energ1	.618	.249	.013	1.856	1.138	3.025
	Drow1	−.549	.246	.026	.578	.357	.936
	worr1	−.764	.260	.003	.466	.280	.775

SPSS multinomial logistic regression dependent variable: Hunger scale. First pooling categories and then transform independent factors so that 1 becomes 0 and 0 becomes 1, using the routine *Transform – Recode into Different Variable*

$P[\chi^2(16) > 19.316] \leq 0.01$ Cox and Snell $R^2 = 0.038$ and Nagelkerke $R^2 = 0.043$

Stata multinomial logistic regression command: mlogit hungryscale energ1 enthus1 drowsy1 tired1 stress1 worried1 quiet1 calm1, baseoutcome(0) rrr

Table 6.22 gives the model for this study around hunger and mood once all of the insignificant variables have been removed though the procedure outlined above. It can be seen that a child who reports being full has a significant likelihood of reporting energetic mood (B=0.618, p=0.013). Having negative B-values the moods of drowsy and worried are associated with a decreased likelihood in a child who has reported they feel full. It can be seen from the table that the B-values associated with 'full' on the hunger scale for drowsy and worried are B=−0.549 (p=0.026) and B=−0.764 (p=0.003) respectively. There is a significant decreased likelihood of children reporting drowsy (B=−0.454, p=0.039), who report feeling fine with regards to hunger. Overall it can be reported from this data that students' moods are related to hunger. The more food they have the more energetic they feel. These full children are also less drowsy and worried.

HOW TO REPORT LOGISTIC REGRESSION

In this chapter we have reported logistic regression output as B-values, EXP(B)-values (odds ratios) and standard errors. As with linear regression we have also given the significance of these values indicating the level with multiple asterisks, such as * p<0.1, ** p<0.05, and *** p<0.01.

■ ■ ■ ■ **REGRESSION**

As in the linear regression chapter we report F-value and R^2-value when testing for the significance of a model. Similarly to the R^2-value in logistic regression there are two commonly reported R^2 values called pseudo R^2 values and these are Cox and Snell R^2 and Nagelkerke R^2. These values are often lower than R^2 and so it can be difficult to use these to give a clearly understandable interpretation around the goodness of fit of the model. In logistic regression the comparable statistic to the F-value is the log-likelihood. The change in the likelihood ratio is used to calculate the difference in the base model that only contains the constant term to the final model. This result is given in the form $P[\chi^2(df)>G] \leq$ significance. The G-value follows a Chi-square distribution and is calculated from minus two times the change in the likelihood ratio. For greater detail on this and other aspects of logistic regression see Appendix 8.

Calculating logistic regression with Stata and SPSS

In SPSS open the binary logistic regression window by selecting *Analyze – Regression – Binary logistic*. Then select the dependent and independent variables you require.

You will also need to inform SPSS which of your independent variables are categorical. To do this click categorical button on the right-hand side of the window and add these variables. Then to analyse your selection by clicking OK. For multinomial logistic regression *Analyze – Regression – Multinomial Logistic Regression*. Then as with binary logistic regression select the dependent and independent variables you require and click OK to analyse your selection.

In Stata as with SPSS there are a few different options that you can select when undertaking logistic regression. For binary dependent variable outcomes select *Statistics – Binary outcomes – Logistic regression, reporting coefficients* OR *Logistic regression, reporting odds ratios*. Then enter the dependent variable in the dependent variable field and independent(s) variables in the independent variable field. Then you can click OK or submit to analyse your selection. For multinomial logistic regression select *Statistics – Categorical outcomes – Multinomial logistic regression*. Then as with the binary case enter the dependent variable in the dependent variable field and independent variables in the independent variable field. A polychotomous factor variable is written by adding i. to the variable name, i.e. i.variable. The regression will then fit estimates for each level and include these results as separate covariate outputs. Specify the value of the base outcome then you can click OK or submit to analyse your selection.

Note that in SPSS Multinomial Logistic Regression to produce the correct output for a base outcome of zero you will need to reverse the values of the independent variable(s). With our 'gender' variable this would mean that 0 becomes 1 and 1 becomes 0. In SPSS you can do this relatively easily by using the routine *Transform – Recode into Different Variable*. Then you

REGRESSION ▓ ▓ ▓ ■

Enter the dependent variable and independent(s) variables

Specify the value of the base outcome for the dependant variable

Click OK or submit to analyse your selection

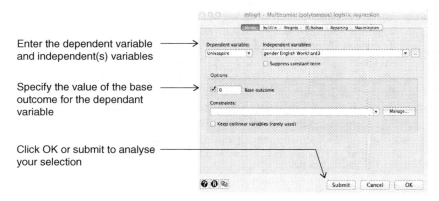

▓ **Figure 6.2** Stata logistic regression

Enter the dependent variable

In Categorical select the variables and reference category to 'first' and select 'change'.

Enter the independent(s) variables

Click OK to analyse your selection

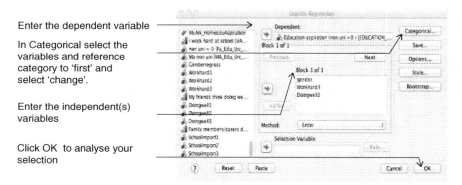

▓ **Figure 6.3** SPSS binary logistic regression

can use the new variable(s) in your analysis. In Stata this transform is not required as the lowest code is set as the base group. To avoid errors in analysis it is always worth checking your logistic regression output using a contingency table as we have demonstrated in this chapter.

NOTES

1 An alternative way of investigating this data could be to pool the hunger scale into two categories. With for example 2 and 1 becoming 'not hungry' and zero being 'hungry'. We are not going to do this in our example.

CHAPTER 7

MAKING CHOICES

Discrete choice theory

In order to determine how choices are made, discrete choice theory sets out an empirical method allowing for probability likelihoods to be determined. Here we build on the method explained in the logistic regression chapter using the logit regression. Examples of models with choice preferences and demographic characteristics will be explored using odds ratio probability likelihoods. Research examples around stated preference and revealed preference data, including some of my own research into parental school choice will be explored in the chapter.

We all love to have choice. Whether it's choice when doing our daily shopping or when making bigger long term life decisions. Choice is very much part of our modern lives. A discrete choice model is a way of analysing the decisions that are made around a range of alternatives. These alternatives could be from different fields of enquiry such as transportation, food, health, education, business, etc.

There are three characteristics that define a set of alternatives when using a discrete choice theory model. This set of alternatives is called the choice set. The first characteristic is that the range of alternatives should be mutually exclusive, in that a person only chooses one of the possible alternatives. Second is that the choice set of alternatives needs to include all possible cases and third there should be a finite number of alternatives (McFadden, 2001).

It would seem that the first characteristics is quite restrictive and does not allow for situations where a decision maker may want to make a range of choices. This is in fact not the case. We can see this by considering an example of research in consumer choice related to fruit products. Given that the consumer has two fruit choices – 'apples' and 'oranges'. These alternatives can be made mutually exclusive by defining them as these four possible choices – 'apples only', 'oranges only', 'apples and oranges' and 'neither apples or oranges'. As you can see from this simple example the researcher just needs to carefully define the choice set of alternatives under investigation to allow for meaningful results to be obtained. You will see how this can be done in practice as we proceed to explore the studies within this chapter.

STATED AND REVEALED PREFERENCE

If a decision maker 'states' their preference this implies that they are making a hypothetical choice. For example, this hypothetical situation could arise with a study that looks at people's choice of dream cars. If when asked which Ferrari they would have the person may reply that they would pick the Daytona as opposed to Testarossa or Moza. Revealed preference on the other hand is a consumer's actual choice. In terms of consumers' choice for different cars then they would be asked what brand and model of car did they own.

Surveys can use questions that elicit revealed or stated preferences in order to inform an outcome. For example, if a new shopping centre was under construction then the local population could be asked about the types of shops they would like in the development. Alternatively, the survey could ask the local population about which shops they visit on a weekly/monthly basis and hence use revealed preference data to develop the shopping centre.

These types of data have advantages and disadvantages. Revealed preference allows for an understanding of customer behaviour, habits and actual choice. The revealed preference is restricted to a limited choice set that the customer is aware of and does not allow for the exploration of new products and services on the market. Stated preference choice allows for new product development, customer price variation considerations and new options. The disadvantage with a stated preference choice survey is whether people's actions are truly reflected in what they say they would do.

A SIMPLE CONSUMER CHOICE MODEL

In order to look at discrete choice theory we will first consider a data set around organic foods. The organic trade association reported in 2017 that in the US more than 82% of households were buying organic food. Organic food sales in the US have been reported to make up 30% of the retail food market (Packaged Facts, 2018). This report also confirms that organic food is thought to be tastier and good for your health. The Global Organic Foods and Beverages Market Industry Report (Grand View Research, 2017) states that in 2015 the organic food market was valued at $77.4 billion and it is estimated that by 2025 it will be worth $110 billion. The variables used in this study have been shown by research to be some of the important factors in determining consumer food choice. Discrete choice theory allows some understanding of what motivates consumers to buy organic food (Huang, 1996; Verhoef, 2005; Yiridoe et al., 2005; Tsakiridou et al., 2006)

This first study illustrates how the discrete choice technique can be applied to choice decisions. As the data set also includes socio demographic information around the consumer this allows for the analysis to take into account a range of factors that affect choice.

The focus of this study is to investigate consumers' knowledge of organic food products as opposed to conventional food. In the design of

■ ■ ■ ■ **MAKING CHOICES**

the study consumers would have been randomly selected, preferably from a household survey, but could also have been interviewed in a shopping centre. If a shopping centre data collection methodology were used then the researcher would need to take care in deciding on the location to administer the face-to-face questionnaire. Bias could be introduced if all of the data were gathered inappropriately say outside an organic food shop!

This organic food questionnaire was designed to analyse consumer attitudes and purchasing behaviour. Consumers were asked questions related to their knowledge of organic foods, how often they eat organic food, price, quality, health benefits, food attributes and their own socio-demographics (gender, age, education level and income). Table 7.1 shows the variables that are included in the organic food choice model.

Table 7.1 Code for variables in the organic food study

Variable name	Variable definition
Choice	2 if the consumer eats organic food on a regular basis. Eating some organic every day of the week; 1 if they eat at least some organic food. Eating some organic food but not every day; 0 if they do not eat any organic food.
Health	1 if the consumer feels that organic food products are beneficial for your health; 0 otherwise
Quality	1 if the consumer feels that organic food products have higher quality than other similar products; 0 otherwise
Taste	1 if the consumer believes that taste is important in their organic food purchase; 0 otherwise
Appearance	1 if the consumer believes that appearance is important in their organic food purchase; 0 otherwise
Knowledge	1 if the consumer reported that they were knowledgeable about organic food; 0 otherwise
Environ	1 if the consumer feels that their organic food purchase is beneficial to the environment; 0 otherwise
Price	1 if the consumer believes that price is important in their organic food purchase; 0 otherwise
Gender	1 if the consumer who answered the questionnaire was female; 0 if male
Income	1 if the consumer earns more than an average yearly wage; 0 if lower
Higheduc	1 if the consumer has completed higher studies; 0 if not
Age	1 if under 21 years of age; 2 if reported to be 21 and up to 25 years; 3 if 25 and up to 40; 4 if 40 and up to 55; 5 if 55 and over.

MAKING CHOICES

Care needs to be taken when defining the choice set to avoid unobserved factors not being correlated over alternatives. An assumption of all logit models is that the error for one of the dependent alternatives contains no information about the error contained in another alternative. This model carefully defines a 'regular buyer' in the choice set to be a consumer saying that they eat some organic food *everyday* of the week. If the consumer is not able to meet this strict criterion – that a day does not go by without eating organic food – then they fall naturally into the second category. The final category is also strict saying that the consumer does not eat any organic food.

A single dichotomous covariate

Before launching into a full analysis using multinomial logistic regression it is advisable to carry out certain practices in order to ensure correct interpretation and understanding of the data set. It is good practice to obtain a rough feel for how a simplified model behaves with one or two variables. This will help with your understanding and allow you to choose the correct default setting within the statistical package you are using. Some hand calculations at the start can help allay any future confusion. Discrete choice analysis is a complex technique and errors can occur easily. Carrying out pre-checks could save time in the long-run.

In order to look at the simplified model for the organic food survey we start by considering a single dichotomous covariate that may affect choice and as shown in Table 7.1 is coded 0/1. For this example we use the variable 'Health'.

Table 7.2 Contingency table: organic food choice

Health		Choice			Total
		Consumer regularly eats organic food (2)	Consumer eats at least some organic food (1)	Otherwise (0)	
Consumer feels that organic food products are beneficial for your health	No (0)	31	66	30	127
	Yes (1)	165	182	26	373
Total		196	248	56	500

Pearson Chi-square (2) = 33.148, p<0.001. Cramer's V = 0.257, p<0.001

■ ■ ■ ■ **MAKING CHOICES**

A contingency table is generated that shows the frequencies around consumer choice of organic food in relation to perceived health benefits. The frequencies in Table 7.2 show that there are 500 consumers, with 373 who feel that organic food is good for their health. Out of these 373, there are 165 consumers who eat organic food on a regular basis, 182 who eat at least some organic food and the remaining 26 consumers who do not eat organic food. Only 127 of the 500 consumers feel that organic food is not beneficial for their health.

Using the contingency table (Table 7.2), as you will remember from Chapter 2, we can calculate the odds ratio using the cross product ratio of the frequencies. Taking the base case of 'otherwise' (0) and the notation for the odds ratio as $\widehat{OR}$, we will work through the calculation step by step below.

First calculate the odds that regular consumers of organic food think that it is beneficial for their health. Use the figures in Table 7.2 thus:

= number of consumers who regularly eat/number otherwise
= 165/26 = 6.3461

Calculate the odds that regular consumers of organic food do NOT think (0) that it is beneficial for their health:

= number regular/number otherwise
= 31/30 = 1.0333

Using these two values it is then possible to calculate the odds ratio $[\widehat{OR}_2$ (regular eat organic(2), otherwise(0))] that regular consumers of organic food think that it is beneficial for their health:

= 6.3461/1.0333

$\widehat{OR}_2$ (regular eat organic (2), otherwise(0)) = 6.142

This result implies that a person who regularly eats organic food is 6.142 times more likely to believe that organic food is good for their health compared to someone who does not eat organic food.

Let's now calculate the odds ratio for consumers who 'eat at least some organic food' (1) following the same principal as above. The odds that they think that it is beneficial for their health is given by:

= number of consumers who eat at least some/number otherwise
= 182/26 = 7.0

Calculate the odds that those who eat at least some organic food do NOT think that it is beneficial for their health:

= number eating some/number otherwise
= 66/30 = 2.2

Odds ratio $[\widehat{OR}_1$ (eat organic, otherwise)] that those who eat at least some organic food think that it is beneficial for their health

= 7.0/2.2

$\widehat{OR}_1$ (eat organic (1), otherwise (0)) = 3.182

MAKING CHOICES

Table 7.3 Model 1 multinomial logistic regression: organic food choice

Choice variable		B	Std. Error	Sig.	Exp(B)	95% Confidence Interval for Exp(B)	
						Lower Bound	Upper Bound
Eat some organic (1)	Intercept	.788	.220	.000			
	Health	1.157	.304	.000	3.182	1.753	5.774
Regularly eat organic (2)	Intercept	.033	.256	.898			
	Health	1.815	.332	.000	6.141	3.205	11.769

SPSS multinomial logistic regression dependent variable: Choice with reference category as otherwise (0) and independent variables covariates. $P[\chi^2(2)>30.821]\leq0.001$. Pseudo R^2 values for Cox and Snell=0.060, Nagelkerke=0.070.

Stata multinomial logistic regression command: mlogit choice health, baseoutcome(0)

This result implies that a person who eats organic food at least some of the time is 3.182 times more likely to believe that organic food is good for their health compared to someone who does not eat organic food. These two odds ratios offer a measure of association between the categories.

Note that to produce this table in SPSS you need to reverse the values in order to calculate a reference category of zero. With our 'Health' variable this would mean that 0 becomes 1 and 1 becomes 0. In SPSS you can do this by using *Transform – Recode into Different Variable*. This new variable can then be used in the analysis. In Stata this is not required.

Running multinomial logistic regression with 'Health' as the independent variable and 'choice' the dependent variable produces the output as set out in Table 7.3. You can see that the figures in the Exp(B) column (apart from some small rounding errors) are the same as those we have just calculated by hand using the contingency table method.

Next let us explore how these odds ratios help to understand the consumer choice data. Looking at the category 'regularly eat organic' the statistically significant coefficient for the variable 'Health' (B = 1.815) is positive and this indicates that consumers who are eating organic food regularly feel that the product has health attributes. The odds ratio of those who regularly eat organic food is 6.141. This means that those consumers who regularly eat organic food are 6.141 times more likely to think that organic food is beneficial to their health than those who do not.

The 95% confidence interval indicates that the odds ratio is in the range from 3.205 to 11.769. Due to the fact that this range is greater than one it indicates that the perceived health benefits are highly significant for consumers who regularly eat organic food.

MAKING CHOICES

Note that 'Health' is also significant at the p<0.001 (0.1% level) with p=0.000 in the 'eat some organic' category. The result shows that consumers who responded that 'organic food products are beneficial to your health' to the survey are 3.182 times more likely to 'eat at least some organic food' than those who said 'they do not eat organic food'.

The 95% confidence range for this likelihood is between 1.753 and 5.774, showing again that we can be very confident about this result. The range values are again, as with the health category for regular eating of organic food, all above the odds ratio value of one indicating that the result is significant. As you will remember from the previous chapter a value greater than 1 for the odds ratio means it has a positive B-value. If the odds ratio is less than 1 then there would be a negative B-value. If the 95% confidence values for the lower and upper bound do not cross the boundary line of 1 this implies that the variable will have a significant p-value.

Expanding on the simple choice model

Using the purposeful selection technique you can then add subsequent variables to the model. For example, we could start with the variable 'Income', so running again multilevel logistic regression we obtain the results set out in Table 7.4. We can see that both 'Health' and 'Income' are significant. Consumers who regularly eat organic food are 3.424 times more likely to be 'earning more than an average yearly wage' than consumers that do not eat organic food. There is a similar significant result for those

Table 7.4 Model 2 multinomial logistic regression: organic food choice

Choice variable		B	Std. Error	Sig.	Exp(B)	95% Confidence Interval for Exp(B)	
						Lower Bound	Upper Bound
organic products (1)	Intercept	.609	.230	.008			
	Income	.844	.351	.016	2.326	1.168	4.631
	Health	.975	.313	.002	2.650	1.436	4.890
regular eating organic (2)	Intercept	−.274	.271	.313			
	Income	1.231	.360	.001	3.424	1.690	6.938
	Health	1.535	.342	.000	4.642	2.375	9.073

SPSS multinomial logistic regression dependent variable: Choice with reference category as otherwise (0) and independent variables covariates. $P[\chi^2(4)>44.22]\leq0.001$ Pseudo R^2 values for Cox and Snell=0.085, Nagelkerke=0.099, McFadden=0.046

Stata multinomial logistic regression command: mlogit choice i.health i.income, baseoutcome(0)

MAKING CHOICES

consumers who only eat some organic food being twice as likely to have earnings more than the average yearly wage. These results seem to imply from our data that more wealthy consumers are eating organic food.

This process of purposeful selection can be continued (as we have seen in previous chapters) in order to obtain a statistical model containing only significant variables. Alternatively, as we have also discussed, an empirical model could be created using past research and literature that has also considered consumer behaviour and organic food choice. In this particular study if we added in all the variables as suggested by the literature the variable 'income' does not feature as significant. This is due to the interaction of all the other variables in the model and illustrates the need for caution and careful exploration of models before merely applying statistical techniques.

In the full model shown in Table 7.5 there are five factors that are significant at the 5% level. The three factors for consumers who eat some organic foods are 'Health' ($p=0.040$), 'Taste' ($p<0.001$) and 'Price' ($p=0.050$). The variable

Table 7.5 Empirical model: organic food choice

Choice variable		B	Std. Error	Sig.	Exp(B)	95% Confidence Interval for Exp(B) Lower Bound	Upper Bound
Some organic food	Intercept	−1.310	.773	.090			
	Female	−.489	.438	.265	.613	.260	1.448
	Income	.620	.400	.121	1.860	.849	4.074
	Higheduc	.346	.472	.463	1.414	.561	3.567
	Age	−.063	.113	.576	.939	.752	1.172
	Health	.702	.342	.040	2.017	1.032	3.943
	Quality	.348	.387	.369	1.416	.663	3.023
	Taste	1.465	.372	.000	4.328	2.087	8.979
	Appearance	.123	.483	.799	1.131	.439	2.916
	Knowledge	.488	.421	.247	1.629	.713	3.719
	Environ	.475	.789	.548	1.607	.342	7.547
	Price	1.190	.607	.050	3.286	.999	10.803
Regular eating organic	Intercept	−1.256	.788	.111			
	Female	.016	.467	.972	1.017	.407	2.540
	Income	.286	.435	.510	1.331	.568	3.122
	Higheduc	.644	.490	.189	1.903	.729	4.969
	Age	.080	.125	.523	1.083	.848	1.382

Choice variable	B	Std. Error	Sig.	Exp(B)	95% Confidence Interval for Exp(B)	
					Lower Bound	Upper Bound
Health	.762	.392	.052	2.142	.994	4.617
Quality	.121	.418	.773	1.128	.498	2.557
Taste	2.030	.420	.000	7.613	3.340	17.354
Appearance	.623	.497	.210	1.865	.703	4.944
Knowledge	.390	.448	.383	1.478	.614	3.553
Environ	1.941	.778	.013	6.966	1.515	32.029
Price	−.640	.574	.265	.527	.171	1.623

SPSS multinomial logistic regression dependent variable: Choice with reference category as otherwise (0) and independent variables covariates. $P[\chi^2(22)>191.813]\leq 0.001$ Pseudo R^2 values for Cox and Snell=0.319, Nagelkerke=0.373.

Stata multinomial logistic regression command: mlogit choice i.health i.income i.quality i.environ i.price i.taste i.appearance i.knowledge i.female age i.highedu, baseoutcome(0)

'Taste' (p<0.001) is also considered highly important by consumer's who regularly eat organic food, along with the variable 'Environment' (p=0.013). It is interesting to note that for consumers who regularly eat organic foods 'Health' is also nearly significant with a p-value of 0.052 and an odds ratio of 2.142. From our early work using just this variable in the contingency table it seems that it would be worth further investigation.

It is clear from our initial exploration of these data that taste is likely to be a major factor for consumers choosing organic food. It is also interesting to note that price is only a concern for non-regular consumers of organic foods and it could be speculated that this is a reason for them not buying more organic foods. This is an interesting finding and mixed methods research using qualitative interviews would be a way for a researcher to investigate these findings further.

There are limitations to the study design we are offering here. It would be good in a mixed methods approach to have some qualitative data from the consumers about their reasons for eating organic foods. This could include daily or weekly diaries detailing consumer's organic food purchases and meals. This information could be used together with the discrete choice analysis to create a rich picture of the decision making process linked to consumer's motivations, background, buying habits and attitudes to organic food shopping.

The next study we are going to investigate uses revealed preference data, which relates to the parents' actual school choices rather than stated preference data, where the parents would have been presented with hypothetical choice situations around school selection.

MAKING CHOICES ▓ ▓ ▓ ■

MULTINOMIAL LOGISTIC REGRESSION MODEL WITH SOCIO-ECONOMIC FACTORS

Over the past few decades research has revealed that in many sub-Saharan African countries a range of school management types exist and have been giving educational choices to parents, including very poor parents, living in informal settlements (Dixon and Humble, 2017; Humble and Dixon, 2017). This research has shown that parents in the Global South are making decisions and choices about where to educate their children. These parents are being offered choices for government, faith based and community schools in the same way that parents are making choices to go to Charter, Academy and faith based schools in the Global North.

In this discrete choice survey parents were asked if it was possible for them to access all school types – government, faith and community. Only those parents who indicated that it was an option for them to choose between all of the school management types were included in this data set. At the start of this chapter we set out criteria that the range of alternatives should be mutually exclusive, in that a person only chooses one of the possible alternatives. Note that these alternatives need to be accessible to all, so in the case of school choice this implies that parents can pick any one of the school management types. This implies choice without restrictions due to cost, location or other limitations. In this particular example it is assumed that all the school management types are 'free'. Yet, as we all know, no form of education is truly free as there are always hidden costs. These hidden costs could be in the form of uniforms, meals, books, stationary and transportation to and from school.

Figure 7.1 shows parental school choice by family income decile. We can use this to illustrate that the parents in this particular data set are not restricted in their choice of schooling alternatives due to financial issues. Within each income category parents are able to choose each of the three

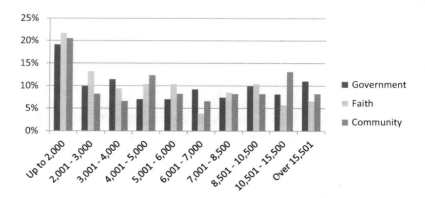

▓ **Figure 7.1** School choice by family income decile

MAKING CHOICES

Table 7.6 Parents' preferences: school characteristics

Preference	Important	Not important
Affordability	25.0	75.0
Strong disciplinary environment	47.2	52.8
Safe and close to home	42.8	57.2
School reputation	70.0	30.0
Academic performance	66.2	33.8
Quality of teaching	78.2	21.8

types of schools under consideration. When looking at the lowest income categories we see that this is not a barrier and all of the three school alternatives are accessible.

In this revealed preference household study the parents were asked to provide the three main reasons for choosing their eldest child's school. The percentage of parents selecting the six most cited preferences is shown in Table 7.6. The three most frequently cited reasons given by the parents in this data set were school reputation, academic performance and quality of teaching with popularity of 70.0%, 66.2% and 78.2% respectively. Table 7.6 is a summary of the parents' school preferences.

In a study such as this where preferences can be subjective, and individuals may interpret questions differently, it is good to ask those being surveyed how they would define the preferences they selected. When writing an article about these data you would want to include a paragraph such as the one that follows that defined these preferences to help the reader understand how the participating parents interpreted these words.

> Quality of assessment is typically made through informal methods and can be quite subjective. First, for parents 'quality of teaching' typically implies that teachers attend school regularly (i.e., are not absent) and are committed and caring towards the children in their charge. Second regarding 'school reputation' the parents place emphasis on the reputation of the school proprietor and leader. Personal relationships within the community also foster reputation around safe environment and discipline. Third, parents believe that schools that are within walking distance for their child are 'close to home' and therefore 'trusted' within the community. Finally, regarding academic performance this is typically based on examination results but parents also value what they are familiar with, such as the amount of homework given and the number of times teachers mark their homework.

MAKING CHOICES

To help to clarify how parents are making these decisions and to show that they are informed decisions it is good to clarify the procedure that they have undertaken in collecting this evidence. This helps to underpin your research and validate the preferences given. It is usual in this type of research to state the range of sources of evidence parents have used to inform their decision making process. These could include talking to relatives, friends and neighbours to find out how they feel about the school and their experiences of sending children to the school. Parents will generally make school visits to a range of alternatives and on these visits they may have the opportunity to observe lessons. They could have also looked at school websites and other sources to find out information on examination performance, extra curricula activities and opportunities gained by past students.

Indeed, some suggest that only between 10% and 20% of parents need to be informed decision makers in order for the market to be competitive (Thorelli and Engledow, 1980; Feick and Price, 1987). In terms of education this implies there is a range of valid school alternatives that offer parents a choice that they believe is appropriate for their child's needs. Schneider et al. (1998) suggest in their paper 'Shopping for Schools: In the Land of the Blind, The One-Eyed Parent Is Enough' that it only requires a subset of parents to be informed decision makers to allow for choice in schooling to be effective.

Socio-economic factors scores

This data set on school choice asked a number of questions around family possessions and wealth. As we saw in Chapter 3 an exploratory factor analysis data reduction technique can be used to collapse these into a smaller set of combined factors. In Table 7.7 the set of items dealing with household wealth have been combined into a smaller set of measures. Principal factor analysis was used with the Varimax procedure to produce an optimal two-factor solution.

When looking at how the household items group together there are two clear themes that emerge which have been termed 'electric' and 'home' as follows:

Factor 1 – Wealth 1 – Electric: Smart Phone, Computer, TV, DVD, Generator.
Factor 2 – Wealth 2 – Home: Fridge, Gas stove, Freezer.

These two factors explain 47.783% of the variation in this set of data. Factor scores for these wealth factors were derived for each pupil in the data set. As we are looking for factor scores that are only correlated with items within that latent factor the Bartlett method was used to produce Wealth 1 and Wealth 2 variables.

Using the parent school choice survey the following items are also incorporated into this model and have been collapsed into two categories to form dichotomous variables using the mean as a cut-off point.

■ ■ ■ ■ MAKING CHOICES

Table 7.7 Data reduction: wealth factors

Rotated Component Matrix

	Component 1	Component 2
TV	.861	
Generator	.829	
DVD Player	.703	
Laptop or Computer	.529	
Car	.457	
Motorbike	.357	
Smart Phone	.382	
Fridge		.864
Gas Stove		.810
Freezer		.769

SPSS extraction method is principal component analysis. Rotation Method: Varimax with Kaiser Normalization. 51.039% variance explained. KMO=0.728, Chi-square(45)=1600.423, p<0.001

Stata command principle component factor: factor tv generator dvdplay computer car motorbike smartphone fridge gasstove freezer, pcf factors(2) blanks(0.38) and postestimation command: rotate, kaiser factors(2) blanks(0.38)

- Family Income: less than the mean $59.85 = 0, greater than the mean $59.85 = 1);
- Family Expenditure: less than the mean of $41.63 = 0, greater than the mean of $41.63 = 1).

Family education and occupation were also reduced to dichotomous variables as follows:

- Highest Level of Education in the Household (no education or primary level only=0, above primary level=1);
- Occupation (unemployed=0, employed=1).

Multinomial logistic regression model

Once the data have been organised then multinomial logistic regression can is used to estimate the empirical model. There are three school choice categories, Government ($s = 0$); Faith-Based Mission ($s = 1$); Community ($s = 2$). Note that the base category for the multinomial logistic regression

MAKING CHOICES

model for this particular study will be government. Parameter estimates can be obtained to estimate the following equation:

$$C_i = \alpha + \beta D_i + \gamma P_i + \varepsilon_i$$

where C_i is the type of school choice that parent i has selected for their child. D_i is the vector controlling for household, parent and child demographic characteristics. These include gender, age, number of children, parent's occupation and highest education, household income and expenditure, two wealth factors and the proportion of non-government schools in the household's community. P_i is a vector of each household's preferences for a set of school characteristics and εi is the unobserved factors.

In Table 7.8 each odds ratio coefficient (Exp(B)) indicates the change in the likelihood that a parent selects a given type of school as opposed to a government school. For a one standard deviation increase in a particular parental preference or school characteristic we can calculate the odds ratio as Exp(SD×B).

Looking in detail at Table 7.9 the results show that there are three parental preferences around school choice that are statistically significant. Parents who stated a preference when selecting schools for their children by them having good 'academic performance' are more likely to send their

Table 7.8 Odds ratio calculations for significant variables

	SD	B×SD	EXP(B×SD)
Academic performance	0.474	0.671×0.474	1.374
Safe	0.495	1.747×0.495	2.374
Reputation	0.495	0.952×0.495	1.602
Affordability	0.433	−0.462×0.433	0.818

Table 7.9 Multinomial logistic regression: school choice study

School type		B	Std. Error	Sig.	Exp(B)	95% Confidence Interval for Exp(B)	
						Lower Bound	Upper Bound
Faith (s=1)	Intercept	−2.282	0.73	0.002			
	Childs_Age	0.127	0.043	0.003	1.135	1.044	1.234
	Gender	−0.355	0.239	0.137	0.701	0.439	1.12
	No. children	0.071	0.053	0.18	1.073	0.968	1.191
	Fam. Income	0.309	0.261	0.236	1.362	0.817	2.27

MAKING CHOICES

School type		B	Std. Error	Sig.	Exp(B)	95% Confidence Interval for Exp(B) Lower Bound	Upper Bound
	Expenditure	−0.309	0.29	0.287	0.735	0.416	1.296
	Occupation	0.112	0.284	0.694	1.118	0.64	1.952
	High. Edu	0.34	0.25	0.174	1.405	0.86	2.293
	Wealth1	−0.248	0.129	0.054	0.781	0.607	1.004
	Wealth2	0.052	0.112	0.642	1.053	0.846	1.312
	Qual. Teach	0.031	0.37	0.932	1.032	0.5	2.13
	Affordability	0.474	0.361	0.190	1.606	0.791	3.262
	Discipline	−0.468	0.345	0.174	0.626	0.318	1.231
	Safe	0.023	0.363	0.948	1.024	0.502	2.087
	Reputation	−0.488	0.351	0.164	0.614	0.309	1.221
	Acad. Perf	−0.133	0.378	0.725	0.876	0.417	1.837
Community (s=2)	Intercept	−1.547	0.664	0.02			
	Childs_Age	−0.102	0.036	0.005	0.903	0.841	0.97
	Gender	−0.416	0.234	0.075	0.66	0.417	1.043
	No. children	0.039	0.058	0.495	1.04	0.929	1.164
	Fam. Income	−0.206	0.244	0.399	0.814	0.504	1.314
	Expenditure	−0.064	0.274	0.814	0.938	0.549	1.603
	Occupation	0.135	0.273	0.62	1.145	0.671	1.954
	High. Edu	0.35	0.242	0.149	1.419	0.883	2.28
	Wealth1	−0.173	0.123	0.159	0.841	0.661	1.07
	Wealth2	0.029	0.111	0.796	1.029	0.827	1.28
	Qual. Teach	−0.543	0.328	0.097	0.581	0.306	1.104
	Affordability	−0.462	0.33	0.161	0.63	0.33	1.203
	Discipline	0.565	0.292	0.053	1.759	0.992	3.119
	Safe	1.747	0.317	0.000	5.737	3.079	10.689
	Reputation	0.952	0.323	0.003	2.59	1.375	4.88
	Acad. Perf	0.671	0.332	0.043	1.957	1.021	3.749

SPSS multinomial logistic regression dependent variable: School type with reference category as Government(0) and independent variables covariates. $P[\chi^2(30)>87.162]\leq0.001$. Cox and Snell=0.160, Nagelkerke=0.185.

Stata multinomial logistic regression command: mlogit schoolchoice gender age numchildren income expenditure occup educat wealth1 wealth2 qualteach afford discipl safe reput acad, baseoutcome(0)

children to a community schools. The results show the likelihood of parents selecting a community school is approximately 1.374 times the likelihood of selecting a government school for every 1 SD increase in the preference rating ($p < 0.05$).

Parents who state that 'safe' is a preference are more likely to send their children to community schools than government. All else equal, a one standard deviation increase in the preference indicator of safe is associated with an increase in the likelihood of selecting community schools instead of government by a factor of 2.374 ($p < 0.001$). Regarding school reputation, parents are also more likely to send their children to a community school when stating these preferences, there is 1.62 times the likelihood of parents selecting a community school for every 1 SD increase in the preference rating ($p < 0.01$).

Individual characteristics show that there is a decrease in the likelihood of parents sending a child to community schools but an increase in the likelihood of attending faith-based schools as the child gets older. The reason it is a decrease for community schools is that the B-value is negative (B=–0.102, p=0.005) and an increase for faith-based schools as the B-value is positive (B=0.127, p=0.003).

The preceding discussion is around the items that are significant ($p<0.05$) and gives odds ratio likelihoods in relation to government schools within the data. We have only discussed here significant variables but researchers may also discuss the variables that are not significant in their reports as these may have played a major part in previous literature or are an important aspect of the present study.

The final study in this chapter illustrates how a discrete choice model can be applied to revealed choice decisions for consumers related to transport. The societal demands around transport for people living in metropolitan areas is constantly growing due to changing life patterns related to work and leisure. Consequences of this are often seen in traffic congestion, increased noise and air pollution and road accidents. Urban environmental planners attempt to avoid these issues by introducing a greater range of transport systems, with the expectation that the public feel more comfortable, happy and safe during journeys for work and pleasure.

ORDERED LOGIT CHOICE MODEL

In this study a group of commuters were asked about their revealed preference choice of transport on their commute to work. The choice is between a bus and underground journey into the city centre. Upon making the decision around the mode of transport they preferred they were then asked what were the important factors that influenced this decision. Ratings were given on a five point Likert scale (see Table 7.10) around the importance of transport affordability, reliability, cleanliness, safety, close

■ ■ ■ ■ **MAKING CHOICES**

■ **Table 7.10** Questionnaire for commuters

	Unimportant (0)	Slightly unimportant (1)	Neither (2)	Slightly important (3)	Important (4)
Cost affordability (Cost)	☐	☐	☐	☐	☐
Service frequency and reliability (Reliable)	☐	☐	☐	☐	☐
Level of overcrowding on the service (Crowding)	☐	☐	☐	☐	☐
Cleanliness and maintenance of service (Clean)	☐	☐	☐	☐	☐
Safety on board (Safety)	☐	☐	☐	☐	☐
Availability of bus stop/ rail station near home (Available)	☐	☐	☐	☐	☐

to home and issues around overcrowding. City planners use this type of model in order to improve transport systems for the future.

Traditionally as you have seen from earlier examples we could tackle this choice decision by using multinomial logistic regression. The predictions from the logistic regression show the likelihood is that cost is more important to rail commuters (rail = 0; bus = 1) as the B-value is negative (B=−0.183) as can be seen from the results in Table 7.11.

All else being equal, the preference indicator for 'cost' is associated with a significant decrease in the likelihood that bus commuters would find the cost an important issue as compared with rail commuters by a factor of 0.833 ($p<0.01$).

As an alternative statistical technique to using multinomial logistic regression we can apply an ordered logit to this kind of model. With this technique it is possible to obtain greater detail about the preferences commuters reveal about transport in this study.

MAKING CHOICES

Table 7.11 Logistic regression: choice and cost

Choice		B	Std. Error	Sig.	Exp(B)	95% Confidence Interval for Exp(B)	
						Lower Bound	Upper Bound
	Intercept	.746	.191	.000			
	cost	−.183	.066	.006	.833	.731	.949

SPSS logistic regression dependent variable: choice and the reference category is Rail(0). $P[\chi^2(1)>7.748]\leq 0.01$. Cox and Snell=0.015, Nagelkerke=0.021.

Stata logistic regression command: logit choice cost

In this survey the respondent has a range of five Likert scale responses. These responses are 'rated' and hence ordered. For example we would say that responses with similar meaning such as 'slightly important' and 'important' are related and those further away such as 'slightly unimportant' and 'important' as less similar. The ordered logit takes into account the ordinal nature of the outcomes and in certain circumstances give greater detail to the analysis (Hausman and Ruud, 1987).

The way in which an ordered logit procedure deals with the range of answers is to represent the respondent's opinion by a utility variable (U). The consumer is said to obtain a certain level of utility or advantage from each of the alternatives. Individual consumers feel that the alternatives offer differing utility. The consumer chooses the alternative that provides the greatest perceived benefit. The paradigm of utility maximization provides a link by which choice probabilities can be estimated (Train, 2009).

This variable (U) takes a range from high being positive to low being negative for the opinions on that particular question. You can think of U as being the range of opinions for a particular question. In this study, for example, the person's response to a question on a Likert scale is broken down into a series of decision cut-off points as follows:

'important' if $U > k_1$
'slightly important' if $k_2 < U < k_1$
'neither' if $k_3 < U < k_2$
'slightly unimportant' if $k_4 < U < k_3$
'unimportant' if $U < k_4$

Figure 7.2 illustrates the probability density function with the four cutoff points k_1 to k_4 that determine the probability distribution. The general shape of the curve is determined by unobserved distribution (ε). Therefore the probability that the commuter answers 'important' is the probability that U is greater than k_1. This is given by the area under the curve in the right hand side of the distribution. The probability that the commuter gives the response to the question asked as 'slightly important' is given by the area

MAKING CHOICES

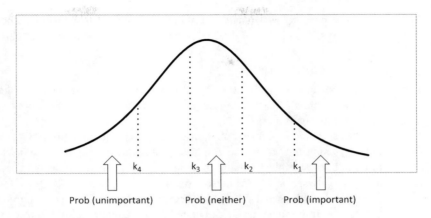

Figure 7.2 Cut-off points for decisions

Table 7.12 Model 1 ordinal logit regression: choice and cost

		Estimate	Std. Error	Odds ratio	Sig.	95% Confidence Interval for odds ratio	
						Lower Bound	Upper Bound
Threshold	[cost = 0]	−2.089	.165		.000	−2.412	−1.767
	[cost = 1]	−1.243	.141		.000	−1.520	−.967
	[cost = 2]	−.527	.131		.000	−.784	−.270
	[cost = 3]	.600	.132		.000	.341	.858
Location	[Choicenew=1]	−.429	.162	0.6509	.008	0.4739	0.8942

SPSS ordinal regression. Dependent variable cost and independent variable choice. $P[\chi^2(1)>7.066]\leq 0.01$ Cox and Snell=0.014, Nagelkerke=0.015. Note to obtain this in SPSS for Ordinal regression you need to change Choice variable from 0 to 1 and 1 to 0 to calculate a reference category of zero. This is the same procedure we highlighted in the logistic regression chapter. Stata does not require you to do this.

Stata ordered logistic regression command: ologit cost choice

under the curve between the cut-off points k_2 and k_1. In the same way the probability for 'neither', 'slightly unimportant' 'unimportant' is calculated from the area under the curve for their respective regions.

In Appendix 10 we discuss in greater detail how these cut-off points can be represented on a distribution of the unobserved factors(ε). The assumption is that the distribution of unobserved factors is distributed logistically. The cumulative distribution function of ε takes the form $F(\varepsilon)=1/(1+\exp(-\varepsilon))$ and is the area under the curve.

MAKING CHOICES ▪ ▪ ▪ ▪

Going back to our discussion about cost related to consumer choice and using the output in Table 7.12 the following model for cost can be written as:

$U = -0.429 \times \text{Choice} + \varepsilon$

The expected value is –0.429 and this result demonstrates as we have previously shown that the rail commuters are more concerned about cost than the bus commuters.

The estimated response probabilities can also be obtained from SPSS and Stata by using the 'estimated response probabilities' option. We will work through two examples by hand in detail to give a clearer understanding of how the software calculates these probabilities.

Using the values in Table 7.12 the response probability that a commuter answers 'unimportant' can be calculated. This is the probability that U is

Prob ('unimportant') = Prob $(U < k_4)$
= Prob $(-0.429 \times \text{Choice} + \varepsilon < -2.089)$ $\quad - (1)$

With choice as bus commuters (choice =1) this gives

Prob $(\varepsilon < -2.089 + 0.429)$ = Prob $(\varepsilon < -1.66)$ = $1/(1+\text{Exp}(1.66))$ = 0.1587

The threshold points tell us how to interpret the score. Setting choice =0 in equation (1) above, gives $\varepsilon < -2.089$ and a resulting probability of 0.11. As noted earlier the calculations for these probabilities have been obtained using the logistic distribution.

The probability a commuter responses to 'slightly unimportant' is the probability that U lies between k_3 and k_4. The probability for the bus commuter (1) is calculated using the following equation:

$$\text{Prob}(\text{'slightly unimportant'}) = \text{Prob}(k_4 < U < k_3)$$

$$= \text{Prob}(-2.089 < -0.429 + \varepsilon < -1.243) = \text{Prob}(-1.66 < \varepsilon < -0.814)$$

$$= 1/(1+\exp(0.814)) - 1/(1+\exp(1.66)) = 0.3070 - 0.1597 = 0.1473$$

Looking at the probability for rail choice (0) gives the probability of 'slightly unimportant' as $-2.089 < \varepsilon < -1.243$
= $1/(1+\exp(-1.243)) - 1/(1+\exp(-2.089))$ = 0.2239 – 0.1102 = 0.1137

Response probabilities

These response probabilities can also be calculated through a contingency table (see Table 7.13). This technique is one we have seen in previous chapters and is useful to help the researcher gain a 'feel' for the data before applying more sophisticated techniques.

Taking an example from Table 7.13 with the variable 'Cost' and the category 'unimportant' we can see that the number of responses from

■ ■ ■ ■ MAKING CHOICES

Table 7.13 Contingency table: choice of transport

		Choice of bus or rail		Total
		Rail (0)	Bus (1)	
Cost relating to affordability	Unimportant	19	50	69
	Slightly unimportant	25	41	66
	Neither	42	38	80
	Slightly important	51	83	134
	Important	77	74	151
Total		214	286	500

Table 7.14 Ordered logit model predictions

	Contingency table probability		Order logit	
	Rail (0)	Bus (1)	Rail (0)	Bus (1)
Unimportant (0)	0.09	0.17	0.11	0.16
Slightly unimportant (1)	0.12	0.14	0.11	0.15
Neither (2)	0.20	0.13	0.15	0.17
Slightly important (3)	0.24	0.29	0.27	0.26
Important (4)	0.36	0.26	0.35	0.26

SPSS command for estimated response probabilities: In ordinal regression output select 'estimated response probabilities'

Stata command for estimated response probabilities: ologit cost choice and then predict var0 var1 var2 var3 var4

commuters stating that they believe cost is unimportant is 19 out of 214 possible rail commuters. Hence the response probability is 19/214 giving a value of 0.09. The number of bus commuters who have the same opinion that the cost of transport is unimportant is 50 out of 286. Hence the response probability can be calculated as 50/286 which is equal to 0.17. Clearly in this particular sample bus commuters show less concern around cost of transport, as this is nearly twice the response probability for rail commuters.

The predictions from the ordered logit model allow for a complete solution as we have seen previously when calculating odds ratios for logistic regression. Table 7.14 shows that comparing the response probabilities from the contingency table and the ordered logit methods are very similar.

MAKING CHOICES ▦▦▦■

Complex ordered logit model

We have seen from this example that the ordered logit provides a technique to look in greater detail at a multiple response Likert scale questionnaire. This technique is not limited to comparing just the one dependent variable of 'cost' to the independent variable 'choice'.

Let us next consider a model with additional independent variables. In addition to the variable 'Cost affordability (cost)' we will add 'Cleanliness and maintenance of service (clean)'. We do this in order to explore whether a respondent's ratings are related. For example a rail commuters rating of cleanliness is probably related to their rating of cost. So we can explore this using multiple ordered response probabilities. It can be seen from Table 7.15 that 'clean' is more important for bus commuters with a positive significant effect (0.154) and choice (−0.429) is still negative. This multivariate model can be written as

$$U = -0.429 \times \text{Choice} + 0.154 \times \text{Clean} + \varepsilon$$

Note the additional term from the previous model of the variable 'clean' is added with its associated coefficient of 0.154. Regarding this study the data suggest that rail commuters (rail=0) are still more concerned about cost as the coefficient is negative (negative B = −0.429). The bus commuters are more concerned about cleanliness and maintenance of service (positive B = 0.154). Prediction for the probability of each of the five categories can be calculated using the same method that we have used in the previous section to obtain the response probability predictions. Again we shall illustrate this by calculating the first few of these probabilities by hand.

▦ **Table 7.15** Model 2 ordinal logit regression: choice, cost and clean

		Estimate	Std. Error	Odds ratio	Sig.	95% Confidence Interval of odds ratio Lower Bound	Upper Bound
Threshold	[cost = 0]	−1.816	.192		.000	−2.192	−1.440
	[cost = 1]	−.963	.174		.000	−1.303	−.622
	[cost = 2]	−.236	.168		.161	−.566	.094
	[cost = 3]	.904	.173		.000	.565	1.243
Location	Clean	.154	.056	1.166	.006	1.042	1.304
	[Choicenew=1]	−.429	.163	0.651	.008	0.4739	0.8944

SPSS ordinal regression with dependent variable cost, independent variable choicenew and covariate clean. P[χ²(2)>14.330]≤0.001 Cox and Snell = 0.028 Nagelkerke = 0.030.

Stata ordered logistic regression command: ologit cost choice clean

■ ■ ■ ■ **MAKING CHOICES**

For bus commuters (choice =1), gives the following:

Prob ('slightly unimportant cost') = Prob ($k_4 < U < k_3$)
= Prob ($-1.816 < -0.429 + 0.154 \times$ Clean $+ \varepsilon < -0.963$)

Using this we can then calculate the relevant probabilities for the different 'clean' responses to the questionnaire. To calculate when the bus commuters responded 'important' concerning cleanliness and maintenance of service (Likert scale value of 4) with the associated cost response of 'slightly unimportant' we proceed as follows:

= Prob ($-1.816 < -0.429 + 0.154 \times 4 + \varepsilon < -0.963$)
= Prob ($-1.816 < 0.187 + \varepsilon < -0.963$)
= Prob ($-2.003 < \varepsilon < -1.15$)
= $1/(1+\exp(1.15)) - 1/(1+\exp(2.003)) = 0.240 - 0.119 = 0.121$

Let us calculate another example for bus commuters (choice =1), who state that cost is 'slightly important' (cost = 3) then following the same procedure:

Prob ('slightly important cost') = Prob ($k_2 < U < k_1$)
= Prob ($-0.236 < -0.429 + 0.154 \times$ Clean $+ \varepsilon < 0.904$)

Then for different 'clean' responses to the questionnaire you can calculate the relevant probabilities. For example, to calculate when bus commuters responded 'neither important or not' concerning cleanliness and maintenance of service (clean = 2) we can produce the following probability:

= Prob ($-0.236 < -0.429 + 0.154 \times 2 + \varepsilon < 0.904$)
= Prob ($-0.236 < -0.121 + \varepsilon < 0.904$)
= Prob ($-0.115 < \varepsilon < 1.025$)
= $1/(1+\exp(-1.025)) - 1/(1+\exp(0.115)) = 0.736 - 0.471 = 0.265$

Table 7.16 is the completed response probability table when bus is the choice variable (1). This allows the researcher to investigate the associations between the variables 'clean' and 'cost'.

The response probability table can also be created when the choice is rail (choice=0). The equation for this is $U = -0.429 \times (0) + 0.154 \times$ Clean $+ \varepsilon$ and hence $U = 0.154 \times$ Clean $+ \varepsilon$

Predictions for the probability of each of the five categories can be obtained from software packages or can calculated by hand following the method illustrated earlier. Table 7.17 shows these response probabilities, it illustrates that the highest probable response is of rail commuters stating that clean and cost are important for them (0.43), with the lowest response being that cost in unimportant and clean is important (0.08).

The results in Tables 7.16 and 7.17 can be obtained from SPSS and Stata by using the functionality 'estimated response probabilities'.

To close this section on the transport study we add two further variables into the model. This model can be written as follows with the addition of the two new variables concerning 'availability of bus stop/rail station

MAKING CHOICES

Table 7.16 Multivariable model: estimated response probabilities (choice =1 (Bus))

Choice = 1 Order logit

Cost			Clean				
			0	1	2	3	4
	Unimportant	0	0.20	0.18	0.16	0.14	0.12
	Slightly unimportant	1	0.17	0.16	0.15	0.13	0.12
	Neither	2	0.18	0.18	0.17	0.16	0.16
	Slightly important	3	0.24	0.25	0.27	0.27	0.28
	Important	4	0.21	0.24	0.26	0.29	0.33

Table 7.17 Multivariable model: estimated response probabilities (choice =0 (Rail))

Choice = 0 Order logit

Cost			Clean				
			0	1	2	3	4
	Unimportant	0	0.14	0.12	0.11	0.09	0.08
	Slightly unimportant	1	0.14	0.12	0.11	0.10	0.09
	Neither	2	0.17	0.16	0.15	0.14	0.13
	Slightly important	3	0.27	0.28	0.27	0.28	0.27
	Important	4	0.29	0.32	0.36	0.39	0.43

near home (available)' and the 'level of overcrowding on the service (crowding)':

$$U = -0.473 \times Choice + 0.113 \times Clean + 0.165 \times Avaliable + 0.200 \times Crowding + \varepsilon$$

Table 7.18 shows the whole multivariate model for the ordered logit. The model shows a highly significant level of fit with a p-value of $P[\chi^2(4) > 38.267] \leq 0.0001$. Notice that all of the four variables – clean, available, crowding and choice – are all significant (p<0.05) with bus commuters being more concerned about cleanliness, availability of services and levels of overcrowding.

■ ■ ■ ■ **MAKING CHOICES**

Table 7.18 Model 3 ordinal logit regression: choice, cost, clean available, crowding

Parameter Estimates

		Estimate	Std. Error	Odds ratio	Sig.	95% Confidence Interval for odd ratio	
						Lower Bound	Upper Bound
Threshold	[cost = 0]	−1.327	.217		.000	−1.751	−.902
	[cost = 1]	−.449	.203		.027	−.848	−.050
	[cost = 2]	.313	.202		.122	−.084	.709
	[cost = 3]	1.496	.213		.000	1.079	1.914
Location	Clean	.113	.057	1.1192	.047	.999	1.254
	Available	.165	.054	1.1794	.002	1.057	1.315
	Crowding	.200	.059	1.2208	.001	1.085	1.373
	[Choicenew=1]	−.473	.164	0.6229	.004	0.4528	0.8569

SPSS ordinal regression with dependent variable cost, independent variable choicenew and covariate clean available crowding. $P[\chi^2(2)>14.330]\leq0.001$ Cox and Snell = 0.028, Nagelkerke = 0.030.

Stata ordered logistic regression command: ologit cost choice clean available crowding

THE RANGE OF DISCRETE CHOICE MODELS

Due to advances in software development the logit model, used throughout this chapter, is one of the most popular and widely used discrete choice modelling techniques as it does not have distribution restrictions. This means that it can be used when the data is not normally distributed. The key assumption of all logit models is that the unobserved factors are not correlated over the alternatives. Putting this a different way, it is saying that the error for one alternative (not defined by the choice set) gives no information about the error contained in another alternative. During the initial stages of the research design the alternatives in the choice set need to be carefully defined. It is important to take care when constructing the empirical model during the design stage of the research as it will help to avoid any of these unobserved factors impacting on results. As we have seen in this chapter, one way of overcoming possible issues with Likert scale responses having dependent errors is to use an ordered logit model. Other discrete choice models have been developed over the years and include probit, GEV (Generalised Extreme Value model) and mixed logit. When the research design cannot compensate for the independence of the

MAKING CHOICES

unobserved factors it is advisable to use one of these techniques (Train, 2009; Hosmer et al., 2013).

The GEV model allows for correlations of unobserved factors over alternatives within a nested group and no correlation for unobserved factors in different nested groups. The most commonly used version of this class of GEV model is called the nested logit. An example of this is when a study is looking at decision makers in different neighbourhoods. An assumption would be that people in the same neighbourhood would come from the same socio-economic background and have access to similar shops and entertainment venues. These neighbourhoods could be 'nested' into groups and decision makers choices within these groups analysed for trends over the whole choice set and also between these groups (Small, 1987; Lee, 1999; Bekhor and Prashker, 2007).

The probit model is particularly useful when decision makers are being investigated over time and they are able to make repeated choices. The restriction of the model is the assumption that the unobserved factors are normally distributed. The probit model is mainly used for cases when choice alternatives vary over time (Haaijer et al., 1998; Greene, 2000; Dow and Endersby, 2004; Chen and Tsurumi, 2010).

A mixed logit model removes the three limitations required by the standard logit model that is 1) allowing for random taste variation, 2) unrestricted substitution patterns and 3) that unobserved factors can be correlated over time. The model has great flexibility around the type of distribution of the unobserved factors with lognormal, uniform, triangular, gamma or any other being able to be used. In recent years the mixed logit model has become more widely used due to improvements in computer processing speeds that allow for the simulation of complex integrations through quadrature (Train, 2009).

HOW TO CALCULATE ORDERED AND ORDINAL REGRESSION

In SPSS open the Ordinal regression (PLUM) window by selecting *Analyze – Regression – Ordinal Regression*. Then select the dependent and independent(s) variables you require in the factor(s) and covariate(s) windows. Then analyse your selection by clicking OK.

Note to obtain values in SPSS for ordinal regression you need to change 'factor(s)' variable from 0 to 1 and 1 to 0 to calculate a reference category of zero. This is the same procedure we highlighted that was required in the logistic regression chapter. In SPSS you can do this by using the routine *Transform – Recode into Different Variable*. Use the new variable(s) in your analysis. This is due to the fact that SPSS default coding is to use the highest code as the reference value. Alternately, Stata uses as a default the lowest code as the reference group.

In Stata as with SPSS there are a few different options that you can select when undertaking ordered logistic regression. The technique we have

■ ■ ■ ■ **MAKING CHOICES**

looked at in this chapter is part of a suite of statistical methods under the heading ordinal outcomes. Select *Statistics – Ordinal outcomes – Ordered logistic regression*. Then enter the dependent variable in dependent variable field and independent(s) variables in the independent variable field. Then you can click OK or submit to analyse your selection.

Calculating ordered and ordinal regression in Stata and SPSS

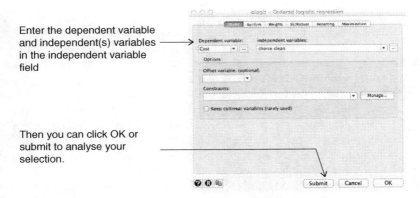

Enter the dependent variable and independent(s) variables in the independent variable field

Then you can click OK or submit to analyse your selection.

■ **Figure 7.3** Stata ordered logistic regression

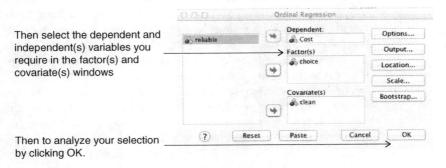

Then select the dependent and independent(s) variables you require in the factor(s) and covariate(s) windows

Then to analyze your selection by clicking OK.

■ **Figure 7.4** SPSS ordinal regression

CHAPTER 8

ITEM RESPONSE THEORY

In this chapter we will explore ways of analysing questionnaires using item response theory. Item response theory is a statistical technique that allows for the analyses of the items in a questionnaire in relation to their latent traits. A questionnaire consists of a series of items related to the proposed research area under investigation. A latent trait cannot be measured directly as it is unobservable and derived from groups of question item responses. These items are collected on a dichotomous (binary) or ordinal scale as we have seen throughout this book. This chapter looks at the fundamentals of item response theory for both dichotomous and polytomous data items and how probabilistic techniques can be used to evaluate the latent structures within questionnaires (Embretson and Reise, 2000; Baker and Kim, 2004).

In the first part of the chapter the study on organic food will be revisited to illustrate how 1-parameter and partial credit models (1PL and 2PL) are used to calculate category and item characteristic curves. The chapter then explores how differential item testing and the information function are used to investigate items in relation to latent model structure. To conclude this chapter, we will investigate validity and reliability issues associated with collapsing Likert scale categories.

Taking forward the study on organic food from the last chapter allows for a closer evaluation of the items in relation to their underlying traits. The questionnaire on organic food was designed to analyse consumers' attitudes and purchasing behaviour. Consumers were asked questions related to their knowledge of organic foods and how often they ate organic food. Data in this study included the consumer's attitudes to price, quality, health benefits and food attributes. There are also socio-demographic data on the respondent's gender, education level, age and income. Income is a binary variable with 1 being if the consumer earns more than an average yearly wage. Education is also given as a binary variable with respondents reporting if they had completed some higher studies.

The hypothesis is that by asking consumers questions about organic food we can conceptualise a latent trait. That trait can be displayed on a straight line and in this case could be thought of as a consumer's perception of organic food.

■ ■ ■ ■ **ITEM RESPONSE THEORY**

ITEM RESPONSE MODEL

First let's set out a definition of item response theory. Item response theory (irt) uses a probability logistic function transform, defined in general as $p = e^{\psi}/{1+e^{\psi}}$ with the value of p lying between 0 and 1. The value p being the probability on a transform of the logit equal to $\ln(p/(1-p))$. This gives the natural logarithm of the odds ratio as a logit function that can be defined for a continuous range of values in the domain $[-\infty, +\infty]$. We can see for example if the probability was p=0.5 this would give a central value of zero for the function, i.e. $\ln[0.5/(1-0.5)]=0$.

The item response theory definition for a probability model is given as the:

Probability of observing the item = trait level of the person – a threshold (difficulty) you need to obtain to get a positive response.

This can be written in a more compact form and is called a 1-parameter or Rasch model.

$$y_{ij} = \theta_j - b_i \text{ with } p_i(\theta_j) = \frac{e^{y_{ij}}}{1+e^{y_{ij}}}$$

We can now show how to use the 1-parameter item response theory model to investigate the health variable in the organic food study. Figure 8.1 is the item characteristic curve. The threshold is marked for this item and has a trait level of −1.5 (b-value for health). This gives the point where 50% of consumer responses believe that organic foods have a health benefit.

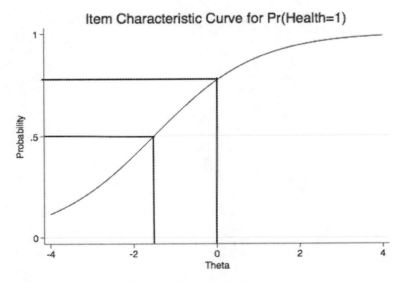

■ **Figure 8.1** Item characteristic curve: health

Stata command: irt 1pl health quality environ price taste appearance knowledge female income highedu and item characteristic curve irtgraph icc health, bcc

ITEM RESPONSE THEORY ▚ ▚ ▚ ■

Partial credit models – 1PL

When looking at ordinal responses with two or more categories then partial credit models (PCMs) are an adaption of the Rasch model for dichotomous items. In our particular organic food study we have a two response scale, with 1 being if the consumer feels positive towards organic food products and related affects and 0 if this is not the case.

In a partial credit model the items vary in their difficulty parameter but share the same discrimination parameter. The advantage of a partial credit model is that it can offer greater information with ordered or categorical items. Looking at the same data the health item has the category characteristic curve as show in Figure 8.2.

The graph in Figure 8.2 shows the curve for consumers feeling that organic food has beneficial health effects (Health=1) and not (Health=0). It can be seen that the cut-off probability of 0.5 is at the intersection of the two curves around −1.5.

Looking at the difference $(\theta - b)$ gives the probability likelihood. Hence when $\theta > b$, the person is more likely to perceive health benefits from organic food. Similarly if $\theta < b$ they are less likely to perceive health benefits.

If we compare the consumers' perceived health benefits with the responses to the environmental question using an item characteristic curve we can see a marked contrast (see Figure 8.3). As the model assumes a normal distribution $(\theta - N(0, 1))$ then the perception of the health benefit item is on a standard normal scale. The theta value is a z-score and is measured in units of standard deviations. In the example in Figure 8.3

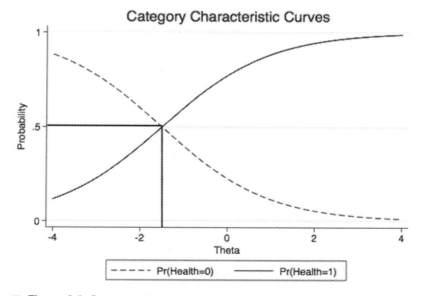

▚ **Figure 8.2** Category characteristic curve: health
Stata category characteristic curve command irtgraph icc health, ccc

■ ■ ■ ■   **ITEM RESPONSE THEORY**

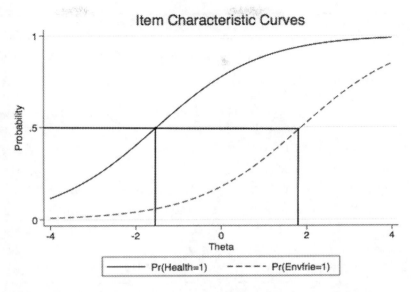

■ **Figure 8.3** Item characteristic curve: health and environment
Stata item characteristic curve command: irtgraph icc health environ, bcc

the perceived point where 50% of the consumers believe that organic food has health benefits has a trait level of −1.5 (b-value for health). This is interpreted as, perceived health benefits are 1.5 standard deviations below the mean on the organic food latent trait. On the same organic food latent trait scale 50% of consumers who believe that purchasing organic foods will be good for the environment are at 1.88 standard deviations above the mean. There is a greater likelihood that these respondents will perceive health benefits for organic food as opposed to the environmental benefits.

Table 8.1 shows numerical output for the 1PL partial credit model, giving the discriminant for the whole model (a), trait level coefficients (b), standard errors (SE) and 95% confidence intervals for the mood variables. The output gives this discrimination parameter (a) for the whole model, which can be thought of as the slope of the curve. This value gives an indication of the relative discrimination between all of the items for this concept. In this model the value 0.8131 implies that the items are moderately discriminating. This suggests that any two people would have similar probabilities when responding to these items.

An item with a larger discrimination value has a higher correlation between the latent trait and the probability of benefit for that particular item. The larger the discrimination parameter the greater the distinguishing power between high and low values of the latent trait. The interpretation of the discrimination values is given in Table 8.2 (Baker, 2001).

ITEM RESPONSE THEORY ▪ ▪ ▪ ■

Table 8.1 Partial credit model: organic food study

	Coef.	SE	95% confidence interval	
Discriminant for whole model (a)	0.8131***	0.0504	0.7142	0.9127
	Coef. (b) difficulty (DIFF)	SE	95% confidence interval	
Health	−1.5069***	0.1614	−1.8233	−1.1906
Quality	0.1009	0.1263	−0.1465	0.3484
Environment	1.8783***	0.1794	1.5266	2.2299
Price	−2.2559***	0.2006	−2.6493	−1.8627
Taste	−1.3651***	0.1554	−1.6696	−1.0605
Knowledge	−1.3374***	0.1543	−1.6397	−1.0350
Appearance	1.7171***	0.1712	1.3814	2.0528

Stata 1PL command: irt 1pl health quality environ price taste appearance knowledge female income highedu choice2

***p<0.001 Log likelihood = −3197.6995

Table 8.2 Discrimination values

0.01–0.34	Very low
0.35–0.64	Low
0.65–1.34	Moderate
1.35–1.69	High
1.70 and above	Very high

Partial credit models – 2PL

Using a 2-parameter model (2PL) $y_{ij} = a_i(\theta_j - b_i)$ there is an additional term a_i which is called a discrimination of item i. Partial credit 2PL models have discrimination factors for each individual item in the model instead of having an overall discrimination factor.

These discrimination factors can be thought of as similar to the factor loadings in factor analysis or as coefficients in regression analysis. They inform how strongly the item associates with this latent trait. As previously in this chapter when we calculated the 1PL model the 2-parameter model also has an adaptation called the graded response model (GRM). The graded response model is for use with ordinal or categorical items. In the 2PL and GRM the items vary in both their difficulty and discrimination.

Using the partial credit model with the organic food study, the discrimination value for the 'health' variable is 1.36 and 'appearance'

ITEM RESPONSE THEORY

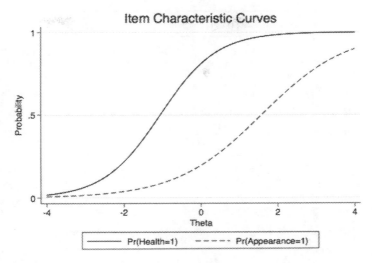

Figure 8.4 Item characteristic curve: health and appearance
Stata item characteristic curve command: irtgraph icc health appearance, bcc

of organic food has a value of 0.90. In Figure 8.4 it can be seen that the 'appearance' variable curve has a flatter shape. The discrimination parameter can be thought of as the slope of the curve and hence the slope for 'health' at 1.36 is steeper than that of 'appearance' at 0.90. The flatter shape in this item characteristic curve means that a smaller proportion of the respondents thought that the appearance of organic food was important.

Using a 2PL or GRM technique with the total model for all the variables in the organic food study gives the numerical output in Table 8.3. For each of the variables we have a discrimination and difficulty coefficient.

Table 8.3 GRM model: organic food study

	Coef.	SE	95% confidence interval	
Health				
Discrim(a)	1.3673***	0.1977	0.9798	1.7549
Diff (b)	−1.0558***	0.1333	−1.3172	−0.7945
Quality				
Discrim(a)	1.4480***	0.18539	1.0847	1.8114
Diff (b)	0.0617	0.0860	−0.1069	0.2302
Environment				
Discrim(a)	1.5312***	0.2186	1.1027	1.9599
Diff (b)	1.2268***	0.1383	0.9558	1.4979

(continued)

ITEM RESPONSE THEORY

Table 8.3 (continued)

	Coef.	SE	95% confidence interval	
Price				
Discrim(a)	−1.3385***	0.2068	−1.7438	−0.9332
Diff (b)	1.5889***	0.1889	1.2186	1.9591
Taste				
Discrim(a)	1.9368***	0.2685	1.4105	2.4631
Diff (b)	−0.8071***	0.0944	−0.9921	−0.6222
Appearance				
Discrim(a)	0.9024***	0.1521	0.6044	1.2005
Diff (b)	1.5822**	0.2437	1.1047	2.0599
Knowledge				
Discrim(a)	−1.1882***	0.1687	−1.5188	−0.8576
Diff (b)	1.0151***	0.1419	0.7369	1.2932

Stata GRM command: irt grm health quality environ price taste appearance knowledge female income highedu choice2.

***$p<0.001$ Log likelihood = −2897.9039

In item response theory the output will not always give a positive discriminant value. To illustrate this let us next consider the variable 'price' and see how important consumers feel that this is related to their own organic purchase. Comparing price to health you can see from Figure 8.5 that the

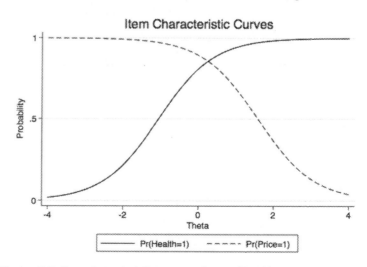

Figure 8.5 Item characteristic curve: price and health

Stata item characteristic curve command: irtgraph icc health price, bcc

■ ■ ■ ■ **ITEM RESPONSE THEORY**

probability curves are very different shapes. This is a surprise as if we look at the discriminant value in Table 8.3 for 'price' it shows that the slope is negative with a value of −1.3385 and has a negative relationship with the latent characteristic trait. Combining this fact with the b-value (1.5889) for 'price' suggests that there is a greater likelihood that most people are placing less importance on price.

DIFFERENTIAL ITEM TESTING

It is possible with item response theory to investigate whether a particular test item behaves differently for people within the same latent trait. This technique can also be used in longitudinal studies to calculate how items change over time (Embretson and Reise, 2000; CFPB, 2017).

To illustrate differential testing with the organic foods study we will divide the data into two consumer groups. One group eats organic food on a regular basis and the other group is made up of those consumers who either eat some organic food or do not eat any. Table 8.4 shows the significant difference of the items in relation to these two groups.

In these two different choice groups there is no significant difference in the respondents' perceptions of health and quality, but all of the other categories show significant differences. The odds ratios show that you are seven times more likely to feel that you are having an effect on the environment if you are a consumer eating organic food on a regular basis. You are nearly three times more likely to believe that the product will taste better if you are in the group who eat organic foods on a regular basis.

The 'knowledge' items odds ratio is less than one, showing that there is a significant decrease in the likelihood for the group who eat organic food on a regular basis to be more knowledgeable. This may seem counterintuitive.

■ **Table 8.4** Differential item test: purchasing groups

Item	Chi-square test	p-value	Odds ratio	95% confidence interval	
Health	0.07	0.7953	1.1226	0.6381	1.9748
Quality	0.01	0.9081	1.0510	0.6805	1.6233
Environment	48.72	0.0000	7.0962	3.9618	12.7102
Price	66.44	0.0000	0.0994	0.0531	0.1861
Taste	13.07	0.0003	2.8846	1.6236	5.1248
Appearance	7.77	0.0053	2.0316	1.2578	3.2813
Knowledge	22.92	0.0000	0.3462	0.2256	0.5314

Stata Mantel-Haenszel DIF Analysis command: difmh health quality environ price taste appearance knowledge, group(choice2)

ITEM RESPONSE THEORY

Table 8.5 Contingency table: knowledge

		Eat some organic food or do not eat any (0)	Regularly eat organic food (1)	Total
Knowledge	0	61	78	139
	1	243	118	361
Total		304	196	500

1 if the consumer reported that they were knowledgeable about organic food; 0 otherwise

When we look at the data using a contingency table (see Table 8.5) it reveals the reason for this result.

There are only 118 people in the group who eat organic foods on a regular basis who feel knowledgeable about organic food products. Yet we have 243 consumers who do not eat organic foods on a regular basis who are saying they are knowledgeable. This is why the odds ratio for regularly eating organic food is less than 1 and thus a decreased likelihood. Using the data given in the contingency table (Table 8.5) we can obtain an estimate for this odds ratio as (118/78)/(243/61)=0.38.

Care always needs to be taken when reporting the findings of your data. Sometimes as in this case where the results do not feel intuitive, a contingency table can be a useful support mechanism to help clarify any confusions. Differential item testing can also be used to calculate gender differences. Using the organic food study we will illustrate how to do this by exploring how gender may affect attitudes to organic food.

In the organic food study gender is coded 1 for female and 0 for male and so the results in Table 8.6 show that females are 3.2 times more likely to believe that organic food is of better quality. There is also a greater likelihood that females believe that organic food will taste better. Other

Table 8.6 Differential item test: gender

Item	Chi-square test	p-value	Odds ratio	95% confidence interval	
Health	2.32	0.1276	1.6115	0.9058	2.8668
Quality	26.25	0.0000	3.2824	2.0830	5.1724
Environment	1.55	0.2131	1.4525	0.8482	2.4872
Price	24.67	0.0000	0.2422	0.1343	0.4370
Taste	12.13	0.0005	2.8373	1.5896	5.0642
Appearance	0.45	0.5022	1.2258	0.7401	2.0304
Knowledge	43.48	0.0000	0.2089	0.1276	0.3419

Stata Mantel-Haenszel DIF Analysis command: difmh health quality environ price taste appearance knowledge, group(female)

■ ■ ■ ■ **ITEM RESPONSE THEORY**

statistically significant results are that there is a decrease in the likelihood that females believe that organic food price is important. These data show that females have a significant likelihood of having less knowledge about organic food then men.

In the next section we will revisit the study on food insecurity to illustrate how item response techniques of boundary values, category characteristics and the information function can be used to allow for greater understanding of items within a questionnaire.

GRADED RESPONSE MODEL (GRM)

In Chapter 6 we explored how children responded to a questionnaire around their moods in a study on hunger. A modified eight item version of a mood check list was used with a polytomous scale. In this section the Graded Response Model (GRM) will be used to illustrate techniques for ordinal items with three categories.

The difficulty parameter represents the point at which a person with trait level $\theta_j = b_{ik}$ has a 50% chance of responding in category k or higher. For example, looking at the estimated parameters of item 'energetic' in the mood data, we see from Table 8.7 that a person with $\theta = -2.1537$ has a 50% chance of answering 1 instead of 2 or 3. This energetic item has a trait level of −2.1537 (b-value), which is 2.1537 standard deviations below the mean for children's mood response on the food latent trait scale. A person with a θ value of 0.4346 has a 50% chance of answering 1 or 2 instead of 3. Therefore related to the latent structure there is a greater probability likelihood that a child will be expressing the opinion that they are undecided (2) or that they feel energetic (3). The estimated discrimination parameter for energetic is 0.7337 and so the curves' slopes are relatively flat (see Figure 8.6).

We can also plot a category characteristic curve to show the probabilities, $Pr(Y = k)$ as a function of θ. Figure 8.7 illustrates the category characteristic curves (CCC) for 'energetic'.

Figure 8.7 shows how the children's energetic mood in the three ordinal responses 'I do not feel like this' (1), 'Undecided' (2) and 'I feel like this' (3) are related to the general mood latent trait level. The boundary characteristic curves show that values of the latent scale below approximately −2.15 are

■ **Table 8.7** GRM model: energetic

	Coef.	SE	95% confidence interval	
Energetic				
Discrim(a)	0.7337***	0.1749	0.3907	1.0767
Diff (b_{i2}) ≥2	−2.1537***	0.4603	−3.0559	−1.2514
Diff(b_{i3})=3	0.4346***	0.1619	0.1173	0.7519

ITEM RESPONSE THEORY ▓ ▓ ▓ ■

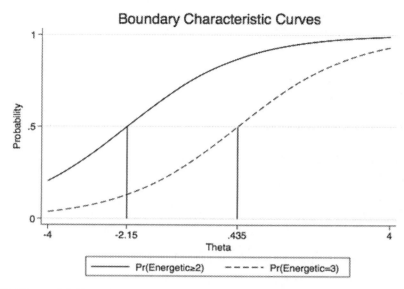

▓ **Figure 8.6** Boundary characteristic curve: energetic
Stata boundary characteristic curve command: irtgraph icc energetic, bcc

most likely to respond in the first category. When the latent trait level lies between −2.15 and 0.43 the most likely response is in the second category. For the third category values on the latent scale above 0.43 are most likely.

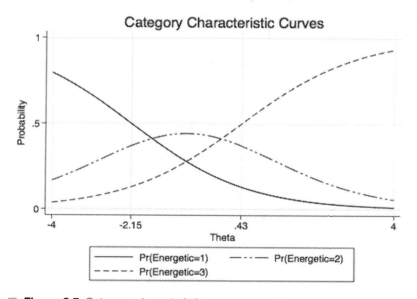

▓ **Figure 8.7** Category characteristic curve: energetic
Stata category characteristic curve command: irtgraph icc energetic, xlabel(−4 −2.15 0.43 4, grid)

PARTIAL CREDIT MODELS (PCM)

To explore this ordinal mood model further we can run a partial credit model (PCM). In a PCM items vary in their difficulty but share the same discrimination parameter. This type of item response model is like a 1PL model but can be used with ordered or categorical items. In the latent mood model we find the discrimination parameter is very low at 0.28 when running a PCM, suggesting that the conceptual model scale is not robust at discriminating for individuals.

Research into ordinal response has shown that as the number of response categories increases then people find it difficult to differentiate between Likert scales with responses such as 'a like true of me' compared to 'somewhat true of me' (Gray-Little et al., 1997). This is not likely in our case as there are only three items that are very distinct. As the low discrimination parameter in our study is not due to the number of categories there must be other underlying reasons for this. In the next section of the chapter we will investigate how to determine possible reasons for our low discrimination parameter and therefore illustrate how to explore the structure of your data using the item information function (IIF).

INFORMATION FUNCTION

The information function checks the reliability of an item in relation to the latent model structure. If the variance of the estimator is σ^2, then the amount of information is given by the formula $I = 1/\sigma^2$.

The amount of information is proportional to the discrimination parameter. The greater the reliability of an item the more precision it has in measuring the latent trait as a discriminating tool. If the value of the information function is large, this means that the person's responses can be estimated with precision. Alternatively, if small then there is less precision in the estimate and responses could be scattered through the latent trait.

Next we illustrate how the information function can give insights into data by considering three studies. The first is the mood study with Figure 8.8 clearly demonstrating how 'drowsy' gives the highest discrimination estimate. The other items offer little discriminatory power as seen from their low information values across the whole of the theta domain. This indicates that the mood questionnaire offers little in the way of a general discriminatory latent construct to assess children's moods overall, implying that the individual items are not forming a single themed construct.

In contrast the organic food data information function, shown in Figure 8.9, shows a much greater range of values for the latent structure. There is a slight bias towards the item information in the negative region of the latent trait. Items featuring significantly have their highest peaks at around negative one. As the graph shows greater item information in the negative region, this suggests that the item responses provide slightly more information about consumers located at the lower end of the organic food latent construct.

ITEM RESPONSE THEORY ▨ ▨ ▨ ■

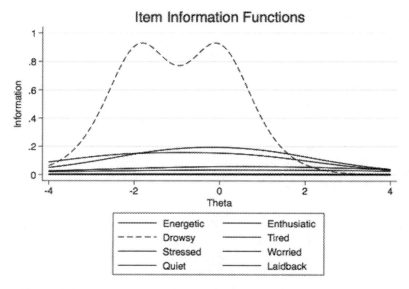

Figure 8.8 Item information function: mood categories
Stata item information function command: irtgraph iif

Overall the item information function suggests that the questionnaire measure provides good information across the latent trait spectrum.

The final data set we will consider is the Roets leadership study where the questionnaire provides a good level of item uniformity. The self-reporting

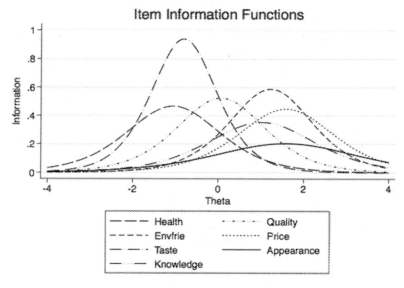

Figure 8.9 Item information function: organic food
Stata item information function command: irtgraph iif

■ ■ ■ ■ **ITEM RESPONSE THEORY**

assessment leadership scale, as we have discovered in previous chapters, is intended to measure leadership, confidence, ambition, desire and team work (Roets, 1997). Thirteen items in this questionnaire are shown in Figure 8.10. The item information function looks at the overall structure and shows a number of peaks across the latent trait spectrum for leadership. It suggests that the questionnaire measure provides a good level of information to help inform the single latent leadership concept. Notice that there is a range of peaks, some with negative theta and other positive. A slightly larger number of these peaks are above zero, suggesting that the questionnaire as a whole provides more information about people at the mid to high end of the leadership latent trait spectrum. Notice in the diagram there is a unity of the amount of information in the item values suggesting that the questions have equality. This supports the work seen earlier in the book when we explored the structure of the responses through exploratory and confirmatory factor analysis. Running PCM for the whole model gives a discrimination value of 1.13 for the whole model. This is classified as moderate discrimination and suggests a good distinguishing power between high and low values of the latent trait, which is supported in Figure 8.10.

Using differential item testing as explored earlier in this chapter we can investigate to see if gender plays a role in the leadership study. From Table 8.8 there is only a significant difference in two of the items concerning gender. These are 'listen to both sides' (T2) and 'promote what is believed' (C3) with $p<0.05$. The odds ratios illustrate that as a female leader you have twice the likelihood to promote what is believed and there is a decrease in the likelihood that you would listen to both sides.

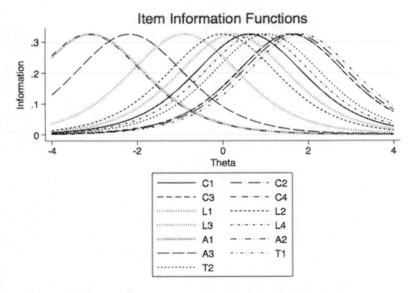

■ **Figure 8.10** Item information function: Roets leadership study
Stata item information function command: irtgraph iif

ITEM RESPONSE THEORY ▨ ▨ ▨ ■

Table 8.8 Differential item test: gender in Roets leadership study

Item	Chi2	p-value	Odds ratio	95% confidence interval	
C1	1.06	0.3034	1.3592	0.8106	2.2791
C2	1.10	0.2945	1.4261	0.7926	2.5660
C3	4.45	0.0349	2.0307	1.0912	3.7791
C4	3.26	0.0708	1.7878	0.9947	3.2131
L1	1.03	0.3105	0.7359	0.4365	1.2406
L2	0.19	0.6666	0.8795	0.5560	1.3912
L3	0.01	0.9378	1.0616	0.6163	1.8285
L4	3.03	0.0817	0.6374	0.3955	1.0270
A1	0.00	0.9603	1.1446	0.3745	3.4986
A2	0.07	0.7889	1.2859	0.4908	3.3687
A3	2.52	0.1128	1.8031	0.9012	3.6076
T1	3.07	0.0796	0.5608	0.3063	1.0267
T2	4.14	0.0419	0.6044	0.3796	0.9622

Stata Mantel-Haenszel DIF Analysis command: difmh C1 C2 C3 C4 L1 L2 L3 L4 A1 A2 A3 T1 T2, group(gender)

Non-uniform difficulty

Continuing to explore the leadership study we can use non-uniform difficulty to investigate if different groups are favoured for certain ranges of a latent trait. We will consider gender with this leadership data but this technique can be used for any defined group, for example with longitudinal data you could define the two groups to be before and after an intervention. Additional information on longitudinal data analysis can be found in Appendix 11.

Table 8.9 gives the results of the non-uniform difficulty test on gender. The two questions, 'promote what is believed' C3 (p=0.0324) and 'admire those who have achieved' A2 (p=0.0007) are the only significant items at the 5% level.

Non-uniform difficulty (DIF) is observed in graphical output when two item characteristic curves cross. In Figure 8.11, for low latent values, just less than −2, females prefer the response 'not very often' (0) to 'quite often' (1). Females have a greater likelihood of giving a positive response to 'admire those who have achieved' (A2) for a greater range of the latent spectrum. Women are much less likely to respond that they would 'promote what is believed' (C3) with virtually zero probability throughout the negative values of theta. It is not until around one standard deviation above the mean that the latent trait for women's attitudes to leadership would respond positively and 1.19 when the likelihood is greater than 0.5.

Table 8.9 Non-uniform difficulty: gender in Roets leadership study

Item	Non-uniform		Uniform	
	Chi-square	p-value	Chi-square	p-value
C1	0.00	0.9770	1.57	0.2102
C2	2.71	0.0999	1.70	0.1921
C3	4.58	0.0324	6.51	0.0107
C4	0.35	0.5560	3.80	0.0512
L1	0.00	0.9876	2.13	0.1440
L2	0.93	0.3344	0.63	0.4278
L3	0.11	0.7389	0.09	0.7677
L4	2.24	0.1346	4.52	0.0336
A1	0.25	0.6158	0.02	0.8768
A2	11.37	0.0007	0.13	0.7173
A3	0.00	0.9748	3.30	0.0693
T1	0.33	0.5663	2.84	0.0917
T2	0.21	0.6489	3.76	0.0524

Stata logistic regression DIF analysis command: diflogistic C1 C2 C3 C4 L1 L2 L3 L4 A1 A2 A3 T1 T2, group(gender)

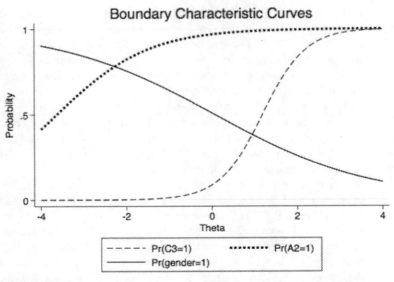

Figure 8.11 Non-uniform boundary curves: gender in Roets leadership study

Stata boundary characteristic curve command: irtgraph icc c3 a2 gender, bcc

ITEM RESPONSE THEORY ▩ ▩ ▩ ■

In this final section of the chapter we will explore how item response theory can be used to check the validity and reliability of collapsing Likert scale data that has already been collected. Throughout the book we have seen examples of where Likert scale variables have been collapsed into a smaller number of categories to aid calculations. As a researcher we could be interested to understand what affects such transformations may have on the results.

RELIABILITY OF MEASURES WHEN COLLAPSING LIKERT SCALE CATEGORIES

In this section we will use the study on intrinsic motivation to demonstrate numerically how item response theory techniques can be used to check and assess the extent to which the latent structure of the measurement outcome is altered by changing the scale. Using four items from both the enjoyment and challenge categories of an intrinsic motivation scale we explore the consequences of changing this scale from a four category Likert scale to a two category binary scale. In Appendix 12 greater theoretical information is discussed around the issue of altering the structure of a questionnaire after the data have been collected.

Intrinsic motivation arises and leads to action, when a person feels both self-determined and competent to pursue an area of interest, feeling both competent and autonomous (de Charms, 1968; Barron, 1969; Zuckerman, 1979; Renzulli, 1986, 2012). The enjoyment and challenge intrinsic motivation items are taken from the Work Preference Inventory (WPI) created by Amabile et al. (1994). It is a short paper and pencil personality instrument that is used to assess various aspects of motivation (Hennessey and Amabile, 1998). The four item Likert scale categories are 'almost never true of you' (1), 'sometimes true of you' (2), 'often true of you' (3) and 'always true of you' (4) and the transformed two-point binary scale is 'not true of you' (0) and 'true of you' (1).

First, we will look at the structural differences of the four-point and two-point item scales using factor analyses. In Table 8.10 the model on the left is binary and on the right the four-point Likert scale. The rank order of these values is the same and there is little difference between the values in these two models, as can be seen in Table 8.10.

The binary model has two rotated factors with eigenvalues 1.980, 1.362 explaining 41.77% of variance, with a correlation between these factors of 0.298. KMO is 0.679 and Chi-square(28)=285.501 (p<0.001). Very similar results are seen with the four-point Likert scale model. The two rotated factors have eigenvalues with slightly stronger factors of 2.285 and 1.355 explaining a greater significance of the variance 45.50%. Again the correlation between these factors, KMO and Chi-squared values are all greater than the four-point category scale at 0.393, 0.725 and 420.975 (p<0.001) respectively.

Notice that in Figure 8.12 the peak of the information function is in roughly the same position just to the left of zero. The curves also demonstrate

Table 8.10 Factor analysis comparison of models

	Binary factors		Four point scale	
	1	2	1	2
Challenge 1: The more difficult the problem, the more I enjoy trying to solve it.	.601		.627	
Challenge 2: I enjoy tackling problems that are completely new to me.	.483		.606	
Challenge3: I prefer work I know I can do well over work that stretches my abilities.	.463		.519	
Challenge4: I enjoy trying to solve complex problems.	.317		.377	
Enjoyment1: I prefer to figure things out for myself.		.568		.616
Enjoyment 2: Curiosity is the driving force behind much of what I do.		.456		.516
Enjoyment 3: It is important for me to be able to do what I most enjoy.		.417		.457
Enjoyment 4: I want my work to provide me with opportunities for increasing my knowledge and skill.		.403		.392

SPSS extraction method for both models was principal axis factoring with rotation method Promax with Kaiser Normalization.

Stata command: factor <variables>, ipf and postestimation of rotate, promax oblique kaiser factors(2) blanks(0.3) gives a similar two factor output.

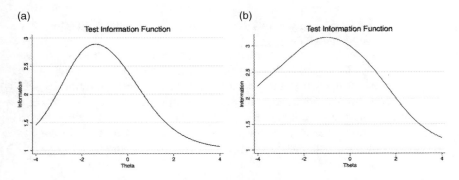

Figure 8.12 Test information function for models
Model on the left is binary and on the right four-point Likert scale

ITEM RESPONSE THEORY

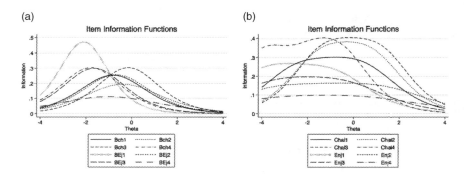

Figure 8.13 Item information function for models
Model on the left is binary and on the right four point Likert scale.

a similar pattern with the binary curve's information dropping lower faster, implying that more information has been lost at the higher end of the latent scale. Next we will explore in detail the individual items and compare item information functions (see Figure 8.13).

Most of the information from the individual items is below 0.3 on the binary scale with only one item above this. This is the item 'intrinsic enjoyment1'. The items having the next highest peaks are 'challenge4' and 'enjoyment3' with negative latent scale values of theta at −2 and 0. This is different in the four-point scale with challenge 2, 3 and 4 all being above 0.3 but with the curves peeking more centrally. Clearly the information resulting from these items is greater but as with the binary items others are below 0.3.

Table 8.11 shows challenge items 1 to 4 for Likert and binary, and illustrates how this technique can be used to test to see if a change of scale still offers a good representation of a model. By looking in greater detail at individual items using the graded response model (GRM) it can be found that the variation in the coefficients show only a small difference in these two models and hence suggest reliability for the change. We can also see this in Table 8.11 by looking at the values for the items difficulty and discrimination parameters.

There are a number of advantages of using item response theory to assess models. We have seen in this chapter how item response theory can be used to explore the detail of items, item information, differential questions, assess the quality of questions and quality of latent structures in questionnaire data. Deriving trait level estimates for items and their properties directly relate to test behaviour in structural analysis. The theory can also be used to assess item category reduction in relation to latent traits (Jansen and Roskam, 1986; Andrich, 1996).

Table 8.11 Graded response model comparison

	Four Likert scale		Binary scale

Chal1

Discrim: 0.9883

Diff for binary =1: −0.8376

4-scale ≥3:

[Boundary Characteristic Curves — Four Likert scale: Pr(Chal1≥2), Pr(Chal1≥3), Pr(Chal1=4); thresholds −2.42, −.828, .448]

1.0090
−0.8191

[Boundary Characteristic Curve for Pr(Bch1=1); threshold −.819]

Chal2

Discrim: 1.1081

Diff for binary =1: −0.3117

4-scale ≥3:

[Boundary Characteristic Curves — Four Likert scale: Pr(Chal2≥2), Pr(Chal2≥3), Pr(Chal2=4); thresholds −1.47, −.312, .838]

0.8814
−0.3875

[Boundary Characteristic Curve for Pr(Bch2=1); threshold −.388]

(continued)

Table 8.11 (continued)

	Four Likert scale	Binary scale
Chal3		
Discrim	1.1455	1.1029
Diff for binary =1	−0.1442	−0.1498
4-scale ≥3		
Chal4		
Discrim	1.1573	1.10287
Diff for binary =1	−1.7257	−1.7842
4-scale ≥3		

■ ■ ■ ■ **ITEM RESPONSE THEORY**

Calculating item response theory with Stata

In Stata the item response theory we have looked at in this chapter is part of a suite of statistical methods under the heading irt – item response theory models. Select *Statistics – irt (item response theory)*. Then select the item model required from the list, either 'Binary item models', 'Ordered item models', 'Unordered categorical item model' or 'Hybrid models'. Then you can click 'Fit model' to analyse your selection.

Selecting *Graph* allows for item characteristic curves, category characteristic curves, item information function and other test information diagrams. Selecting *DIF* allows for differential item functioning using the Mantel-Haenszel test with a differential grouping variable.

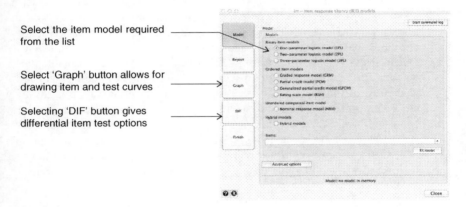

■ **Figure 8.14** Stata item response theory

APPENDIX

This appendix is designed to support the reader who wishes to have a greater depth of understanding of statistical techniques employed in this book. The idea of the appendix is to answer some of the additional background questions that the reader may have in relation to the statistics employed. Due to space the appendix can only offer a starting point, a glimpse into the wonderfully fascinating world of statistics. The appendix is supplementary to the rest of the book and is not required reading to be able to perform any of the statistical data analysis that is carried out. Contained is greater detail on the statistical methods employed, offering the reader a range of statistical tests, their mathematical equations, proofs and calculations. Statistical topics covered are regression, correlation, distribution fitting, factor analysis, longitudinal data, discrete choice theory and item response theory.

1 MULTIPLE IMPUTATION

As discussed in Chapter 1 there is a range of methods to deal with missing data. The most sophisticated of these is called multiple imputations. Imputation methods predict the missing data using weighted evidence from other items in the survey. The imputation assumption is that the missing values depend on the observed (collected) data not on unobserved data. Univariate imputation is used to impute missing data for a single variable using such techniques as linear regression for continuous variables. In the case of binary or categorical variables then logistic regression should be used. When imputing multiple variables it is advised to impute them simultaneously using a multivariate technique. A multivariate normal data augmentation technique is most often used as typically the missing values are distributed randomly. This imputation technique can also be used with binary and categorical data with the results being rounded to whole numbers when necessary (Rubin, 1987; Allison, 2002).

To illustrate the concept of imputation the screenshot from Stata (Figure A.1) shows a small data set of ten respondents each having data on three variables (var1, var2, var3). The first variable 'var1' contains two missing

■ ■ ■ ■ **APPENDIX**

	var1	var2	var3	_mi_m	_mi_id	_mi_miss	var4
1	2.23	1	3.5	0	1	0	1.738525
2	3.72	4	6.04	0	2	0	4.590877
3	3.54	3	5.22	0	3	0	3.544056
4	6.09	7	8.49	0	4	0	7.767356
5	6.53	5	6.86	0	5	0	5.637698
6	.	5	6.71	0	6	1	6.177909
7	8.28	7	8.49	0	7	0	7.767356
8	.	4	5.92	0	8	1	5.023046
9	10.74	9	10.13	0	9	0	9.860998
10	17.1294	5	6.71	1	6	.	.
11	12.28224	4	5.92	1	8	.	.
12	5.271137	5	6.71	2	6	.	.
13	5.825009	4	5.92	2	8	.	.

■ **Figure A.1** Stata imputation screenshot

values in row six and eight. An imputation technique in Stata is used by selecting *Statistics – Multiple Imputation (Control Panel)*. In the control panel select *Setup* and *Impute* options to estimate missing data. Figure A.1 shows the output from the Stata code commands:

mi set mlong: mi register imputed var1: mi register regular var2 var3
mi impute mvn var1 = var2 var3, add(10)
mi estimate, saving(mit1): regress var1 var2 var3
mi predict var4 using mit1

Variable 'var4' in the seventh column gives the prediction for 'var1' using our imputed data and the other variables. For the first missing variable the prediction is 6.177909. This value is smaller than 6.53 as seen in row five. This would be expected due to similarities between these rows. An analogous argument can be made around the missing value in row eight.

As we have discussed in Chapter 1, imputation of data is not the best option but if needs must and as a researcher you feel that it is appropriate to augment your collected data to make it complete, then there are a great range of highly sophisticated imputation techniques at your disposal in both Stata and SPSS (Carpenter and Kenward, 2013).

2 DISTRIBUTION FITTING

As we have seen by calculating the skewness and kurtosis of data you can gain some insight into the relative normality of the data. A value of zero is said to be perfectly normal. Deviations of less than ±1 from zero are considered very good. If the values lie outside of this range between ±1 and ±2 then this is considered acceptable.

An alternative way to determine if your data is normally distributed is to use a test that compares the distance between your distributions cumulative function and a comparable normal distribution. A non-parametric statistical test that can be used to compare distributions is the Kolmogorov-Smirnov

APPENDIX

Table A.1 One sample Kolmogorov-Smirnov distribution test of normality

Smaller group	D	p-value
Home support:	0.1386	0.000
Cumulative:	−0.2342	0.000
Combined K-S:	0.2342	0.000

test (Goodman, 1954; Stephens, 1974; Gregoire and Driver, 1987; Royston, 1991, 1992; Conover 1999).

If the Kolmogorov-Smirnov test gives a significant result with p<0.05 then the distributions tested differ. A significant result means the data is not normally distributed. The only limitation of this kind of test is as the sample size increases there is a tendency for the test to give a significant result, implying a difference in the data.

As an example we will use the Kolmogorov-Smirnov test to see if 'home support' from the parental involvement education study is distributed normally. The variable 'home support' has 500 observations with a mean value that is approximately zero and a standard deviation of one, hence an approximation to N(0,1). Using the Stata command ksmirnov HomeSupport = normal((HomeSupport-0)/1) gives the output shown in the Table A.1.

The output from Stata for this data states that there are 78 matching unique values out of the 500 observations. It is a significant result with a p-value of 0.000, suggesting that the sample data set differs from the normal distribution.

The Kolmogorov-Smirnov test is said to be highly effective when used to compare two sample data sets to establish if they have a similar distribution pattern. The maximum absolute difference between the two cumulative distribution functions [$F_n(x)$ and $G_m(x)$] is D. Given that D_α is the critical value calculated from the Kolmogorov-Smirnov distribution tables, then $p(D \leq D_\alpha) = 1 - \alpha$ can be used to test the hypothesis that $F_n(x)$ and $G_m(x)$ are similar distributions of data.

If $\max_{x} |F_n(x) - G_m(x)| \leq D_\alpha$ then the samples are a good fit, i.e. $D \leq D_\alpha$

The proof of this statement comes from the Glivenko-Cantelli theorem that states that if $F_n(x)$ is made of samples from the same distribution as $G_m(x)$ then this statistic will converge to zero in the limit as n goes to infinity (Darling, 1957; Conover, 1999). The Kolmogorov distribution has a value of:

$$F(x) = \frac{\sqrt{2\pi}}{x} \sum_{k=1}^{\infty} e^{-\frac{(2k-1)^2 \pi^2}{(8x^2)}}$$ and approximated by $\frac{1.3581}{\sqrt{n}}$ for $\alpha = 0.05$

when n > 50

To illustrate how to use the Kolmogorov-Smirnov test we will compare two 5-point Likert scale data sets. First we will calculate the

■ ■ ■ ■ **APPENDIX**

■ **Table A.2** Two sample Kolmogorov-Smirnov test

Likert scale	Before	Cumulative/500	After	Cumulative/500	Difference (D)
1	48	0.096	50	0.1	0.004
2	46	0.188	50	0.2	0.012
3	107	0.402	100	0.4	0.002
4	155	0.712	200	0.8	0.088
5	144	1	100	1	0
Total	500		500		

■ **Table A.3** Stata Model 1: two sample Kolmogorov-Smirnov test

Smaller group	D	p-value
1:	0.0020	0.998
2:	−0.0880	0.021
Combined K-S:	0.0880	0.042

ksmirnov var, by(group), with group being before=1 and after=2

Kolmogorov-Smirnov test by hand and compare the result with the output from Stata. Table A.2 shows the distribution of the responses to a Likert scale question asked before and after an intervention. The cumulative totals have been calculated in order to find the largest absolute difference (D). The maximum difference is 0.088 and the approximate Kilmogorov-Smirnov critical value at the 5% level is $1.3581/\sqrt{500} = 0.0607$

Therefore $D = 0.088 > 0.0607 = D_{0.05}(p = 0.042)$ and hence the data sets are not similar. We can therefore say that this intervention has had an effect and that there is a statistically significant change in the respondent's Likert scale answers.

The output in Table A.3 shows the three different tests produced by Stata. The first test is the hypothesis that group 1 (before intervention) contains smaller values than group 2 (after intervention). This is found not to be true as the p-value is 0.998 and so we reject this hypothesis. The second test is of the hypothesis that group 1 (before) contains larger values than group 2 (after). This is significant with a p-value of 0.021 and so we accept the hypothesis. The final test gives the same answer as the calculation we preformed showing that the data sets are not similar.

Finally in this section we will look at two data sets when two distributions are similar. As in the first example we will use data from five hundred

APPENDIX ▓ ▓ ▓ ■

Table A.4 Kolmogorov-Smirnov test calculation

Likert scale	Before	Cumulative/500	After	Cumulative/500	Difference (D)
1	48	0.096	50	0.1	0.004
2	46	0.188	50	0.2	0.012
3	107	0.402	100	0.4	0.002
4	176	0.754	200	0.8	0.046
5	123	1	100	1	0
Total	500		500		

Table A.5 Stata Model 2: two sample Kolmogorov-Smirnov test

Smaller group	D	p-value
1:	0.0020	0.998
2:	−0.0460	0.347
Combined K-S:	0.0460	0.665

responses given to a question before and after an intervention. Table A.4 shows cumulative totals calculated in order to find the largest absolute difference (D). The maximum difference is 0.046 and the approximate Kolmogorov-Smirnov critical value at the 5% level is $1.3581/\sqrt{500} = 0.0607$

$D = 0.046 < 0.0607 = D_{0.05}(p = 0.665)$ and hence the data sets are similar. In this second example of equality of distribution functions we can say that the intervention has not had a statistically significant effect on the way people responded.

The Stata output in Table A.5 demonstrates that all three tests are not significant and hence there is no significant difference between the two data samples.

3 FACTOR ANALYSIS

In this section in order to aid the understanding of how factor models are derived we calculate a factor solution by hand using a set of simultaneous equations (Loehlin, 2004; Brown, 2006). Firstly we will set out the notation required to formulate equations in exploratory and confirmatory factor analysis. The covariance or correlation between variables is associated to factor loadings by the equation $COV(X1, X2) = \lambda_1 \phi_{11} \lambda_2$ where X_j are the

■ ■ ■ ■ APPENDIX

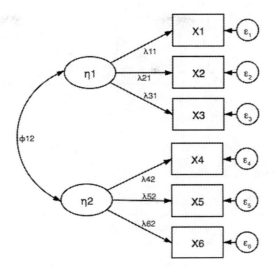

■ **Figure A.2** Factor model

individual items, λ_j are the eigenvalue factor loadings and ϕ_{11} is the factor variance of latent factor η_1. In the completely standardised solution the latent factor is equal to 1.00. The variable ϕ_{12} is the covariance between the two latent variables and ε_j represents the variance that is unique to the indicator X_j. Figure A.2 illustrates this model.

From this diagram we can construct the following equations:

$$COV(X1, X2) = \lambda_{11}\phi_{11}\lambda_{21}$$

$$VAR(X1) = \lambda_{11}^2 \phi_{11} + \varepsilon_1$$

$$COV(X3, X4) = \lambda_{32}\phi_{12}\lambda_{42}$$

The errors (residual variances) can be calculated as one minus the square of the factor loading as $\varepsilon_1 = 1 - \lambda_{11}^2$. The square of the factor loading represents the proportion of the variance in a variable item that is explained by the latent factor $\eta_1^2 = \lambda_{11}^2$

Considering the study around parental involvement in education, Figure A.3 shows the latent factor 'general school invitations' (L1) accounting for 94.09% ($0.97^2 = 0.9409$) of the variance in 'I feel welcome at school' (GSI1). The smallest eigenvalue factor loading in this model is 0.45 and accounts for only 20.25% ($0.45^2 = 0.2025$) of the variance in 'the teachers at the school keep me informed about my child's progress in school' (GSI3).

We will use the simple one factor model in Figure A.3 as an example to illustrate how factor analysis calculations are performed. Using the

APPENDIX ▨ ▨ ▨ ■

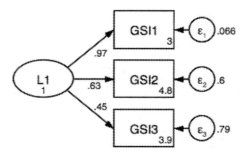

▨ **Figure A.3** Factor loading

▨ **Table A.6** Correlations for parental education motivation

	GSI1	GSI2	GSI3
I feel welcome at school (GSI1)	1.000		
The school lets me know about special school events and meetings (GSI2)	0.609	1.000	
The teachers at the school keep me informed about my child's progress in school (GSI3)	0.440	0.287	1.000

equations of the form COV $(X1, X2) = \lambda_{11}\phi_{11}\lambda_{21}$ we can write the following non-linear simultaneous equations:

$$COV\left(GSI1, GSI2\right) = \lambda_{11}\phi_{11}\lambda_{21} = ab = 0.609$$

$$COV\left(GSI1, GSI3\right) = \lambda_{11}\phi_{11}\lambda_{31} = ac = 0.440$$

$$COV\left(GSI3, GSI2\right) = \lambda_{31}\phi_{11}\lambda_{21} = bc = 0.287$$

Letting $\lambda_{11} = a, \lambda_{21} = b, \lambda_{31} = c,$ and $\phi_{11} = 1.00$

The parent's educational motivation correlations that we considered in Chapter 5 are given in Table A.6.

Using the values from Table A.6, the COV equations, the 3 factor loadings ($\lambda_{11}, \lambda_{21}, \lambda_{31}$ changed to a, b, c), 3 error terms ($\varepsilon_1, \varepsilon_2, \varepsilon_3$), the factor variance fixed at 1.00 (ϕ_{11}) we can write the following six equations:

$$ab = 0.609 - (1)$$
$$ac = 0.440 - (2)$$

APPENDIX

$$bc = 0.287 - (3)$$
$$\varepsilon_1 = 1 - a^2$$
$$\varepsilon_2 = 1 - b^2$$
$$\varepsilon_3 = 1 - c^2$$

Rearranging equations (1) and (2) to give b =0.609/a and c =0.440/a and then substituting these into equation (3) gives:

$$(0.609/a)(0.440/a) = 0.287$$

Solving gives $a^2 = 0.9337$ and $a = 0.96626 \approx 0.97$
Using this result and $b = 0.609/a$ gives $b = 0.63025 \approx 0.63$
Similarly, with $c = 0.440/a$ we can calculate $c \approx 0.45$
Hence
$\varepsilon_1 = 1 - 0.97^2 \approx 0.06, \varepsilon_2 = 1 - 0.63^2 \approx 0.6$, and $\varepsilon_3 = 1 - 0.45^2 \approx 0.79$
Note that we can see that these are the factor loading values and error terms in Figure A.3.

Eigenvalues and eigenvectors

Eigenvalues and eigenvectors allow us to gain an insight into the structure of matrices (Thurstone, 1935; Tabachnick and Fidell, 2001; Anthony and Harvey, 2012). In this section will look at how to calculate eigenvalues and eigenvectors from a simple two by two matrix: $A = \begin{pmatrix} 5 & 3 \\ -\frac{3}{2} & -\frac{1}{2} \end{pmatrix}$

The matrix A is made up of numerical values that could represent in a data set the responses from two people to two items in a survey. Generally research data could produce much larger matrices. For example, ten survey items with responses from 200 people would produce a matrix with 200 rows by 10 columns. The first step in calculating eigenvalues and eigenvectors is to calculate the determinant of matrix A.

$$det(A - \lambda I) = 0 = det\left(\begin{bmatrix} 5 & 3 \\ -\frac{3}{2} & -\frac{1}{2} \end{bmatrix} - \lambda \begin{bmatrix} 1 & 0 \\ 0 & 1 \end{bmatrix}\right) \text{ where}$$

$I = \begin{bmatrix} 1 & 0 \\ 0 & 1 \end{bmatrix}$ is called the identity matrix.

$$det(A - \lambda I) = \begin{vmatrix} 5-\lambda & 3 \\ -\frac{3}{2} & -\frac{1}{2}-\lambda \end{vmatrix} = (5-\lambda)\left(-\frac{1}{2}-\lambda\right) + \frac{9}{2} = \left(\lambda - \frac{1}{2}\right)(\lambda - 4)$$

179

APPENDIX ▪ ▪ ▪ ■

From this $\left(\lambda - \frac{1}{2}\right)(\lambda - 4)$ we obtain the two eigenvalues as $\lambda = 4$ and $\lambda = \frac{1}{2}$ for matrix A. To find the eigenvectors we use the equation $Ax = \lambda x$ with $x = \begin{bmatrix} a \\ b \end{bmatrix}$ being the vector we are looking to calculate that goes with each eigenvalue. To find the eigenvector when the eigenvalue is 4 we can write this equation as

$$Ax = \begin{pmatrix} 5 & 3 \\ -\frac{3}{2} & -\frac{1}{2} \end{pmatrix} \begin{pmatrix} a \\ b \end{pmatrix} = \begin{pmatrix} 5a + 3b \\ -\frac{3}{2}a - \frac{1}{2}b \end{pmatrix} = 4 \begin{pmatrix} a \\ b \end{pmatrix}$$

This results in two equations which are the same $a + 3b = 0$ and $-3a - 9b = 0$. The solution is $a = -3b$. This means that there is an infinity of solution vectors that could represent this, all of which take the form of the vector in the direction $\begin{pmatrix} -3 \\ 1 \end{pmatrix}$ Similarly you can calculate the eigenvector as $\begin{pmatrix} -2 \\ 3 \end{pmatrix}$ for the eigenvalue $\frac{1}{2}$.

The combination of eigenvalues and eigenvectors is given as $4\begin{pmatrix} -3 \\ 1 \end{pmatrix} + \frac{1}{2}\begin{pmatrix} -2 \\ 3 \end{pmatrix}$. Notice that the eigenvalue of 4, simply due to its magnitude, has a greater impact on the resulting vector direction.

Using these eigenvalues as a representation of matrix A we can write this as a combination of vectors $X_j = \lambda_j \eta_1$ and their relationship to the single η_1 the latent factor in this case.

Item 1: $\lambda_1 \eta_1 + \varepsilon_1 = 4\eta_1 + \varepsilon_1$
Item 2: $\lambda_2 \eta_1 + \varepsilon_2 = \frac{1}{2}\eta_1 + \varepsilon_2$

In general terms we are looking to solve $Ax = \lambda x$ to find eigenvalues (λ) and eigenvectors (x) for our matrix (A). First let $(A - \lambda I)x = 0$, as x is only zero for a trivial solution then this implies that $\det(A - \lambda I) = 0$ for non-trivial solutions. As we have seen in the example above this allows us to calculate the eigenvalues and eigenvectors of the matrix A. Eigenvalues and eigenvectors are the mathematics used to determine the components in exploratory and confirmatory factor analysis.

4 CORRELATION

Linear Pearson correlation coefficient r

In the formula for Pearson correlation the value of $\Sigma(x - \bar{x})(y - \bar{y})$ is influenced by the strength of the correlation between and the spread of the

APPENDIX

variables. If there is a positive correlation between the points the value is positive and negative if there is a negative correlation. If there is no correlation between the variables then the sum of the products of positive and negative values tend to cancel each other out and result in a sum near zero.

The addition to the formula of the number of values (n) gives the average deviation from the bivariate centroid, known as covariance:

$$Cov(x,y) = \frac{1}{n}\sum(x-\bar{x})(y-\bar{y})$$

If we then divide this by the standard deviations for x and y we obtain the linear correlation coefficient r defined as $r = \frac{\sum(x-\bar{x})(y-\bar{y})}{\sqrt{\sum(x-\bar{x})^2}\sqrt{\sum(y-\bar{y})^2}}$ in a slightly amended form this can be written as $r = \frac{\sum xy - n\bar{x}\bar{y}}{\sqrt{(\sum x^2 - n\bar{x}^2)}\sqrt{(\sum y^2 - n\bar{y}^2)}}$

Dividing by the standard deviations of x and y removes the issue of the size of r being dependent on the measurement units being used and allows for r to lie between -1 and $+1$. If $r = +1$ then this means there is a perfect positive correlation and $r = -1$ then a perfect negative correlation. A value $r = 0$ implies that there is no linear correlation.

The following example illustrates how correlation can be calculated by hand for a data set containing two variables (mathematics and English scores) for seven sets of scores (a-g). As can be seen from Table A.7 the variables are multiplied together (xy), squared and the totals of these rows are then calculated.

The mean of x is $\bar{x} = 4$ and y is $\bar{y} = 4$. The calculated values are then substituted into the following formula for the Pearson correlation coefficient:

$$r = \frac{\sum xy - n\bar{x}\bar{y}}{\sqrt{(\sum x^2 - n\bar{x}^2)}\sqrt{(\sum y^2 - n\bar{y}^2)}} = \frac{133 - 7 \times 4 \times 4}{\sqrt{140 - 7 \times 16}\sqrt{140 - 7 \times 16}} = \frac{21}{28} = 0.75$$

Table A.7 Worked example Pearson correlation calculation

Item	a	b	c	d	e	f	g	Total
Mathematics (x)	5	1	7	3	2	4	6	28
English (y)	4	3	7	1	2	6	5	28
xy	20	3	49	3	4	24	30	133
x²	25	1	49	9	4	16	36	140
y²	16	9	49	1	4	36	25	140

APPENDIX ▨ ▨ ▨ ■

This result of 0.75 shows that there is a strong positive linear correlation between these two variables. In SPSS and Stata the calculation for this data gives the result as r=0.75, with a significance of p=0.052

Note that you can prove that r will only take values in the range $-1 \leq r \leq +1$ by using u, v, $\Sigma(x - \bar{x})^2$, and $\Sigma(y - \bar{y})^2$

As a hint on how to do this let $U = u / \Sigma(x - \bar{x})^2$ and $V = v/\Sigma(y - \bar{y})^2$ and then show that $\sum(U+V)^2 = 2n(1+r)$ hence prove that $r \gg -1$

Then by considering both $\sum(U+V)^2$ and $\sum(U-V)^2$ use these to prove the result that $-1 \leq r \leq +1$

Spearman rank correlation coefficient r (Spearman's rho (ρ))

The Spearman rank correlation coefficient is calculated in a very similar fashion to the Pearson correlation coefficient but using ranks assigned to the data. We assume that the ranks of x and y in the data take integer values from 1, 2, 3, ..., n. The total of these integer ranks are made for the n integers $\Sigma x = \Sigma y = \frac{1}{2}n(n+1)$ and for the sum of the squares of the integers $\Sigma x^2 = \Sigma y^2 = \frac{1}{6}n(n+1)(2n+1)$

Hence $\bar{x} = \bar{y} = \frac{1}{2}(n+1)$

The difference (d) between x and y is given as $d = x - y$. Hence the difference squared can be written as, $\Sigma d^2 = \Sigma(x-y)^2 = \Sigma x^2 + \Sigma y^2 - 2\Sigma xy$

From this equation we can write $\Sigma xy = \frac{1}{6}n(n+1)(2n+1) - \frac{1}{2}\sum d^2$

Using the Pearson correlation coefficient

$$r = \frac{\sum(x-\bar{x})(y-\bar{y})}{\sqrt{\sum(x-\bar{x})^2}\sqrt{\sum(y-\bar{y})^2}}$$ in this slightly amended form we can write

$$r = \frac{\sum xy - n\bar{x}\bar{y}}{\sqrt{(\sum x^2 - n\bar{x}^2)}\sqrt{(\sum y^2 - n\bar{y}^2)}}$$

Substituting from the above equations we can obtain the Spearman rank correlation coefficient r_s

$$r_s = \frac{\frac{1}{6}n(n+1)(2n+1) - \frac{1}{2}\sum d^2 - \frac{1}{4}n(n+1)^2}{\frac{1}{6}n(n+1)(2n+1) - \frac{1}{4}n(n+1)^2}$$

$$r_s = 1 - \frac{6\sum d^2}{n(n+1)\left[2(2n+1) - 3(n+1)\right]}$$

APPENDIX

$$r_s = 1 - \frac{6\sum d^2}{n(n^2-1)}$$

The following example shows how the Spearman rank correlation can be calculated for two rankings of n paired data items. The example in Table A.8 shows data from two judges in a cookery competition. The judges have given a rank score for seven scones in the cookery competition. From Table A.8 we can see that n = 7 and calculate

$\Sigma\ d^2 = 1+4+0+4+0+4+1 = 14$

These values can then be used in the Spearman rank correlation formula to calculate the coefficient $r_s = 1 - \frac{6\sum d^2}{n(n^2-1)} = 1 - \frac{6 \times 14}{7 \times 48} = 1 - \frac{84}{336} = 0.75$

The value of 0.75 shows that there is a strong positive linear correlation between these judge's scores. The software packages SPSS and Stata give the result for this data as r=0.75, with p=0.052

Kendall rank correlation coefficient (Kendall's Tau (τ))

Kendall correlation coefficient is a different measure of rank correlation to Spearman correlation. This correlation technique has less restrictions on the data, with no need for there to be an equal distance between the ranks. The way that Kendall correlation works is to look at identifying the amount of rank disarray in the reference column. To calculate the Kendall rank correlation coefficient every pair of items needs to be taken into consideration.

To illustrate how this technique is calculated we will look again at the scone cookery competition example (Table A.8). Letting the reference column be the first judge (x) and we rearrange the table so that the first judge's ranks are in order. There are 7 items and so 21 pairs (6+5+4+3+2+1) to look at. These pair are ab, ac, ad, ae, af, ag, bc, bd, be, etc. The first rank in the column for the second judge is 3 and below this there are 4 ranks greater than 3. These are the pairs bf, ba, bg, and bc. There are only 2 ranks less than 3 and these are the disagreements. The second entry for the second judge is 2 and below this there are 4 ranks greater than this. These are the

Table A.8 Worked example of Spearman rank correlation

Item	a	b	c	d	e	f	g
1st Judge(x)	5	1	7	3	2	4	6
2nd Judge (y)	4	3	7	1	2	6	5
d	1	−2	0	2	0	−2	1
d²	1	4	0	4	0	4	1

APPENDIX ▨ ▨ ▨ ■

Table A.9 Worked example of Kendall correlation

Item	1st judge(x)	2nd judge(y)	Agreements	Disagreements
b	1	3	4	2
e	2	2	4	1
d	3	1	4	0
f	4	6	1	2
a	5	4	2	0
g	6	5	1	0
c	7	7		
Total			16	5

pairs ef, ea, eg and ec. With only one disagreement being ed. Continuing to work down the table using this same method results in the figures in Table A.9. Hence r_k = (number of agreements − number of disagreements)/(total number of pairs)

= (16−5)/21 = 0.52

The formula for Kendall's rank correlation can be written as

$$r_k = \frac{A-D}{\frac{1}{2}n(n-1)}$$

where A is the number of agreements and D is the number of disagreements. In SPSS and Stata the data gives the result as r=0.524, with p=0.099

5 LINEAR REGRESSION

Linear regression models the relationship between two variables. Although points may not fall exactly on a straight line, linear regression involves the fitting of a best-fit straight line for a set of data points. The regression line is said to be a perfect fit when all of the points lie on a straight line. The Pearson correlation coefficient for this is either r = −1 (negative correlation) or r = +1 (positive correlation).

The square of the correlation coefficient is called the coefficient of determination (r^2). When $r^2 = 0$ then the goodness of fit is poor and $r^2 = 1$ the goodness of fit is perfect. This r^2 value implies the share of the y variance explained by the x variance. For example if $r^2 = 0.82$ then this means that 82% of the variance in y is explained through the variance in x.

In this section we will look at the details of how the regression technique works in two dimensions. Consider a set of paired data observations (x_i, y_i) plotted on a scatter graph we can estimate the straight line that passes close to these observations as $y_i = a + bx_i + \varepsilon_i$. The goal of regression is to create

■ ■ ■ ■ APPENDIX

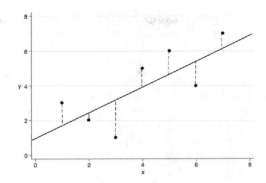

■ **Figure A.4** Regression line with errors

the equation of a line with gradient (b) and intercept on the y-axis (a) for a set of paired data observations (x_i, y_i). The position of this regression line being such that it minimises the errors (ε_i). One method of achieving a linear model for bivariate data is by minimizing the sum of the squares of these errors using a technique called method of least squares.

To illustrate the method of least squares we will use a set of seven points shown in Figure A.4. The line is an estimate, which has been drawn as close to as many of the points as possible in order to minimise the error.

The dotted lines are shown as the errors (ε_i) and the aim of the least squares method is to a minimise these distances above and below the line. Given that (x_i, y) are the straight line regression point estimates and (x_i, y_i) are the actual values, then the error quantity is the amount of deviation from the true score value. It can be written as $y - (a + bx_i) = \varepsilon_i$ and is called the

■ **Table A.10** Calculating regression residuals

Coordinates of the seven points on the graph (x_i, y_i)	Regression line y-value	Residual error ε_i-value $y - (a + bx_i) = \varepsilon_i$	Error squared $(\varepsilon_i)^2$-value $(y-(a+bx_i))^2 = (\varepsilon_i)^2$
x_i y_i	$y = 1 + 0.75x_i$	Error $y - (1 + 0.75x_i) = \varepsilon_i$	Residual $(y-(1+0.75x_i))^2 = (\varepsilon_i)^2$
1 3	1.75	1.25	1.5625
2 2	2.5	−0.5	0.25
3 1	3.25	−2.25	5.0625
4 5	4	1	1
5 6	4.75	1.25	1.5625
6 4	5.5	−1.5	2.25
7 7	6.25	0.75	0.5625
Total		0	12.25

APPENDIX ▨ ▨ ▨ ■

residual. Classical test theory (CTT) states that any measured score consists of two parts, a true score and an amount of error (Gulliksen, 1950; Novick, 1966; Lord and Novick, 1968).

When SPSS and Stata are used to calculate this line for the seven points shown in Figure A.4 they give the variable output B-value of 0.75 and a constant value of 1. Hence the equation of the line is $y = 1 + 0.75x_i$

The output will also give the standard error of the B-value and the constant. The smaller the standard error value the greater confidence we have in the regression line being a good fit to the points. The sum of the squares of the residuals in this example has a value of 12.25 (see Table A.10).

This residual will be reflected in the p-value significance and the 95% confidence interval bounds. Using the standard error you can calculate these confidence interval bounds as Coef ± 1.96 SE. The upper 95% confidence interval bound is 0.75 +1.96x0.295 = 1.32 and the lower bound as 0.75– 1.96x0.295 = 0.17

Method of least squares

The following is the derivation of method of least squares for the two dimensional case.

The sum of squares can be written as $S = \Sigma(y - (a+bx))^2 = \Sigma(\varepsilon)^2$

To simplify the algebra we can write this as

$y - (a + bx) = (y - \bar{y}) - b(x - \bar{x}) + (\bar{y} - a - b\bar{x})$ where $\bar{y}$ and $\bar{x}$ are the mean values of y_i and x_i

Letting $u = x - \bar{x}$, $v = y - \bar{y}$, and $c = \bar{y} - a - b\bar{x}$ to give

$$S = \Sigma(v - bu + c)^2$$
$$= \Sigma(v^2 + b^2u^2 + c^2 - 2buv - 2bcu + 2cv)$$
$$= \Sigma v^2 + b^2\Sigma u^2 + nc^2 - 2b\Sigma uv - 2b\Sigma u + 2c\Sigma v$$

As $\Sigma u = 0$ and $\Sigma v = 0$ then

$$S = \Sigma v^2 + b^2\Sigma u^2 + nc^2 - 2b\Sigma uv$$

Completing the square

$$S = \Sigma u^2 \left(b - (\Sigma uv / \Sigma u^2)\right)^2 + \Sigma v^2 - ((\Sigma uv)^2 / \Sigma u^2) + nc^2$$

If S takes a minimum value $\Sigma v^2 - ((\Sigma uv)^2 / \Sigma u^2)$ when $b = (\Sigma uv / \Sigma u^2)$ and c =0

Hence obtaining $\bar{y} - a - b\bar{x} = 0$

The least squares regression line for the equation y = a + bx with values of a and b calculated from the following formulas

$$b = (\Sigma uv / \Sigma u^2) = (\Sigma(x - \bar{x})(y - \bar{y})) / \Sigma(x - \bar{x})^2 \text{ and } a = \bar{y} - b\bar{x}$$

■ ■ ■ ■ **APPENDIX**

Note that by definition the regression line will always pass through the point $(\bar{x}, \bar{y})$

Multivariate regression coefficients

It is often the case that there is not just one independent variable that is the influencing factor. Multivariate analysis is comparable to using bivariate regression as the technique to find a solution for the vector **b**$_i$ such that the sum of square residuals is a minimum. The general form in the multivariate case, for n observations with i independent variables is a vector equation $\mathbf{Y_n} = \mathbf{x_{in} b_i} + \mathbf{\varepsilon_n}$ which can be written in its expanded matrix form as a set of n linear equations;

$$\begin{bmatrix} y_1 \\ y_2 \\ \vdots \\ y_n \end{bmatrix} = \begin{bmatrix} 1 & x_{11} & x_{21} & \cdots & x_{i1} \\ 1 & x_{21} & x_{22} & \cdots & x_{i2} \\ \vdots & \vdots & \vdots & & \vdots \\ 1 & x_{1n} & x_{2n} & \cdots & x_{in} \end{bmatrix} \begin{bmatrix} b_0 \\ b_1 \\ \vdots \\ b_i \end{bmatrix} + \begin{bmatrix} \varepsilon_1 \\ \varepsilon_2 \\ \vdots \\ \varepsilon_n \end{bmatrix}$$

To find the least squares estimates for all b_i the sum of squares is a minimum when

$$\sum \varepsilon_n^2 = \mathcal{E}'\mathcal{E} = \left(y_n - x_{in} b_i\right)^T \left(y_n - x_{in} b_i\right)$$

The smallest sum of squares could be when all ε_n are zero and then $\mathbf{Y_n} = \mathbf{x_{in} b_i}$. By using the fact that $x^T x b_i = x^T y$ then it is possible to estimate b in the vector form $\left(x^T x\right)^{-1} x^T y$ where x^T is the transpose matrix and $()^{-1}$ is the inverse matrix (Fox, 1997; Draper and Smith, 1998; Sen and Srivastava, 2011)

Adjusted R²

The aim of linear regression as we have seen in the previous sections is to use independent variables to help explain a predicted model in relation to a dependent variable. As the number of independent variables increases this can improve the coefficient of determination but there is also a greater risk of some variables having little explanatory ability. This is called over parameterization. There is an R^2 value that compensates for this called adjusted R^2. As additional variables are added the adjusted R^2 formula takes this into account.

$$\text{Adjusted } R^2 = 1 - \left(1 - R^2\right)(n-1)/(n-k)$$

In this formula k is the number of variables in the model and n is the number of observations. For the researcher it is worth bearing in mind that additional variables can increase the quality of the model but they can also reduce it. This reduction will be visible by using the adjusted coefficient of determination comparing models with different numbers of variables.

APPENDIX ▨ ▨ ▨ ■

Goodness of fit F-test

As we have seen the coefficient of determination (R^2 value) is not the only measure of whether independent variables give a more accurate representation of a model. The F-test is a goodness of fit measure that uses the mean square sums of squares rather than the sum of squares in R^2 test. The F-test is the ratio of improvement in the model, giving a value that tells us how much variation is explained by the model and how much is left unexplained. In general for multivariate regression the F-value is calculated as the mean sum of squares or the explained variance divided by the residual mean squares or the unexplained variance.

F = (explained variance)/(unexplained variance)

$$F = \frac{\sum_{i=1}^{K}\left(\overline{Y}_i - \overline{Y}\right)^2 n_i \Big/ (K-1)}{\sum_{i=1}^{K}\sum_{j=1}^{n_i}\left(Y_{ij} - \overline{Y}_i\right)^2 \Big/ (N-K)}$$

With $\overline{Y}_i$ as the sample mean in the i-th group, n_i is the number of observations in the i-th group, $\overline{Y}$ is the overall mean of the data, K is the number of groups within the data. The variable Y_{ij} is the j-th observation in the i-th group out of K, and N is the total sample size.

6 SAMPLE SIZE

Deciding on a significant sample size is important for research validity. In this section we will first consider conditions related to normally distributed data and then more general cases. To illustrate this we will take an example where we wish to be 95% certain that the sample mean is within ten units of the population mean ($\overline{x} \pm 10$). Then this implies that $\overline{x} \pm 1.96\frac{\sigma}{\sqrt{n}}$ for a sample with known variance (σ^2). The upper bound for this limit has to be less than or equal to ten and can be written as $10 \geq 1.96\frac{\sigma}{\sqrt{n}}$ Solving this inequality gives the minimum size for the sample under these conditions as $n \geq (0.196\sigma)^2$

In the general case for non-parametric tests these can be approximated by a normal distribution with mean np and variance np(1–p), with $X = N(np, np(1-p))$. The sample proportion is found by dividing the number observed by the size of the sample (x/n). We can use this to write

$$\frac{x}{n} = N\left(\frac{np}{n}, \frac{np(1-p)}{n^2}\right) = N\left(p, \frac{p(1-p)}{n}\right)$$

indicating that the distribution of the sample proportion is approximately normal with population proportion

APPENDIX

(p) and the variance depends on the size of the sample and p. Using this result we can define a 95% confidence interval as $\hat{p} \pm 1.96\sqrt{\dfrac{p(1-P)}{n}}$ with $\hat{p}$ being the sample proportion. It can be seen from this that any given confidence interval has a maximum width when p=0.5. Proof of this is simply shown by differentiating p(1–p) to give a stationary value condition of 0=1–2p. This 95% confidence interval gives an upper bound and allows for the calculation of the minimum sample size as approximately

$$\hat{p} \pm 1.96\sqrt{\dfrac{0.5(1-0.5)}{n}} \approx \hat{p} \pm \sqrt{\dfrac{1}{n}}$$

For example this can be used to determine the minimum sample size for a required specific degree of accuracy. Suppose we wish to determine the proportion of consumers from a total population who select a certain preferential choice to within 10% of accuracy. The inequality $0.1 \geq \dfrac{1}{\sqrt{n}}$ shows that the sample size (n) needs to be greater than 100 for us to be 95% confident that we will get an appropriate sample.

Bartlett et al., (2001) is a good starting point for readers interested in obtaining more detail on the range of techniques for determining sample sizes for surveys. The paper calculates the minimum samples size for various populations. It states that at the 5% level of significance the minimum sample size should be 119 for continuous data and 370 for categorical data for a population of size ten thousand. For the same population size, the 1% level of significance for these minimum sample sizes increase to 209 for continuous data and 623 for categorical data.

7 CONFIRMATORY FACTOR ANALYSIS (CFA)

A CFA model can be expressed in matrix form as $X = \Lambda_x \eta + \varepsilon$, where X is the relationship among observed variables, η the latent factors and ε unique variances. The expanded form of this matrix equation is $X_j = \lambda_{j1}\eta_1 + \lambda_{j2}\eta_2 + \ldots + \lambda_{jm}\eta_m + \varepsilon_j$ where X_j represents the j th of p indicators obtained from n independent subjects (n is the number of people in your sample), λ_{jm} represents the eigenvalue factor loadings relating variable j to the m th eigenvector factor η (if m = 2 this means that the number of grouping relationships, latent factors is two), and ε_j represents the variance that is unique to the indicator X_j and is independent of all η's and all other ε's.

With general assumptions that there is no correlation between constructs and an expected value of zero for ε and η the variance–covariance matrix for the indicators X denoted as $\Sigma = \Lambda_x \Phi \Lambda_x' + \theta\varepsilon$ where Φ is the covariance matrix of latent constructs (η) and $\theta\varepsilon$ is a diagonal matrix of the variance errors. It is this set of matrices that are used with Stata's CFA procedure to generate maximum likelihood estimates.

APPENDIX ▨ ▨ ▨ ■

In order to establish which model provides the best fit the χ^2 test and the fit indices can be calculated in Stata.

Formally, the null and alternative hypotheses of a confirmatory model are specified as:

$H_0: \Sigma = \Sigma(\theta)$
$H_a: \Sigma = \Sigma\alpha$

where Σ is the population matrix estimated by the observed correlations between indicators, $\Sigma(\theta)$ is the implied correlation matrix that results from the pattern matrices and $\Sigma\alpha$ is any positive definite matrix. Retaining H_0 implies that the observed correlations among the indicators are well modelled by the specified pattern matrices (Λ_x, Φ, $\theta\varepsilon$). Conversely, rejection of H_0 implies poor model fit. A range of fit and comparison-based indices, including the Chi-square test, is used to determine which model provides the best fit for these data (Bentler, 1990; Steiger, 1990; Browne & Cudeck, 1993; Brown, 2006). The fit indices include Root Mean Square Error of Approximation (RMSEA), Standardised Root Mean Square Residual (S-RMR), Coefficient of Determination (CD), Tucker-Lewis Index (TLI) and Comparative Fit Index (CFI). Hu and Bentler (1999) suggest various cut offs for these fit indices. To minimize Type I and Type II errors one should use a combination with S-RMR or the RMSEA. In general good models should have an S-RMR <0.08 or the RMSEA <0.06 with the fit index values > 0.9.

8 LOGISTIC REGRESSION

The distribution of the logistic regression can produce very meaningful estimates of effects due to the functions simplicity of use. These estimates are called odds ratios and are obtained from the expected distribution function:

$$E(Y|x) = \pi(x) = Exp(g(x))/(Exp(g(x)) + 1)$$

With $g(x) = b_0 + b_1 x$ (1)

This transformation is important as it gives properties of a continuous function with linear parameters. The outcome variable is $y = \pi(x) + \varepsilon$ for dependent variable x. The quantity ε is one of two possible values depending on the value of y:

y=1 then $\varepsilon = 1 - \pi(x)$ with probability $\pi(x)$

y=0 then $\varepsilon = -\pi(x)$ with probability $\varepsilon = 1 - \pi(x)$

Therefore ε has a binomial distribution with mean of 0 and variance of $\pi(x)/1 - \pi(x)$

Logistic regression produces an estimate for $\pi(x)$ from a 2 by 2 contingency table as shown in Table A.11.

APPENDIX

Table A.11 Expected distribution contingency table

		Dependant variable $y = \pi(x) + \varepsilon$	
		No (0)	Yes(1)
Independent variable x	No (0)	$1-\pi(0)$	$\pi(0)$
	Yes(1)	$1-\pi(1)$	$\pi(1)$

Table A.12 Example data for expected distribution contingency table

	Male	Female
No	105	154
Yes	153	88

Chi-square= 26.316, p=0.001. Cramer's V=0.229 with p=0.001.

Odds ratio for 'yes' is identified as $\pi(1)/1-\pi(1)$ and for 'no' is $\pi(0)/1-\pi(0)$ giving the ratio for 'yes' relative to 'no' as

$$\widehat{OR} = [\pi(1)/1-\pi(1)] / [\pi(0)/1-\pi(0)] = Exp(b_1) \quad (2)$$

This result is obtained by substituting values for $\pi(x)$ from equation (1) above into (2), thus producing the standard odds ratio exponential for the independent variable to the dependent variable (Rothman et al., 2008; Hosmer et al., 2013)

In this next example we will explore in greater detail the contingency table (Table A.12) which illustrates data on males and female coffee-drinking habits to give an idea how calculations are performed for standard errors and confidence limits.

The odds of the number of males that drink Americano, latte and espresso to females who drink the same = number males/number of females = 153/88 = 1.74

The odds of the number of males that did not drink Americano, latte and espresso divided by the number of females who also did not = number males that did not/number of females who did not = 105/154 = 0.68

Odds ratio of males drinking Americano, latte and espresso to females = 1.74/0.68 = 2.56

Giving the $\widehat{OR}$ of 2.56 implies that a male is 2.56 times more likely to drink Americano, latte and espresso in a coffee shop than a female. By taking the natural log of the odds ratio, B-values can be calculated. In this example the B-value is $b_1 = \ln(2.56) = 0.94$ and standard error $= [1/105 + 1/154 + 1/153 + 1/88]^{1/2} = 0.034$.

APPENDIX ■ ■ ■ ■

The 95% confidence interval can be calculated for this case as b_1 as 0.94 ± 1.96×0.034. The general form of the 95% confidence interval for B-values are of the form B± 1.96×SE. The 95% confidence interval for the Odd ratios are EXP(B± 1.96×SE).

For continuous independent variables as discussed Chapter 6 these limits need to include either a constant change value (in the chapter we gave the example using 10 units) or one standard deviation (SD). This means that the confidence limits can be calculated as follows:

The 95% confidence interval for B-values are of the form B± 1.96× SD×SE. The corresponding limits in general the 95% confidence interval for Odd ratios are EXP(B± 1.96× SD ×SE).

Log-likelihood test

There are two stages to assessing models, firstly building a model and making sure that it contains the required variables. Secondly, assessing the goodness of fit so that the model reflects the 'true' outcomes and is an accurate representation of the observed values. Tests for assessing the significance of variables in a model need to consider whether the inclusion of a variable improves the model. This is not a measure of whether these variables give a more accurate representation as this is called a measure of goodness of fit that will be discussed below.

The log-likelihood test is a measure that compares observed to predicted values in a similar approach to that of the F-test for linear regression. The log-likelihood test is based on the G statistic which is defined as G = D(model without the variables) – D(model with variables) where D is given by D = –2ln [(likelihood of fitted model)/(likelihood of the saturated model)].

In linear regression the method used for estimating the unknown parameter values of a and b is called least squares. This is used to calculate these parameters that minimise the error of $S = \Sigma (y- (a+bx))^2 = \Sigma (\varepsilon)^2$. Since the outcome of logistic regression is dichotomous a different method is required to calculate the unknown parameter values b_0 and b_1 in the equation below. This method is called maximum likelihood and it calculates the values of b_0 and b_1 that maximise the probability of obtaining the observed data set. The logistic regression model is this transform of $\pi(x)$

$$E(Y|x) = \pi(x) = Exp(g(x))/(Exp(g(x)) + 1)$$
$$\text{with } g(x) = b_0 + b_1 x$$

The importance of this transform is that g(x) is linear and continuous over a range of x. With the above expected distribution function the log-likelihood function can be written

$$\text{as } L = \sum_{i=1}^{n} \{y_i \ln[\pi(x_i)] + (1-y_i)\ln(1-\pi(x_i))\} \quad (3)$$

APPENDIX

derived from the expression $\pi(x_i)^{y_i}[1-\pi(x_i)]^{1-y_i}$

Where this expression π(x) is the conditional probability that y_i is equal to 1 given x, and similarly 1 − π(x) is the quantity that y_i is equal to 0 given x.

To calculate the values of b_0 and b_1 equation (3) is differentiated with respect to b_0 and b_1 to give these two equations

$$\sum[y_i - \pi(x_i)] = 0$$
$$\sum x_i[y_i - \pi(x_i)] = 0$$

These equations are nonlinear and an iterative procedure is required to solve these in SPSS and Stata (McCullagh and Nelder, 1989). Note that some software packages report the value of the deviance of D rather than the log-likelihood of the fitted model.

We will illustrate the log-likelihood test with an example of an improved model, where adding variables gives a larger value of the log-likelihood than a base model with no variables.

Using the G-statistic G = D(model without the variables) − D(model with variables) and log-likelihoods calculated by a software package of:

L(model without the variables) = −16.764 and L(model with variables)=−9.679.
Calculating G = −2(−16.764 − (−9.679)) = 14.17. Where the value 14.17 is a Chi-square value, whose significance can then be accessed to evaluate the model, as we have seen in Chapter 6, to give a p-value associated with this test.

Wald test

The Wald test (W) assesses the individual contributions of the independent variables. The Wald value is calculated by using slope parameter (B) divided by the standard error (W= B/SE). The significance of the Wald value is given as a p-value.

Hauck and Donner (1977) carried out a detailed investigation around the performance of this test and found that it behaved in an 'aberrant manner'. Their paper suggests that the test often rejects the null hypothesis when the coefficient is actually significant. The advice from this research is to use the test with caution. If used it should be in conjunction with other tests such as the likelihood ratio. The likelihood ratio test is particularly recommended to assess the significance of coefficients due to its consistent reliability (Hauck and Donner, 1977; Hosmer, et al, 2013).

Goodness of fit test

Goodness of fit tests are used to assess whether the probabilities obtained from a logistic regression truly reflect the outcome data set. In goodness of fit tests we are comparing the fitted values to the observed values. It has

APPENDIX

been found that these tests are most reliable with samples over four hundred (Hosmer et al., 1997; Canary 2013).

If observed sample outcome variables are $\mathbf{y}' = (y_1, y_2, y_3, \ldots y_n)$ and the models estimated fitted values are $\hat{\mathbf{y}}' = (\hat{y}_1, \hat{y}_2, \hat{y}_3 \ldots \ldots \hat{y}_n)$ then the model can be said to fit under the follow criteria:

(1) if the distance between $\mathbf{y}'$ and $\hat{\mathbf{y}}'$ are small and (2) if each pair $(y_i, \hat{y}_i)$ for i=1,2,3…n contribute a small error related to the structure of the model.

Note that p-values in goodness of fit tests are not a good measure to differentiate between models. For example when two different models have p-values greater than 0.05, the model with a higher p-value does not imply that this model is a better fit. The researcher should think that both models fit and look into other considerations to determine, if appropriate, which is preferred. Alternatively if goodness of fit results provides one model with a p-value below 0.05 and another with one above 0.05, then the one above is preferred. Yet even in this case caution needs to be taken (Hosmer et al., 1997). It should be noted that goodness of fit tests should not be used to help build models as likelihood ratio tests are better in judging the significance of coefficients.

Pseudo R² value measures

These measures offer a comparison between the fitted model and the empty model. The three pseudo R^2 measures considered in this book are:

- Hosmer and Lemeshow $R^2 = LL(Model) / LL$ (Original)
- Cox and Snell $R^2 = 1 - Exp(-(2/n)(LL(Model) - LL\text{ (Orginal)}))$
- Negelkerke $R^2 = \left[Cox\ and\ Snell\ R^2 \right] / \left[1 - Exp\left((2/n) LL \text{ (Original)}\right) \right]$

LL stands for the log-likelihood. The measure can vary between 0 and 1, with 1 indicating that the model predicts the outcome variable perfectly and zero not at all. The number of items in the sample is defined by n.

Care needs to be taken when considering pseudo R^2 values as these are often low and do not always provide a clear understandable interpretation around the goodness of fit of the model.

Receiver Operating Characteristic (ROC)

The classification accuracy can be measured by looking at the area under the Receiver Operating Characteristic (ROC) curve. This curve shows the ability of the model to discriminate between yes outcomes (1) and no outcomes (0). This is used to measure the model's fit to assign a higher probability to the outcome with value 1 rather than to value 0. The technique does this by looking at the probability of sensitivity (true=1) related to 1-specificity (false=0) for all possible values.

■ ■ ■ ■ **APPENDIX**

General guidelines for discrimination values of the area under the ROC curve are:

ROC = 0.5	No discrimination
0.5 < ROC < 0.7	Poor discrimination
0.7 ≤ ROC < 0.8	Acceptable discrimination
0.8 ≤ ROC < 0.9	Excellent discrimination
ROC ≥ 0.9	Outstanding discrimination

(Source: Hosmer et al., 1997, p.177)

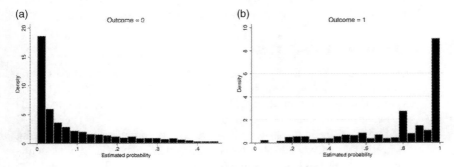

Figure A.5 Histograms illustrating excellent discrimination

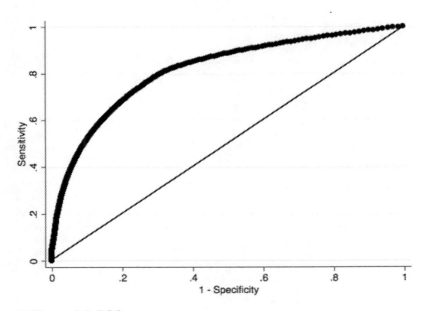

Figure A.6 ROC curve

APPENDIX

The histograms with excellent discrimination would look similar to those shown in Figure A.5. We can clearly see from these plots the estimated probabilities discriminating towards lower probability values for an outcome of zero and higher probability values for an outcome of one.

The ROC curve shown in Figure A.6 is an example of excellent discrimination having a ROC value of 0.88. Such ROC curves are created by plotting Sensitivity against 1- Specificity. The ROC graph can be drawn in SPSS and Stata once logistic regression has been performed.

Alternatively if the probability distributions for both outcome one and zero have been determined from the statistical package then a ROC curve can be drawn using these outputs. This can be obtained by plotting the cumulative distribution function for outcome = 1 on the y-axis against cumulative distribution function for outcome = 0 on the x-axis.

9 MARGINAL EFFECTS

In Chapter 6 we used the command 'margins' in Stata as a way of estimating marginal effects. The example was used in relation to logistic regression as an estimate of the predictive margins for males and females to levels of English test results from 40 through 90 at intervals of 10. The graph in Figure A.7 was used to illustrate how useful this command can be showing the probability of having aspirations to go to university related to student's gender and their English test score results.

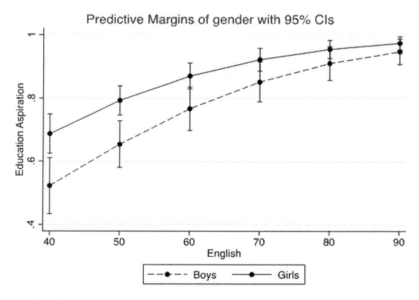

Figure A.7 Stata margins plot

■ ■ ■ ■ APPENDIX

The code used in Stata to produce this graph is as follows:

logit Univaspire English Doingwell3 Workhard3 Schoolimport2 Schoolimport3 i.gender
margins: margins gender, at(English=(40(10)90))
marginsplot

This margins technique can also be used for longitudinal data. In the example shown in Figure A.7 the variable gender could be replaced with a longitudinal variable, coded as 0 for baseline results and 1 for results after the intervention.

10 DISCRETE CHOICE THEORY

Discrete choice theory is used to help to understand the process that leads individuals to make choices and factors that collectively determine or cause this choice. A consumer decision maker, labelled n, faces choices among j alternatives. We assume that the consumers have certain preferences that maximise their utility. By utility we mean how much usefulness a consumer thinks that they obtain by making the choice. This paradigm of utility maximization provides a link by which choice probabilities can be estimated. The utility that the decision maker n obtains from alternative j is U_{nj}, j=1, ... J. This utility is known to the decision maker but not the researcher. Therefore the behaviour model is stated as – choose alternative i if and only if $U_{ni} > U_{nj}\ \forall\ j \neq i$.

The researcher does not observe the decision makers' utility. The researcher merely observes some attributes of the alternatives as faced by the decision maker, labelled $X\ \forall\ j$ and some attributes of the decision maker, labelled S_{nj}. The function, called the representative utility, that relates these observed factors to the decision maker's utility is $V_{nj} = V(X_{nj}, S_{nj})\ \forall\ j$ as there are aspects that the researcher does not observe $V_{nj} \neq U_{nj}$. The utility is decomposed as $U_{nj} = V_{nj} + \varepsilon_{nj}$ where ε_{nj} is the unknown factor. As the decision maker's choice is not deterministic, as ε_{nj} is not observed, then the probability of any particular outcome is derived. The probability that the decision maker chooses a particular preference i from the set of all possible outcomes is $P_{ni} = \text{Prob}(V_{ni} + \varepsilon_{ni} > V_{nj} + \varepsilon_{nj}\ \forall\ j \neq i)$ and hence, $P_{ni} = \text{Prob}(\varepsilon_{nj} < \varepsilon_{ni} + V_{ni} - V_{nj}\ \forall\ j \neq i)$

In the logit choice probability model, the cumulative distribution over all $j \neq i$ is the product of the individual cumulative distributions:

$$P_{ni} \setminus \varepsilon_{ni} = \prod_{j \neq i} e^{-e^{-(\varepsilon_{ni} + V_{ni} - V_{nj})}}$$

The probability that the decision maker chooses outcome U_{nj} is the expected value of this over all possible values of the unobserved factors (ε_{ni}) weighted by its density:

APPENDIX

$$P_{ni} = \int (P_{ni} \backslash \varepsilon_{ni}) f(\varepsilon_{ni}) d\varepsilon_{ni}. \text{ Giving } P_{ni} = \frac{e^{V}_{ni}}{\Sigma_j e^{V}_{nj}} \quad (1)$$

The relationship of the logit probability to the representative utility (V_{nj}) is sigmoid. If the representative utility of an alternative is very low compared with other alternatives, a small increase in the utility has little effect on the probability of it being chosen. The point at which the increase has the greatest effect on the probability of it being chosen is when the probability is close to 0.5. In this case a small improvement creates a large change in the probability.

For example, to investigate different consumers' choices, the following discrete choice theory model could be used to estimate the following equation:

$$U_{ni} = \alpha_r + \beta_r S_{ni} + \gamma_r X_{ni} + \varepsilon_{ni} \quad (2)$$

U_{ni} is the discrete choice groups under consideration in the research. An advantage of using the logit model for discrete choice is that it accounts for individual taste variation, that is the fact that different people are different. Two people may have the same income, education, etc., and yet they could make different choices, reflecting their individual preferences and concerns. Logit models can capture these taste variations. Tastes that vary systematically with respect to some attributes of the decision maker are incorporated into the model as the vector controlling for household, parent and child demographic characteristics (S_{ni}). These could include the consumer's gender, age, occupation, education, wealth factors, income and other relavent demongraphics. X_{ni} is a vector of the consumer preferences for a set of alternative choices as faced by the decision maker and ε_{ni} is the unobserved factors. Importantly, McFadden (1974) demonstrated that the log-likelihood function with these choice probabilities is globally concave in parameters β and γ, which helps in the numerical maximisation procedures.

Such a logit choice probability model can be expressed as follows from equations (1) and (2) above as:

$$\Pr(U_{ni} = r) = \exp(\alpha_r + \beta_r S_{ni} + \gamma_r X_{ni}) \Big/ \sum_{s=0}^{1} \exp(\alpha_r + \beta_r S_{ni} + \gamma_r X_{ni})$$

where r is the different discrete choice groups under consideration in the research. By estimating this model it is possible to see how preferences and demographics affect the different choice groups.

■ ■ ■ ■ APPENDIX

Derivation of a choice model

In this next section we will derive a simple choice model to illustrate its relationship to logistic regression. Assuming that a person only takes on an action if some linear function (U) is positive where $U = \beta x + \varepsilon > 0$. Let the unobserved actions be considered random, with density $f(\varepsilon)$, where the function 'f()' is logistic.

Defining, a binary function 'I()' to take the values of one and zero, with I(U)=1 if the value of ε and x have a person choosing the 'selected outcome' and I(U)=0 the person makes a different choice.

The probability of choosing the outcome is the expected value of I(U) over all possible unobserved factors can be written as the following integral.

$$P(I(U)=1) = \int I(U) F(\varepsilon) d\varepsilon = \int I(\beta x + \varepsilon > 0) f(\varepsilon) d\varepsilon$$

Assuming that the function f() is logistic then $f(\varepsilon) = \dfrac{e^{-\varepsilon}}{(1+e^{-\varepsilon})^2}$ and $F(\varepsilon) = \dfrac{1}{(1+e^{-\varepsilon})}$

Using these facts in our integral gives the probability of choosing the outcome as $P(I(U)=1) = \int I(\varepsilon > -\beta x) f(\varepsilon) d\varepsilon$ and hence we can set limits of integration as

$$\int_{\varepsilon=-\beta x}^{\infty} f(\varepsilon) d\varepsilon = 1 - F(-\beta x) = 1 - \dfrac{1}{1+e^{\beta x}} = \dfrac{e^{\beta x}}{1+e^{\beta x}}$$

Evaluating this choice integral above gives the resulting form of the odds ratio in logistic regression.

In 1974, McFadden proposed a modification to this model to include multiple cases. This is called a discrete choice model or multinomial logistic regression. McFadden was awarded the Noble prize for economics for this work in 2000.

11 LONGITUDINAL DATA ANALYSIS

In this section we will give some specialised examples of how the techniques in this book can be used to investigate longitudinal data.

Intent to treat (ITT) estimate

The intent to treat estimating equation can be written as:

$$Y_{is} = \beta_0 + \beta_1 Y_0 + \beta_2 \text{Intervention}_i + \beta_3 X_i + \varepsilon_{is}$$

and may be used to analyse the impact of an intervention (treatment group) using linear regression. Where Y_{is} represents a continuous measure for

APPENDIX ▨ ▨ ▨ ■

Table A.13 Intent to treat

Outcome	Control group mean	Intervention group mean	Difference (Estimated impact)	Effect size	p-value of estimate
Continuous outcome measure	Mean	Mean + β_2	β_2	β_2/SD	p-value from β_2 regression

student i in subject s. To improve the precision of the estimates, we control for baseline measure given by the variable Y_0. The equation includes a vector that controls for student background characteristics, X_i. This would include such variables as student gender; age; household characteristics – mother's and father's highest level of educational attainment; mother's job status; average monthly income for the household; and the number of adults and children living in the household, etc. Although interventions will generally have random assignment of participants it is still a good policy to include baseline covariates in the impact estimation to make the estimation more precise and therefore increase the power of the analysis. Doing so also controls for the handful of differences between the treatment and control groups on observable characteristics apparently generated by chance. The primary coefficient of interest is β_2, which provides an unbiased estimate of the intervention controlling for baseline measures and background characteristics. Table A.13 illustrates how that calculation would be performed. It is also usual when calculating intent to treat to give the linear regression output to illustrate which variables significantly contribute to the model.

The intervention group mean is calculated as the mean of the control group plus the estimated difference value taken from regression analysis. The Cohen's d measure of effect size can be calculating as β_2/SD.

Wilcoxon signed rank test

Longitudinal repeated measures such as Likert scale data, that come from the same participants, can be analysed using statistical techniques such as the dependent t-test and Wilcoxon signed rank test (de Winter and Dodou, 2010).

To illustrate how to interpret a Wilcoxon signed rank test we will use an example from a Likert scale question that has been asked to two groups of 500 participants before and after an intervention.

> For group A 192 of the 500 participants gave a higher Likert response after the intervention, with 275 of the ranks tied. In contrast for group B only 113 of the 500 cases gave a higher response with 313 tied. For group B the Wilcoxon shows no statistically significant change in rank order ($z = 3.626$, $p > .05$, $r = 0.115$) but for group A the change in

APPENDIX

rank order was statistically significant (z = 10.463, p < .01, r =0.330). As the Cohen's effect size in this case is a mark between 0.3 to 0.5 and represents a moderate change in group A's responses.

Note that the r-value effect size in a Wilcoxon signed rank test is calculated by dividing the Z-score by the square root of the number of observations. In this case there are 1000 observations, as we have 500 participants being tested at two points in time.

Generalised estimating equations (GEE)

Marginal models provide a natural way of extending generalised linear models (GLM) to longitudinal data. The marginal models do not require distributional assumptions for observations and are known as generalised estimating equations (GEE). The GEE approach offers a general and unified approach to analysing correlated responses that can be discrete or continuous. Both Stata and SPSS can analyse data using the GEE method of estimation (Karlstrom, 2001; Fitzmaurice et al., 2011).

12 ITEM RESPONSE THEORY

Item response theory can be used to check the validity and reliability of collapsed Likert scale categories that have already been collected. For example, we may wish to collapse categories in a data set having collected Likert scale responses 'strongly agree', 'agree', 'disagree' and 'strongly disagree'. We want to check the reliability of collapsing this data to a dichotomous scale consisting of only 'disagree' and 'agree'.

This can be expressed mathematical as one of invariance. By altering the structure of the questionnaire after the data has been collected we wish to know how much we have altered the latent structure of the measurement outcome.

Using a 1-parameter model (1PL) $y_{ij} = (\theta_j - b_i)$ for polytomous items as $p_{ij} = \dfrac{\exp(\theta_{jy} - b_{iy})}{\sum_k \exp(\theta_{jk} - b_{ik})}$ with j people answering the Likert scale questions (Rasch, 1960; Jansen and Roskam, 1986; Andrich, 1996). Each item i having y categories. For example if you had j=500, i=10 and y=4, this would be 500 people answering 10 Likert scale questions with each question having 4 response categories. To explore this we will firstly look at a proof by Jansen and Roskam (1986) that states for the compressed Likert scale to represent the initial scale the parameter weights for the categories need to be equal. This is a very strong restriction as it is basically saying the two categories that are being collapsed need to have the same item response profile.

APPENDIX ▨ ▨ ▨ ■

Collapsed Likert scale categories

What follows is the proof and a perturbation of this strong restriction, to see how much variation is allowed to produce a valid response. Using the following item response model:

$$p_{ij} = \frac{\exp(\theta_{jy} - b_{iy})}{\sum_k \exp(\theta_{jk} - b_{ik})}$$

The first step in the proof is to make a unidemensional reduction, this assumes that θ_{jy} and b_{iy} are linearly dependent. $\Theta_{jy} = \phi_y \theta_j + \psi_y$ and $b_{iy} = \phi_y b_i$

The parameter ϕ_y weights each of the subject parameters differently for each category. A similar idea to what we have seen before in the 2PL model. The parameter ψ_y gives the measure of how the person assesses the easiness in responding to each category, either positive or negative.

Substituting these into the Rasch model gives the following uni-dimensional polychotomous model.
$$p_{ij} = \frac{\exp\left(\psi_y + \phi_y(\theta_j - b_i)\right)}{\sum_k \exp\left(\psi_k + \phi_k(\theta_j - b_i)\right)}$$

Using this model we wish to assess what conditions are required when joining two categories. Let us assume that we are jointing category 3 and 4 to create category 2. In terms of probabilities we can write:

Prob(choosing category 2) = Prob(choosing category 3) +Prob(choosing category 4)

Using the uni-dimensional polychotomous model we created above and substituting into our probability statement we obtain.

$$\exp(\psi_2)\exp(\phi_2(\theta_j - b_i)) = \exp(\psi_3)\exp(\phi_3(\theta_j - b_i)) + \exp(\psi_4)\exp(\phi_4(\theta_j - b_i))$$

Taking $\theta_j = b_i$ in this equation above gives $\exp(\psi_2) = \exp(\psi_3) + \exp(\psi_4)$

Next to allow for ease of solution the following transformations are made:
$$\exp(\theta_j - b_i) = x$$

$$\phi_2 = p, \phi_3 = q, \phi_4 = r$$

$$\exp(\psi_2) = A_2,\ \exp(\psi_3) = A_3,\ \exp(\psi_4) = A_4$$

This gives $(A_3 + A_4)x^p = A_3 x^q + A_4 x^r$

re-writing this as $(A_3 + A_4) = (A_3 x^q + A_4 x^r)/x^p$

As the left-hand side of this equation is constant for all x the derivative is zero.

$$A_3(q-p)x^{q-p-1} A_4(r-p)x^{r-p-1} = 0$$

APPENDIX

which can be written as $A_3(q-p)x^{q-r} + A_4(r-p) = 0$
Taking $\theta_j = b_i$ this gives x=1 and this equation then becomes
$\phi_2 = p = (A_3 q + A_4 r)/(A_3 + A_4)$

Substituting back into $A_3(q-p)x^{q-r} + A_4(r-p) = 0$ gives $(q-r)x^{q-r} - (q-r) = 0$ hence $q = r$ and substituting back into $(A_3 + A_4)x^p = A_3 x^q + A_4 x^r$ gives the condition $\phi_2 = \phi_3 = \phi_4$ required for collapsing the two categories into one.

Perturbing for a small change in $x = x_0 + \varepsilon x_1$ gives this for $p(x_0 + \varepsilon x_1)^p \approx (x_0)^p + \varepsilon p x_1 (x_0)^{p-1}$ with similar results with q and r.

Substituting into $(A_3 + A_4)x^p = A_3 x^q + A_4 x^r$ and looking ε terms gives $(A_3 + A_4) p x_1 = A_3 q x_1 + A_4 r x_1$ and hence $\left|\dfrac{\phi_2 - \phi_3}{\phi_2 - \phi_4}\right| = \left|\dfrac{e^{\psi_4}}{e^{\psi_3}}\right|$ showing that when there is a slight difference between the two categories then there is slight difference in the final collapsed. This difference is proportional in relative size to the easiness in responding to each category. These results support that care needs to be taken when collapsing categories but that under certain conditions valid and reliable outcomes can be obtained.

Computing likelihoods and trait levels

In this section an example is taken from the organic food study with seven items. The difficulty level for each of these items is given in Table A.14 along with one set of responses to these. For this person the response pattern can be written as (1,1,1,0,1,0,1). If the trait levels and the item difficulty are known for a person (person 'a' in this case) then the probability can be calculated for all the probabilities P_{ia} by using the relevant irt equation, in

Table A.14 Calculating likelihoods and trait levels

Item	Coef. (b) difficulty (DIFF)	Persons response	Term	Trait level Θ=0	Trait level Θ=2
Health	−1.5069***	1	P_{1a}	0.8186	0.9709
Quality	0.1009	1	P_{2a}	0.4748	0.8698
Environment	1.8783***	1	P_{3a}	0.1326	0.5304
Price	−2.2559***	0	P_{4a}	0.9052	0.9860
Taste	−1.3651***	1	P_{5a}	0.7966	0.9666
Knowledge	−1.3374***	0	P_{6a}	0.7921	0.9657
Appearance	1.7171***	1	P_{7a}	0.1522	0.5703

APPENDIX

this case the PCM. Table A.14 shows the calculations for the probabilities at trait levels 0 and 2.

$$p_1(\theta_a) = \frac{\exp(0-(-1.5))}{1+\exp(0-(-1.5))} = 0.8186 \qquad p_7(\theta_a) = \frac{\exp(2-1.7)}{1+\exp(2-1.7)} = 0.5703$$

From these values it is also possible to calculate the probability of the likelihood of a response pattern. Responses are of a probability of 1 being P or the probability of not a 1 being 1-P. In this example the likelihood of response pattern is given as $L(X_a) = P_{1a}P_{2a}P_{3a}(1-P_{4a})P_{5a}(1-P_{6a})P_{7a}$ Hence for trait level theta equals zero it is $L(X_a | \Theta = 0) = 0.81 \times 0.47 \times 0.13 \times (1-0.90) \times 0.79 \times (1-0.79) \times 0.15$ = 0.000123.

Then you can if you wish, calculate response patterns for individual people in your sample. The same idea can be used to calculate 2PL models.

REFERENCES

Allison, P. D. (2002). *Missing data*. Thousand Oaks, CA: Sage.
Amabile, T. M., Hill, K. G., Hennessey, B. A., and Tighe, E. M. (1994). The Work Preference Inventory: Assessing intrinsic and extrinsic motivational orientations. *Journal of Personality and Social Psychology, 66,* 950–967.
Andrich, D. (1996). Theoretical and empirical evidence on the dichotomization of graded responses. In G. Engelhard and M. Wilson (Eds.). *Objective measurement III: Theory into practice.* Norwood, NJ: Ablex.
Anthony, M., and Harvey, M. (2012). *Linear Algebra. Concepts and Methods.* New York: Cambridge University Press.
Archer, L., DeWitt, J., and Wong, B. (2014). Spheres of influence: What shapes young people's aspirations at age 12/13 and what are the implications for education policy?. *Journal of Education Policy, 29*(1), 58–85.
Argyle, M., and Hills, P. (2002). The Oxford Happiness Questionnaire: a compact scale for the measurement of psychological well-being. *Personality and Individual Differences, 33,* 1073–1082.
Baker, F. B. (2001). *The basics of item response theory.* College Park, MD. Clearinghouse on Assessment and Evaluation.
Baker, F. B., and Kim, S. (2004). *Item Response Theory: Parameter Estimation Techniques.* 2nd ed. New York: Dekker.
Bartlett, J. E., Kotrlik, J.W, and Higgins, C. C. (2001). Organizational Research: Determining Appropriate Sample Size in Survey Research. *Information Technology, Learning and Performance, 19*(1), 43–50.
Barron, F. (1969). *Creative person and creative progress.* New York: Holt, Rinchart & Winston.
Bartolucci, F., Bacci, S., and Gnaldi, M. (2016). *Statistical Analysis of Questionaires. A Unified Approach Based on R and Stata.* NW, USA: CRC Press.
Bekhor, S., and Prashker, J. N. (2007). GEV-based destination choice models that account for unobserved similarities among alternatives. *Transportation Research Part B: Methodological, 42*(3), 243–262.
Bendel, R. B., and Afifi, A. A. (1977). Comparison of stopping rules in forward regression. *Journal of American Statistical Association, 72,* 46–53.
Bentler, P. M. (1990). Comparative fit indices in structural models. *Psychological Bulletin, 107*(2), 238–246.
Bowerman, B. L., and O'Connell, R. T. (1990). *Linear statistical models: an applied approach.* Belmont, CA: Duxbury.

REFERENCES

Brown, T. A. (2006). *Confirmatory Factor Analysis for Applied Research*. New York, NY: The Guilford Press.

Browne, M. W., and Cudeck, R. (1993). Alternative Ways of Assessing Model Fit, In: K. A. Bollen, and J. S. Long. (Eds.), *Testing Structural Equation Models*. (pp. 132–162). Sage, Newbury Park, California.

Bursac, Z., Gauss, H. C., Williams, D.K., and Hosmer, D.W. (2008). Purposeful selection of variables in logistic regression. *Source Code for Bioloogy and Medicine*, *16*, 3–17.

Canary, J. (2013). *Grouped goodness of fit tests for binary regression models.* Doctorial dissertation, University of Tasmania, Hobart, Tasmania, Australia.

Carifio, J., and Perla, R. (2008). Resolving the 50 year debate around using and misusing Likert scales. *Medical Education*, *42*, 1150–1152.

Carpenter, J., R., and Kenward, M. G. (2013). *Multiple Imputation and its Applications*. New York: Wiley.

CFPB. (2017). *CFPB Financial Well-being Scale: Scale development technical report*. [online] Accessed at www.consumerfinance.gov/data-research/research-reports/financial-well-being-technical-report/

Chan, D. (1998). The conceptualization and analysis of change over time: An integrative approach incorporating longitudinal and covariance structure analysis and multiple indicator latent growth modeling. *Organizational Research Methods*, *1*, 421–483.

Chen, G., and H. Tsurumi, H. (2010). Probit and logit model selection. *Communications in Statistics - Theory and Methods*, *40*, 159–175.

Chenoweth, E. (2003). *Factors that influence the college attendance decisions of Appalachian students*. Master's thesis, UMI Number 1415126. Ann Arbor, MI: ProQuest Information and Learning Company.

Chou, C. P., and Bentler, P. M. (1995). Estimates and test in the structural equation modeling. In R. H. Hoyle. (Ed.). *Structural equation modeling: Concepts, issues, and applications* (pp.37–55). Thousand Oaks, CA: Sage.

Cohen, L., and Manion, L. (2000). *Research Methods in Education*. London and New York: Routledge.

Cohen, J. (1988). *Statistical power analysis for behavioural sciences*. New York: Academic Press.

Conover, W. J. (1999). *Practical Nonparametric Statistics*. New York: Wiley.

Conway, J. M., and Huffcutt, A. I. (2003). A review and evaluation of exporatory factor analysis practices in organizational research. *Organizational Research Methods*, *6*(2), 147–168.

Creswell, J. W. (2002). *Educational research: Planning conducting, and evaluation quantitative and qualitative research*. Upper Saddle River: Merrill Prentice Hall.

Creswell, J., and Plano Clark, V. (2011). *Designing and Conducting Mixed Methods Research* (2nd Edition). Thousand Oaks, CA: Sage.

Cromer, B. A., Tarnowski, K. J., Stein, A. M,, Harton, P., and Thornton, D. J. (1990). The school breakfast program and cognition in adolescents. *Development and Behavior Pedagogy*, *11*, 295–300.

Curran, P. J., West, S. G., and Finch, J. F. (1996). The robustness of test statistics to nonnormality and specification errors in confirmatory factor analysis. *Psychological Methods*, *1*, 16–29.

REFERENCES

Darling, D. A. (1957). The Kolmogorov-Smirnov, Cramer-von Mises Tests. *The Annals of Mathematical Statistics*, *28*(4), 823–838.

David-Kacso, A., Haragus, P. T., and Roth, M. (2014). Peer influences, learning experiences and aspirations of Romanian high school students in their final school year. *Procedia-Social and Behavioral Sciences*, *141*, 200–204.

de Charms, R. (1968). *Personal Causation: The internal Affective Determinants of Behaviour*. New York: Academic Press.

de Winter, J. C. F., and Dodou, D. (2010). Five-Point Likert Items: t test versus Mann-Whitney-Wilcoxon. *Practical Assessment, Research and Evaluation*, *15*(11), 1–16.

Di Stefano, C., Zhu, M., and Mindrila, D. (2009). Unerstanding and using factor scores: Considerations for the applied researcher. *Practical assessment, research and evaluation*, *14*(2), 1–11.

Dixon, P., Humble, S., and Chan, D. W. (2016). How children living in poor areas of Dar Es Salaam, Tanzania perceive their own multiple intelligences, *Oxford Review of Education*, *42*(2), 230–248.

Dixon, P., and Humble, S. (2017). How school choice is framed by parental preferences and family characteristics: A study of Western Area, Sierra Leone. *Journal of School Choice: International Research and Reform*, *11*(1), 95–110.

Dodd, B. G., De Ayala, R. J, and Koch, W. R. (1995). Computerized adaptive testing with polytomous items. *Applied Psychological Methods*, *19*, 5–22.

Dolan, C. V. (1994). Factor analysis of variables with 2, 3, 5, and 7 response categories: A comparison of categorical variable estimators using simulated data. *British Journal of Mathematical and Statistical Psychology*, *47*, 309–326.

Dow, J. K., and Endersby, J. W. (2004). Multinomial probit and multinomial legit: a comparison of choice models for voting research. *Electoral Studies*, *23*, 107–122.

Draper, N. R., and Smith, H. (1998). *Applied Regression Analysis* (3rd ed.). John Wiley.

Dwyer, J. T., Evans, M., Stone, E. J., Feldman, H. A., Lytle, L., and Hoelscher, D. (2001). Adolescents' eating patterns influence their nutrient intakes. *Journal of American Dietary Association*, *101*, 798–802.

Embretson, S. E., and Reise, S. P. (2000). *Item Response Theory for Psychologists*. Mahwah, NJ: Lawrence Erlbaum.

Epstein, J. L., and Salinas, K. C. (1993). *School and family partnerships: Surveys and summaries*. Baltimore: Johns Hopkins University, Center on Families, Communities, Schools and Children's Learning.

Feick, L. F., and Price, L. L. (1987). The Market Maven: A Diffuser of Marketplace Information. *Journal of Marketing*, *51*, 83–97.

Field, A. (2000). *Discovering statistics using SPSS for windows*. London-Thousand Oaks-New Delhi: Sage publications.

Fitzmaurice, G.M., Laird, N. M. and Ware, J. H. (2011). *Applied Longitudinal Analysis*. New Jersey: John Wiley.

Fox, J. (1997). *Applied Regression Analysis, Linear Models and Related Methods*. Sage.

Furnham, A., and Brewin, C. R. (1990). Personality and Happiness. *Personality and Individual Differences*, *11*(10), 1093–1096.

REFERENCES

Glass, G. V., Peckham, P. D., and Sanders, J. R. (1972). Consequences of failure to meet assumptions underlying the analyses of variance and covariance, *Review of Educational Research*, *42*, 237–288.

Golembiewski, R. T., Billingsley, K., and Yeager, S. (1976). Measuring change and persistence in human affairs: Types of change generated by OD designs. *Journal of applied Behavioural Science*, *12*, 133–157.

Goodman, L. A. (1954). Kolmogorov-Smirnov tests for psychological research. *Psychological Bulletin*, *51*(2), 160–168.

Grand View Research. (2017). *Global Organic Foods and Beverages Market, Industry Report 2018 – 2025* Accessed online at www.grandviewresearch.com/industry-analysis/organic-foods-beverages-market

Gravetter, F., and Wallnau, L. (2014). *Essentials of statistics for the behavioral sciences*, (8th ed.). Belmont, CA: Wadsworth.

Gray-Little, B., Williams, V. S. L., and Hancock, T. D. (1997). An item response theory analysis of the Rosenburg Self-esteem Scale. *Personality and Social Psychology Bulletin*, *23*(5), 443–451.

Green, S. B. (1991). How many subjects does it take to do a regression analysis? *Multivariate Behavioral Research*, *26*, 499–510.

Green, C. L., Walker, J. M. T., Hoover-Dempsey, K. V., and Sandler, H. M. (2007). Parents' motivations for involvement in children's education: An Empirical Test of a Theoretical Model of Parental Involvement, *Journal of Educational Psychology*, *99*(3). 532–544.

Greene, W. (2000). *Econometric Analysis*. Prentice Hall: Upper Saddle River, NJ.

Gregoire, T. G., and Driver, B. L. (1987). Analysis of ordinal data to detect population differences. *Psychological Bulletin*, *101*(1), 159–165.

Grice, J. W. (2001). Computing and evaluating factor scores. *Psychological Methods*, *6*, 430–450.

Guadagnoli, E., and Velicer, W. (1988). Relation of sample size to the statbility of component patterns. *Psychological Bulletin*, *103*, 265–275.

Gulliksen, H. (1950). *Theory of mental tests*. New York: Wiley.

Haaijer, M., Wedel, M., Vriens, M., and Wansbeck, T. (1998). Utility covariances and context effects in conjoint MNP models. *Marketing Science*, *17*, 236–252.

Hauck, W. W., and Donner, A. (1977). Wald's test as applied to hypotheses in logit analysis. *Journal of American Statistical Association*, *72*(360), 851–853.

Hair, J. F., Black, W. C., Babin, B. J., and Anderson, R. E. (2006). *Mutlivariate Data Analysis*. Upper Sddle River, NJ: Prentice Hall International.

Harman, H. H. (1976). *Modern factor analysis*. Chicago: University of Chicago Press.

Hershberger, S. L. (2005). Factor scores. In B. S. Everitt and D. C. Howell (Eds.) *Enclopedia of statistics in behavioural science*. (pp. 636–644). New York: John Wiley.

Hausman, J., and Ruud, P. (1987). Specifying and testing econometric models for rank ordered data. *Journal of Econometrics*, *34*, 83–103.

Havlicek, L. L., and Peterson, N. L. (1976). Robustness of the Pearson correlation against violation of assumption. *Perceptual and Motor Skills*, 43, 1319–1334.

Hennessey, B. A., and Amabile, T. M. (1998). Reward, Intrinsic Motivation, and Creativity. *American Psychologist, June 53*(6), 674–675.

▪ ▪ ▪ ■ REFERENCES

Hershberger, S. L. (2005). Factor scores. In B. S. Everitt, and D. C. Howell (Eds.), *Encyclopedia of statistics in behavioral science* (pp. 636–644). New York, NY: John Wiley.

Hills, P., and Argyle, M. (2002). The oxford Happiness Questionnaire: a compact scale for the measurement of psychological well-being. *Personality and Individual Differences, 33,* 1073–1082.

Hoover-Dempsey, K. V., and Sandler, H. M. (1995). Parental involvement in children's education: Why does it make a difference? *Teachers College Record, 97,* 310–331.

Hoover-Dempsey, K. V., and Sandler, H. M. (1997). Why do parents become involved in their children's education? *Review of Educational Research, 67,* 3–42.

Hoover-Dempsey, K. V., and Sandler, H. M. (2005, March 22). *Final performance report for OERI Grant # R305T010673: The social context of parental involvement: A path to enhanced achievement.* Final report, submitted to Institute of Education Sciences, U.S. Department of Education, Washington, D.C.

Hosmer, D. W., Lemeshow, S., and Sturdivant, R. X. (2013). *Applied Logistic Regression.* Toronto: John Wiley and Sons, Inc.

Hosmer, D. W., Hosmer, T., Le Cessie, S., and Lemeshow, S. (1997). A comparison of goodness of fit tests for logistic regression model. *Statistics in Medicine, 16,* 965–980.

Howell, W. G., and Peterson, P. E., with Wolf, P. J., and Campbell, D. E. (2006). *The Education Gap: Vouchers and Urban Schools.* Revised Edition, Washington, DC: The Brookings Institution Press.

Hu, L., and Bentler, P. M. (1999). Cut off criteria for fit indexes in covariance structure analysis: Conventional criteria versus new alternatives. *Structural Equation Modelling, 6,* 1–55.

Huang, C. L. (1996). Consumer's preferences and attitudes towards organically grown produce. *European Review of Agricultural Economics, 23*(3), 331–342.

Humble, S., and Dixon, P. (2017). School choice, gender and household characteristics: Evidence from a household survey in a poor area of Monrovia, Liberia. *International Journal of Educational Research, 84,* 13–23.

Hunter, J. E., and Schmidt, F. L. (1990). Dichotomization of continuous variables: The implications for meta-analysis. *Journal of Applied Psychology, 75*(3), 334–349.

Hutcheson, G., and Sofroniou, N. (1999). *The multivariate social scientist.* London: Sage.

Jansen, P. G. W., and Roskam, E. E. (1986). Latent Trait Models and Dichotomization of Graded Presponses. *Psychometrika, 51*(1), 69–91.

Johnson, D. R., and Creech, J. C. (1983). Ordinal measures in multiple indicator models: A simulation study of categorization error. *American Sociological Review, 48*(3), 398–407.

Kaiser, H. F. (1970). A second-generation little jiffy. *Psychometrika, 35,* 401–415.

Kanarek, R. (1997). Psychological effects of snacks and altered meal frequency. *British Journal of Nutrition, 77,* 105–120.

Karlstrom, A. (2001). *Developing generalized extreme value models using the Piekands representation theorem.* Infrastructure and Planning. Royal Institute of Technology, Stockholm.

REFERENCES

Khoo, S. T., and Ainley, J. (2005). *Attitudes, intentions and participation. Longitudinal Survey of Australian Youth.* Victoria: Australian Council for Educational Research.

Ivankova, N. V., Creswell, J. W., and Stick, S. (2006). Using Mixed-Methods Sequential Explanatory Design: From Theory to Practice. *Field Methods, 18*(1), 3–20.

Jamieson, S. (2004). Likert scales: how to (ab)use them. *Medical Education, 38,* 1212–1218.

Johnson, R. B., Onwuegbuzie, A. J., and Turner, L. A. (2007). Toward a Definition of Mixed Methods Research. *Journal of Mixed Methods Research, 2,* 112–133.

Jolliffe, I. T. (1986). *Principal component analysis.* New York: Springer-Verlag.

Lee, B. (1999). Calling patterns and usage of residential toll services under self-selecting tariffs'. *Journal of Regulatory Economics, 16,* 45–82.

Loehlin, J. C. (2004). *Latent variable models.* Mahwah, NJ: Erlbaum.

Lord, F. N., and Novick, M. R. (1968). *Statistical theories of mental test scores.* Reading, MA: Addison-Wesley.

Lubke, G. H., and Muthen, B. O. (2004). Applying Multigroup Confirmatory Factor Models for Continuous Outcomes to Likert Scale Data Complicates Meaningful Group Comparisons. *Structural Equation Modeling, 11,* 514–534.

Lumley, T., Diehr, P., Emerson, S., and Chen, L. (2002). The importance of Normality assumption in large public health data sets. *Annu. Rev. Public Health, 23,* 151–169.

Mahoney, C. R., Taylor, H. A., Kanarek, R. B., and Samuel, P. (2005). Effect of breakfast composition on cognitive processes in elementary school children. *Physiological Behavior, 85,* 635–645.

Mason, H. D. (2015). Meaning, Happiness and Psychological distress: correlates and qualitative reflections. *Journal of Psychology in Africa, 25*(1),15–19.

McCullagh, P., and Nelder, J. A. (1989). *Generalised linear models.* Chapman and Hall: London.

McFadden, D. (2001). Economic choices. *American Economic Review, 91*(3), 351–378.

Meyers, R. (1990). *Classical and modern regression with applications.* Boston, MA: Duxbury.

Mickey, J., and Greenland, S. (1989). A study of the impact of confounder selection criteria on effect estimation. *American Journal of Epidemiology, 129,* 125–137.

Miles, J., and Shevlin, M. (2001). *Applying regression and correlation: a guide for students and researchers.* London: Sage.

Muijs, D. (2010). *Doing Quantitative Research in Education. Second Edition.* London: Sage Publications.

Norman, G. (2010). Likert scales, levels of measurement and the "laws" of statistics. *Advances in Health Science Educational Theory Practice, 15*(5): 625–632.

Novick, M. R. (1966). The axioms and principal results of classical test theory. *Journal of Mathematical Psychology, 3,* 1–18.

Owen, F., and Jones, R. (1982). *Statistics.* Polytech Publishers Ltd. UK: Stockport.

Packaged Facts. (2018). *Organic and Clean Label Food Consumer in the U.S.* Accessed online at www.packagedfacts.com/Organic-Clean-Label-Food-Consumer–11410671/

■ ■ ■ ■ REFERENCES

Pearson, N., Biddle, S. J. H., and Gorely, T. (2009). Family correlates of breakfast consumption among children and adolescents. Systematic review. *Appetite*, *52*, 1–7.

Pottorff, D. D., Phelps-Zientarski, D., and Skovera, M. E. (1996). Gender perceptions of elementary and middle school students about literacy at school and home. *Journal of Research and Development in Education*, *29*(4), 203–211.

Rasch, G. (1960). *Probabilistic Models for Some Intelligence and Attainment Tests*. Copenhagen: Danish Institute of Educational Research.

Renzulli, J. S. (1986). The three-ring conception of giftedness: A developmental model for creative productivity. In R. J. Sternberg and J. E. Davidson (Eds.), *Conceptions of giftedness* (pp. 53–92). New York: Cambridge University Press.

Renzulli, J. S. (2012). Re-examining the Role of Gifted Education and Talented Development for the 21st Century: A Four-Part Theoretical Approach. *Child Gifted Quarterly*, *56*(3), 150–159.

Roderick, J. A., Little, R. C., and Schenker, N. (1995). Missing data. In G. Arminger, C. C. Clogg, and M. E. Sobel (Eds.), *Handbook of statistical modeling for the social and behavioral sciences* (pp. 39–75). London/New York: Plenum Press.

Roets, L. F. (1997). *Leadership: Askils training program*. Des Moines, IA: Leadership Publishers.

Rothman, K. J., Greenland, S., and Lash, T. L. (2008). *Modern Epidemiology*. Lippincott-Raven, Philadelphia.

Royston, P. (1991). Estimating departure from normality. *Statistics in Medicine*, *10*, 1283–1293.

Royston, P. (1992). Approximating the Shapiro–Wilk W-test for non-normality. *Statistics and Computing*, *2*, 117–119.

Rubin, D. B. (1987). *Multiple Imputation for Nonresponse in Surveys*. New York: Wiley.

Schafer, J. L., and Graham, J. W. (2002). Missing data: Our view of the state of the art. *Psychological Methods*, *7*, 147–177.

Schagen, I., and Elliot, K. (2004). *What does it mean? The use of effect sizes in educational research*. Slough, Berks: National Foundation for Educational Research.

Schneider, M., Teske, P., Marshall, M., and Roch, C. (1998). Shopping for Schools: In the Land of the Blind, The One-Eyed Parent is Enough. *American Journal of Political Science*, *42*(3), 769–793.

Sedlmeier, P., and Gigerenzer, G. (1989). Do studies of statistical power have an effect on the power of the studies? *Psychological Bulletin*, *105*, 309–316.

Sen, A., and Srivastava, M. (2011). *Regression Analysis — Theory, Methods, and Applications*, Springer-Verlag, Berlin.

Sheather, S. (2009). *A modern approach to regression with R*. New York, NY: Springer.

Siega-Riz, A. M., Popkin, B. M., and Carson, T. (1998). Trends in breakfast consumption for children in the United States from 1965 to 1991. *American Journal of Clinical Nutrition*, *67*, 748S–756S.

Small, K. (1987). A discrete choice model for ordered alternatives. *Econometrica*, *55*(2), 409–424.

REFERENCES

Stevens, S. S. (1946). On the theory of scales of measurement, *Science*, *103*, 677–680.

Stevens, J. P. (1992). *Applied multivariate statistics for the social sciences*. Hillsdale, NJ: Erlbaum.

Stephens, M. A. (1974). EDF Statistics for Goodness of Fit and Some Comparisons. *Journal of the American Statistical Association. American Statistical Association*, *69*(347), 730–737.

Strand, S., and Winston, J. (2008). Educational aspirations in inner city schools. *Educational Studies*, *34*(4), 249–267.

Suissa, S. (1991). Binary methods for continuous outcomes: a parametric alternative. *Journal of Clinical Epidemiology*, *44*, 241–248.

Sullivan, G. M., and Artino, A. R. (2013). Analyzing and Interpreting Data From Likert-Type Scales. *Journal of Graduate Medical Education*, *5*(4), 541–542.

Steiger, J. H. (1990). Structural model evaluation and modification: an interval estimation approach. *Multivariate Behavioral Research*, *25*(2), 173–180.

Strand, S., and Winston, J. (2008). Educational aspirations in inner city schools. *Educational Studies*, *34*(4), 249–267.

Tabachnick, B. G., and Fidell, L. S. (2001). *Using multivariate statistics*. Boston: Allyn and Bacon.

Thayer, R. E. (1989). *The biopsychology of mood and arousal*. New York: Oxford University Press.

Thompson, B. (2007). Effect sizes, confidence intervals, and confidence intervals for effect sizes. *Psychology in the Schools*, *44*, 423–432.

Thorelli, H., and J. Engledow (1980). Information Seekers and Information Systems: A Policy Perspective. *American Economic Review*, *64*(3), 373–390.

Thurstone, C. (1935). *The vectors of mind*. Chicago: University of Chicago Press.

Trochim, W. M., and Donnelly, J. P. (2006). *The research methods knowledge base*, (3rd ed.). Cincinnati, OH:Atomic Dog.

Trusty, J., Robinson, C. R., Plata, M., and Ng, K. M. (2000). Effects of gender, socioeconomic status, and early academic performance on postsecondary educational choice. *Journal of Counseling & Development*, *78*(4), 463–478.

Train, K.E. (2009). *Discrete Choice Methods with Simulation*. New York: Cambridge University Press.

Tsakiridou, E., Konstantinos, M., Tzimitra-Kalogianni, I. (2006). The influence of consumer's characteristics and attitudes on the demand for Organic Olive Oil. *J. Int. Food Agribus. Market.*, *18*(3/4), 23–31.

Verhoef, P.C. (2005). Explaining purchase of organic meat by Dutch consumers'. *Eur. Rev. Agr. Econ.*, *32*(2), 245–267.

Walker, J. M. T., Wilkins, A. S., Dallaire, J. P., Sandler, H. M., and Hoover-Dempsey, K. V. (2005). Parental involvement: Model revision through scale development. *Elementary School Journal*, *106*, 85–104.

Yiridoe, E. K., Bonti-Ankomah, S., Martin, R. C. (2005). Comparison of consumer's perception towards organic versus conventionally produced foods: A review and update of the literature. *Renew. Agr. Food Syst.*, *20*(4), 193–205.

REFERENCES

Zientek, L. R., Yetkiner, Z. E., and Thompson, B. (2010). Characterizing the mathematics anxiety literature using confidence intervals as a literature review mechanism. *Journal of Educational Research, 103*, 424–434.

Zuckerman, H. (1979). The scientific elite: Nobel laureates' mutual influences. In R. S. Albert (Ed.) *Genius and eminence*, (pp.241–252). Elmsford, NY: Pergamon Press.

Zimmerman, D. W., and Zumbo, B. D. (1993). The relative power of parametric and nonparametric statistical methods. In G. Keren & C. Lewis (Eds.), *A handbook for data analysis in the behavioral sciences: Methodological issues* (pp. 481–517). Hillsdale, NJ, US: Lawrence Erlbaum Associates, Inc.

INDEX

aspirations to attend university study 10–11, 100–102, 106–114

Bartlett's test 35, 46–47, 58–59, 61, 134

Chi-square test 24–27, 85–87, 105, 166
confirmatory factor analysis 79–80, 189–190; first order models 80–87; multi-dimensional models 87–95, 90–91
contingency tables 21–28, 75, 101–107, 115–116, 126–127, 142–143, 158, 191; Cramer's V test 25–26; see also odds ratio
correlation 5, 51, 85–86, 180–184; Kendall 64–65, 183–184; Pearson 54–55, 62–63, 180–182; Spearman 64, 182–183

data 5–6; binary 10, 102–104, 113, 121, 150, 166–170; categorical data 26, 30, 121–122, 152, 154, 161, 172, 189; continuous 54–55, 66–67, 100, 108–109, 111–113, 172, 189; dichotomous 100–102, 110, 118, 126, 135, 150, 152, 192; discrete 5–6, 62, 123; ordinal 5–6, 30, 51, 64–66, 111–112, 144–147, 150–153, 159–160; polychotomous 100–103, 108, 121, 202
differential item testing 157–158; non-uniform difficulty 164–166
discrete choice theory 123, 197–199
distribution 4–5, 173–176; Kolmogorov-Smirnov 174–176; normal 4, 25, 39, 173, 188–189; unobserved 19, 126, 136, 140–141, 147–148, 199

effect size 26–27, 54, 77, 199–201
eigenvalue 35–37, 42–43, 47, 166, 177, 179–180
exploratory factor analysis 30–32, 80; communality 32–34; data reduction 41–44, 56–61, 90, 135–136; factor score extraction 45–46; Kaiser-Meyer-Olkin (KMO) 35; maximum likelihood 32, 39–41, 46–47, 192; principal components 41–43, 47, 56–61, 90–91; principal factor (principal axis factoring) 32, 37–38, 47, 87, 135; stable 39

F-test 70, 76, 105–106, 188, 192
factor analysis 176–179; see also exploratory and confirmatory
food insecurity study 11–12, 114–120, 159–160; hunger scale 114; mood questionnaire 11–12, 113–117

goodness of fit test 84–85, 193–194

happiness study 6–7, 30–40, 78–87

information function 161–164, 167–168
intrinsic motivation study 15–16, 166–170
item response models 150–151, 201–203; graded response 159–160; likelihood of response 203–204; partial credit 152–157, 161; Rasch 151–152, 202; trait level 203

INDEX

kurtosis 4, 39–40, 173

latent structure 31, 43, 56, 62–63, 79, 83, 87, 91–93, 150, 166–168; invariance 95–96, 201; *see also* factor score extraction
likelihood ratio test 105–106, 120–121, 192–193
Likert scale 4–6, 30–31, 55–56, 62–64, 68, 79, 111, 115, 140, 174–175, 200–201; collapsing 166–170, 202–203
linear regression 44–45, 67–70, 184–186; adjusted R^2 187; multicollinearity 71; multivariate 71–74, 187; sample size 77
logit models 123, 126, 197–198; Generalised Extreme Value model (GEV) 147–148; mixed 148; ordered 138–147; probit 148
logistic regression 100–109, 190–192; continuous approximations 111–113; goodness of fit test 193–194; Log-likelihood test 192–193; multinomial 113–120; multivariable 110–111; Pseudo R^2 values 106, 110, 194; receiver operating characteristic (ROC) 194–196
longitudinal analysis 95–96, 157, 164, 197; Generalized Estimating Equations (GEE) 201; intent to treat (ITT) 199–200; Wilcoxon signed rank test 200–201

marginal effects 109–110, 196–197
missing data 16, 19, 46; imputation 16–19, 46, 172–173

negatively worded (reversed) 30–31, 106–108, 112

non-parametric tests 4–5, 25, 64, 188–189, 200–201

odds ratio 26–27, 102–108, 115–117, 126–129, 157–158, 190–192
organic food study 12–13, 124–131, 150, 154–162, 203–204
Oxford happiness questionnaire 6–7, 32–40, 44–46, 80–87

p-value 20–21
parametric tests 4–5, 25
parental involvement in education study 7–9, 55–65, 90–95
pattern matrix 38–39, 189–190
post estimation tools 84–85, 89–91
preference, stated and revealed 124, 135–138, 197–199

reference cell coding 103–106
Roets rating scale for leadership 10, 87–90, 162–165
rotation methods 37–39; Promax (oblique) 37–38, 41, 47, 56, 80, 87; Varimax (orthogonal) 41, 47, 134; *see also* exploratory and confirmatory

sample size 4, 25–26, 39, 71, 77, 173–174, 188–189
scatter diagram 51–54
school choice study 14–15, 132–138
skewness 4–5, 39–40, 173–174
structural equation modeling (SEM) 79–85

transportation study 15–16, 138–147

variable selection 74–75; purposeful 75–76, 117–120, 129–131; stepwise 74–75

Printed in the United States
by Baker & Taylor Publisher Services